Literary Research: Strategies and Sources
Series Editors: Peggy Keeran & Jennifer Bowers

Individual volumes in the Literary Research: Strategies and Sources *series have supporting Web pages that can be reached by consulting the series listing on the Scarecrow Press home page, www.scarecrowpress.com.*

1. *Literary Research and the British Romantic Era: Strategies and Sources* by Peggy Keeran and Jennifer Bowers, 2005.
2. *Literary Research and the British Renaissance and Early Modern Period, 1500–1700: Strategies and Sources* by Jennifer Bowers and Peggy Keeran, due 2007.
3. *Literary Research and British Modernism: Strategies and Sources* by Alison Lewis, due 2007.

D1519332

Literary Research and the British Romantic Era

Strategies and Sources

Peggy Keeran
Jennifer Bowers

Literary Research:
Strategies and Sources, No. 1

The Scarecrow Press, Inc.
Lanham, Maryland • Toronto • Oxford
2005

SCARECROW PRESS, INC.

Published in the United States of America
by Scarecrow Press, Inc.
A wholly owned subsidary of
The Rowman & Littlefield Publishing Group, Inc.
4501 Forbes Boulevard, Suite 200, Lanham, Maryland 20706
www.scarecrowpress.com

PO Box 317
Oxford
OX2 9RU, UK

British Library Cataloguing in Publication Information Available

Library of Congress Cataloging-in-Publication Data
Keeran, Peggy, 1959-
  Literary research and the British romantic era : strategies and sources / Peggy
Keeran ; Jennifer Bowers.
    p. cm. -- (Literary research ; no. 1)
  Includes bibliographical references and index.
  ISBN 0-8108-5209-8 (pbk. : alk. paper)
  1. Romanticism--Great Britain--Research--Methodology. 2. Romanticism--
Great Britain--Bibliography--Methodology. 3. English literature--18th century--
Research--Methodology. 4. English literature--19th century--Research--
Methodology. 5. English literature--18th century--Bibliography--Methodology.
6. English literature--19th century--Bibliography--Methodology. 7. English
literature--Bibliography--Methodology. 8. English literature--Research--
Methodology. I. Bowers, Jennifer, 1962- II. Title. III. Series.

PR457.K44 2005
820.9'145'072--dc22   2005014537

Contents

vi   Contents

Acknowledgments

We would like to thank our editors at Scarecrow Press, Sue Easun for accepting our book proposal and for her early encouragement and good humor, and Martin Dillon for his valuable help when he took over as editor for the project.

Sylvia Tufts was invaluable getting the manuscript formatted for publication. We don't know what we would have done without her.

Barbara Berliner, Chris Brown, Michael Levine-Clark, Stefanie Berliner, Kathy Keeran, Nonny Schlotzhauer, Steve Fisher, Lois Jones, and Betty Meagher all provided us with feedback about the content of the book as well as expert advice when we needed to clarify certain details.

We'd like to thank Christy Gillette for allowing us to use her research question for Chapter 11, and for providing feedback on the content. We found, as we were working with Christy to discover the information about book sales, Mary Brunton, and Jane Austen, that we were employing almost all the techniques discussed in this book; her topic provided us with a practical way to wrap up the book and describe a microcosm of the whole research process.

Finally, but most importantly, we'd like to thank our families, friends, and colleagues for their patience as we wrote the book, especially at the end when we made the push to finish, were double-checking to make sure everything was as accurate as possible, and seemed to be working on the manuscript constantly. A very special thanks to Mary and Gary Younger and Scott, Nathaniel, and Gwen Howard.

Any errors or omissions are ours alone, and we hope we kept those to a minimum.

Introduction

Every literary age presents scholars with both predictable and unique research challenges. As librarians, we work with literary scholars to help them use standard and specialized reference tools to identify primary and secondary sources of value for their specific projects. Our goal in this volume is to explain the best practices for conducting literary research in the British Romantic era and to address the challenges scholars working in this era face. Learning sound research practices and knowing standard resources will empower scholars to solve those questions that can be answered by routine procedures, as well as enabling them to know when to consult with librarians on more esoteric issues. In addition to learning effective research skills, we believe that scholars can benefit from placing the research process in a larger context, by taking into account the era in which the literature was published along with today's research environment.

We have chosen to write about the British Romantic era for this guide because of the interesting challenges it presents to both scholar and librarian. Our main focus is on England but we include Scotland, Ireland, and Wales. This was an era of contradictions, of growth, and diversity in all aspects of English life. The Romantic era, roughly 1775–1830, was characterized by great societal, political, and economic shifts in England and abroad. During these years the population of England doubled. By the beginning of the Romantic era, the general population had become literate with widely varying taste in reading matter. Reading became a widespread activity and publishing and bookselling expanded to respond to the needs and interests of all classes. Advances in binding and paper-making technology made publishing less expensive. Lending libraries flourished for those who could not afford to purchase books or periodicals. Review journals, initially intent on comprehensively identifying and reviewing all books and then upon identifying and reviewing those considered high quality, grew in importance and influence. What appears to be a cohesive age with a single identifying title, "The Romantic Era," is actually far more complex.

The literary era dubbed "Romanticism" originally referred narrowly to the works of six male poets: Wordsworth, Blake, Coleridge, Keats, Shelley, and Byron. As current scholarly endeavors aim to illustrate, however, the time encompasses a rich and varied range of poets, essayists, and novelists of both genders. The term itself is under debate as relevant, while at the same time being redefined to be more inclusive in order to reflect the diversity of literature published. Researchers of canonical figures will find overwhelming amounts written on the original six poets, including websites devoted to their works and academic studies about them. On the other hand, there may be limited information about the lesser-known authors, with few if any contemporary or critical discussions. For example, a search in *MLA International Bibliography* on Keats will retrieve hundreds of records while a search on Mary Tighe or Winthrop Mackworth Praed will result in less than 10 hits each. How does a scholar find relevant materials when too many or too few citations are found? What else is there beyond *MLA* and the library catalog to unearth as much as possible? What sources exist to help identify the authors, books, periodicals, pamphlets, and essays of this time? Without indexes, what techniques can be used to find articles by topic within periodicals or newspapers? How can useful manuscript and archival collections be identified? What were the reputations of various authors at the time? Which journals reviewed their writing and what were the political biases of those journals? Who read their works? How can the researcher discover the political forces which permitted or discouraged particular types of writings? How can contemporary views about particular genres, such as Gothic novels, novels of sentiment and romantic love, or historical novels, be found? Does the relationship between review publications and authors affect the research process? And, finally, how do issues such as these affect literary research during the Romantic era? We will address these and other questions in this volume.

In the following guide to research within the Romantic era, we discuss the various research resources available to the scholar for both primary and secondary research. Our advice is directed specifically at the scholar of the Romantic era and provides clues for identifying relevant materials. The sources discussed include: general literary research guides; union library catalogs; print and online bibliographies; manuscripts and archives; microfilm and digitization projects; eighteenth- and nineteenth-century journals and newspapers; contemporary reviews; and electronic texts, journals, and Web resources. Some of these resources are all-inclusive and need to be mined to find relevant works, and others have been created specifically with the Romantic researcher in mind. In each chapter we will address how the research tools are best used to extract relevant information. In addition, we will examine, when pertinent, how the electronic era has enriched literary research in general and for this era specifically.

The research methodology itself is crucial to the success of finding relevant materials. Without strong searching skills, scholars may waste a great deal of time and energy simply trying to figure out how to use a tool, effort which could be used to read and integrate research materials into a scholarly work. In this volume we will emphasize the process, thereby enabling scholars to become effective researchers. Both search strategies and evaluation and comparison of sources will be addressed because, although scholars may be familiar with one or two basic electronic sources, often they do not take full advantage of the sources they know, nor realize there are other resources which may be more appropriate to use. We will also discuss core and specialized electronic and print research tools and standard search techniques, describe strengths and weaknesses of each, and explain how the varying tools relate to each other. For example, we will explain how to find contemporary reviews of literary works, which resources exist which will help identify the reviews, and how the various tools compare.

This volume is intended to be read as a narrative to provide an overall coherence to the research process, but can also be used as a recommendation guide to specific types of reference tools. By weaving together the literary world in which British Romantic literature was produced, the reference research tools available to enter that world, and the search techniques to make the research process as effective and rewarding as possible, the scholar will be able to work knowledgeably with the tools available and to build a solid foundation of primary and secondary evidence supporting their research.

Chapter 1
Basics of Online Searching

Before we begin, it is important to learn and to understand the basic rules of online searching. Too often the authors of this book see library patrons type a string of words into a database without realizing how the commands are being interpreted. For, indeed, whenever words are entered into a database, the search engine used by that database is receiving a string of commands to execute. There are some very practical steps to take which will help you search consistently across online database resources, and which will ensure you find relevant sources. Understanding the content of this chapter is vital to the successful Romantic scholar. These techniques are the foundation for the information detailed in the chapters which follow.

Step 1: Write Research Question as Topic Sentence

By writing down the research question as a topic sentence, you are defining the core ideas about your project and therefore you can clearly see the central concepts to be explored. From this step you can develop search strategies to find relevant sources. For example, if you are curious about the reputation of Milton during the Romantic era, you could write the following topic sentence: "I want to discover what Milton's reputation was during the Romantic era." The main concepts are *Milton*, *reputation*, and *romantic*. Perhaps you are interested in how scientists were depicted in literature during this time: "I want to explore the role of the scientist in literature during the Romantic era." The main concepts are *scientist*, *literature*, and *romantic*.

Step 2: Brainstorming Keywords

The next step is to take the main concepts and think of other keywords which could be used to find relevant materials. This step will allow you to think about the different ways your topic can be described, so that if the first search doesn't work, you have other terms to try. The Milton example above looks very straightforward, but the concepts of *reputation* and *romantic* may not be broad enough to find anything on the topic. The same is true with the second topic: what if instead of *romantic* the term *romanticism* is used, or the term *romantics*, or *gothic*? Maybe, instead of the name of the movement, *19th century* is used in a bibliographic record. You may want to know about *science* in this era, as well as *scientists*. Is the term *literature* adequate? What about *fiction*, *novels*, or *literary works*? Would these additional terms help locate relevant sources? By asking questions about your project, you can expand on the keywords you can search.

To help visualize this step of the process, create a table of concepts. As shown in Table 1.1, put the different concepts across the top of the table and then synonyms or related terms listed underneath.

Table 1.1. Possible keywords for searching topic about the role of the scientist in Romantic-era literature

Concept #1	Concept #2	Concept #3
scientist(s)	literature	romantic(s)
science(s)	fiction	romanticism
	novel(s)	18th century
	literary	19th century

Step 3: Structure of Electronic Records: The Example of MARC

Search engines retrieve information from databases using certain internal rules established for identifying and extracting relevant records. The researcher executes a search—for example, a title, author, or keyword search—and the search engine retrieves materials based upon the command received. In Step 4 we will discuss a variety of search strategies, but before that it is valuable to understand the structure of a record within a database because then the results of a search strategy become more logical. This section will explain this process, using the MARC record as the example.

The most common record any scholarly researcher will encounter is that found in library catalogs: the MARC (**MA**chine **R**eadable Cataloging) record, established by the Library of Congress. Most libraries which provide Web access to their catalogs contract with a commercial vendor, such as Innovative Interfaces, Voyager, DRA, or Dynix, to provide an integrated software package which allows the data entered to be cataloged, organized, and accessed. Librarians use the integrated software to catalog materials in MARC, to organize the MARC coding into indexes, and to provide access to the contents of the database via a Web-based interface. The Web-based interface is the library catalog you see when searching for books and other materials: this library catalog interface generally allows patrons to employ a variety of search options to retrieve the data from the indexes, such as title, subject, author, and keyword searches.

   To illustrate how a MARC record is organized, and therefore retrieved using the search interface, let's look at two records: a periodical and a book. In MARC cataloging, each part of the bibliographic record is divided into fields and subfields. Each field is assigned a three-digit numeric tag, which can be used by the search engine to retrieve the record from a designated index. For example, if the library decides to have a separate periodical index, the MARC tag 222, which identifies the record as a periodical, may be placed in the periodical title index. Figure 1.1 below illustrates the features of a MARC record for a periodical, *The Edinburgh Review*. When you search for *The Edinburgh Review* by periodical title in a library catalog in which the 222 has been placed into the periodical title index, you will find the periodical, if, of course, the library owns the periodical.

Figure 1.1. Modified *MARC* record for *The Edinburgh Review*, with tag 222 highlighted

---

001 1567494
010 89026669
090 AP4|b.E3
130 0 Edinburgh review (1802)
222 04 The Edinburgh review.
245 04 The Edinburgh review.
260 Edinburgh :|bA. and C. Black,|c1803–1929.
310 Quarterly
362 0 Vol. 1, no. 1 (Oct. 1802)–v. 250, no. 510 (Oct. 1929).
500 Sydney Smith, though not formally an editor, superintended
 the first three numbers. Cf. Dict. nat. biog., v. 53, p.
 120.
700 1 Smith, Sydney,|d1771–1845.

Source: University of Denver, Penrose Library catalog

   Figure 1.2 shows a modified MARC record for William St Clair's book *The Reading Nation in the Romantic Period*. Tag 245 identifies the title field for monographs. If a title index is created which contains

the 245, then, when a patron executes a title search in the library catalog, this book will be found. To further explain this MARC record, the
100 tag is the tag for the author, the 020 tag designates the International
Standard Book Number (ISBN), the 260 the publications information,
and the 650s the Library of Congress subject headings. Each of these
tags would have their own indexes so that you would be able to search
by author, ISBN, publisher, or subject. However, the keyword index is
much more flexible and will allow a variety of tags to be included, so
that information from different parts of the record can be combined.
For example, the 100, 245, 260, and 650 tags could all be included in a
library catalog keyword index, to allow you to search for *st clair* and
romantic together. Keyword searching will be explained in greater
depth below.

**Figure 1.2. Modified *MARC* record for *The Reading Nation in the
Romantic Period*, with tags 100, 245, 260, and 650s highlighted**

---

001 52886917
010 2003060795
020 052181006X
049 DVPP
050 00 Z1003|b.S77 2004
100 1 St. Clair, William.
245 14 The reading nation in the Romantic period /|cWilliam St
Clair.
260 Cambridge ;|aNew York :|bCambridge University Press,
|c2004.
300 xxix, 765 p. :|bill. ;|c24 cm.
504 Includes bibliographical references (p. 724–742) and
index.
650 0 Books and reading|xSocial aspects|xHistory.
650 0 English literature|xHistory and criticism.
650 0 Books and reading|xSocial aspects|zEngland|xHistory.
650 0 Book industries and trade|zEngland|xHistory.
650 0 Literature and society|zEngland|xHistory.
651 0 England|xIntellectual life.

Source: University of Denver, Penrose Library catalog

This brief overview of the MARC record helps illustrate how standard structure for records allows individual records to be retrieved during a search. Once the indexes within this library catalog have been set
up so that the relevant MARC tags can be retrieved when a specific
search has been executed, then the researcher can use established

search strategies, described in Step 4, to retrieve relevant sources. Although it isn't necessary to understand how each record in every database is coded, it is very important for the researcher to understand how a search engine is retrieving records and which search techniques to use.

Step 4: Creating Search Strategies

Field Searching

In the discussion about the MARC record above, we discovered that different indexes are created to search for specific fields within a record. The most recognizable searches are searching by author or by title in a library catalog where you know the author of the book, or the title of the book, and you use the appropriate search option offered by the library catalog to find the resource. This is called *field searching* in which you are telling the search engine to focus on a specific part of the record to find the information you seek. Depending upon the search engine, almost any part of the record can be searched using the field search: title, author, abstract, full text, publication type, publication date, language, or subject. Each of these types of searches will be restricted to specific parts of the record. Generally, the most flexible type of search in an online database is the *keyword*, sometimes called the *default*, search, because it can retrieve almost any part of the record, depending upon how the search engine has been set up to retrieve records.

Boolean Searches

Whether you realize it or not, almost every online database or search engine uses some form of Boolean logic to allow relevant information, based upon the keywords searched, to be retrieved. If you type a string of words into a database which uses strict Boolean operators to retrieve records, then you may get no results. It is important to understand how Boolean operators work.

Boolean logic and Boolean operators are named for George Boole, a nineteenth-century British mathematician. His theory for logic is the basis for the design of modern computers and for retrieving data from databases. The three operators used to search online databases are *and*, *or*, and *not*. These operators are used to define the relationships between the concepts listed in Step 2 above, which enable the researcher to narrow the search, broaden the search, or to exclude a concept from the search.

1) Boolean Operator "And"

And narrows the search.

Look at Table 1.1 in Step 2. To focus in on all aspects of your topic, type the word *and* between the keywords listed under the separate concept headings:

scientist and literature and romantic

If you type this combination of keywords and Boolean operators into an online bibliographic database which requires Boolean logic, you will find records containing all these terms. Figure 1.3 is a diagram to help you visualize how the concepts are combined.

Figure 1.3. Boolean *and* search

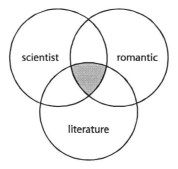

The shaded area indicates where the three concepts overlap, and illustrates that all three concepts must be present in a library catalog record for the record to be retrieved. This keyword search retrieved the following record, Figure 1.4, found in *MLA International Bibliography* (*MLAIB*). We've put the keywords in bold and in italics to illustrate where in the record the keywords were found: the title field and the subject field.

Figure 1.4. Modified record retrieved from *MLAIB* using Boolean *and* to combine separate concepts

Title:	The ***Romantic*** and the ***Scientist*** Revisited
Author(s):	Tomlinson, Richard S.
Source:	The Friend: Comment on Romanticism 1993 Oct; 2 (2): 9–26.
General Subject Areas:	*Subject Literature:* English ***literature***; *Period:* 1800–1899;
Subject Terms:	Romanticism; relationship to science
Document Information:	*Publication Type:* journal article *Language of Publication:* English

Source: *MLAIB*, via EbscoHost.

2) Boolean Operator "Or"

Or broadens the search.

Refer back to Table 1.1 above. Each concept has several keywords associated with it. Those keywords can be strung together using the operator *or* to allow all to be searched at one time:

*literature **or** fiction **or** novel*

Type this into a library catalog which uses Boolean operators and all records with any of the terms present will be located. The diagram in Figure 1.5 illustrates this point.

Figure 1.5. Boolean *or* search

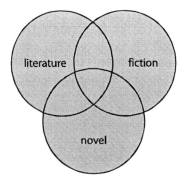

3) Boolean Operator "Not"

Not excludes unwanted concepts.

Perhaps, during your research, you discover that an unwanted concept keeps appearing. For example, you want sources on *England* but *New England* is found in half the records. You can exclude that concept as follows:

england **not** *new*

Figure 1.6. Boolean *not* search

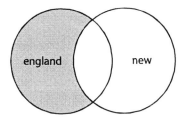

This search will eliminate all records with *New England*. However, this operator can be problematic because, if combined with our first search, it will also discard a record for a book in which *new* observations about the role of the *scientist* in *Romantic literature* are examined. So while *not* does rid the results of unwanted citations, it may also block something valuable. Therefore, be cautious when using the *not* operator.

Truncation/Wildcards

Some search engines allow keywords to be truncated with a designated symbol, such as *, ?, !, #, or others, to find the stem of the word and all variant endings. Use the help screens within the database you are searching to discover which truncation symbol to use. One standard truncation symbol is the asterisk (*). The stems of two of our keywords are *romantic* and *scien*; using the asterisk to truncate, *romantic** retrieves *romantic, romantics, romanticism* while *scien** retrieves *science, sciences, scientist, scientists, scientific.*

Be careful when truncating the word to be searched, because if the keyword is truncated too much unwanted sources will be retrieved. For example, truncating *roman** will retrieve *roman, romans*, and *Romania*, as well as *romantic, romantics*, and *romanticism*, but records with the first set of results are probably irrelevant to the research question. *Romantic** is a much more effective truncation strategy. If your interest is specifically about *scientists*, then truncating the word *scientist** will find records with the singular and plural of the word only and ignore *science, sciences, scientific.*

Some databases allow wildcard symbols to be used within a word to find singular and plural forms of words: *wom?n* will find *women, woman,* and *womyn.* Check the help screens in the database being search to find out all methods for using truncation and wildcard symbols.

Nesting

Complex Boolean operator and truncation searches can be combined using a strategy called *nesting*. The use of parenthesis allows similar concepts to be grouped together. The content within the parenthesis will be processed by the database first, and then the rest of the search terms, moving from left to right, will be processed. Nesting permits more sophisticated searching. For example, all of the following searches, using the keywords from Concept #2 in Table 1.1, can be executed separately:

> *romantic* and scientist* and novel*
> *romantic* and scientist* and poetry*
> *romantic* and scientist* and fiction*

However, keywords listed under one concept can be grouped together using parenthesis:

romantic* and scientist* and (poetry or fiction or novel*)

Nested searches help eliminate duplicate records, and therefore is a more efficient means of searching than the individual searches above.

Phrase Searching/Proximity Operators

This section addresses some very complicated issues about searching, and it may take practice to understand. Essentially, the search engine for a database will determine how the content of that database will be retrieved, while the structure of the record within the database will determine if the record can be found doing the search entered. To illustrate this, let's search for sources about the author Mary Shelley, sometimes known as Mary Wollstonecraft Shelley. The Library of Congress Subject Heading for this author is *Shelley, Mary Wollstonecraft, 1797–1851*. We will review how different searches entered will affect the list of results retrieved.

If a concept is represented by a phrase, check the help screens to see if the database allows phrase or proximity searches to retrieve relevant records. Some search engines require the use of quotation marks around the phrase to inform the system that the terms are to be located next to each other: *"romantic era"*. Some search engines require the use of proximity operators instead: *romantic w era*.

WorldCat, discussed in Chapter 3, uses an interface called *First-Search* as its search engine. We will go into more depth about the differences between databases and search engines later in this chapter, but for now it is important to understand that the search engine, *First-Search*, allows the content of the database, *WorldCat*, to be searched and relevant records retrieved. *FirstSearch* allows phrases to be searched using either quotation marks or proximity operators. If the phrase is not set apart using either quotation marks or proximity operators, then the *FirstSearch* search engine interprets the words as separate keywords and, as a default, will employ the Boolean operator *and* to retrieve records containing the keywords (see Table 1.2 below).

The *FirstSearch* search engine allows you to search for a phrase using quotation marks: *"mary shelley"*. However, at times, phrase searching isn't effective and proximity operators, which allow more flexible relationships between words to be established, work better. The following *proximity operators* are used in *WorldCat*, when *FirstSearch* is the search engine:

w   *with*—use to indicate required word order; use *wn* (where *n* is a number) to indicate number of words between the words being searched: *mary w2 shelley*.

n   *near*—use to indicate flexible word order; use *nn* (where the second *n* is a number) to indicate number of words between the words being searched: *mary n2 shelley*.

Table 1.2 illustrates the results in *WorldCat*, using the *FirstSearch* search engine, using various search strategies.

Table 1.2. Search strategies and records retrieved in *WorldCat*

Search strategy	Retrieves	Number of results
"mary shelley"	mary shelley	1002
mary w2 shelley	mary shelley mary wollstonecraft shelley	2384

mary n2 shelley	mary shelley
	mary wollstonecraft
	  shelley
	shelley mary
	  wollstonecraft
		2435

mary shelley	mary and shelley (defaut search = and)	2981

- The last search, *mary shelley*, retrieves the most records because the two terms are searched separately. As a result, the search will retrieve "false drops," meaning both the words are present in the record but the records are not about Mary Shelley. For example, the search retrieved the book *Skeletal Biology of Past Peoples: Research Methods*, written by Shelley Rae Saunders and Mary Anne Katzenberg.
- The first search, *"mary shelley"*, is the most restrictive because it does not make allowances for the author's middle name.
- The second search, *mary w2 shelley*, allows *Mary Shelley* and *Mary Wollstonecraft Shelley* to be retrieved, but not records where the author's last name comes first, such as in the Library of Congress subject heading field.

- Although you may still get false drops, the most accurate and the most flexible method for finding records with the author's name present is the third option, *mary n2 shelley*, because it allows the records to be retrieved whether the first name is first or the last name appears first, and it allows the middle name to be present or not.

Subject versus Keyword Searches

Once you have executed a search and found relevant citations, look to see which subject headings have been assigned to the source. *Subject headings*, also called *descriptors*, are controlled terms, or controlled vocabulary, used to describe all sources of a like nature. The most widely used subject headings in library catalogs are those established by the Library of Congress. The 26th edition is the most current edition available of *Library of Congress Subject Headings*, a multi-volume set which should be available for consultation in most reference sections of academic libraries. For example, in the *LCSH* volumes, we discover the Library of Congress subject heading for Mary Shelley is *Shelley, Mary Wollstonecraft, 1797–1851*, which would be assigned to materials where Mary Shelley is one of the core subjects. *WorldCat* and most academic libraries use these standard LC headings. To further illustrate the usefulness of subject headings, if you find a book on the depiction of scientists in Romantic literature, look at the subject headings to see if you have been searching the most relevant terms. The book *Romantic Science: the Literary Form of Natural History*, edited by Noah Heringman, was found in the library catalog using the keyword search *scienc* and romantic* and literature* (see Figure 1.7).

Figure 1.7. Modified record illustrating the Library of Congress subject headings used to describe *Romantic Science*

Title	**Romantic science : the literary forms of natural history** / Noah Heringman, editor.		
Publ info	Albany : State University of New York Press, c2003.		

LOCATION	CALL #	STATUS
Books Upper Level	PR468.N3 R66 2003	AVAILABLE

Description	xiii, 281 p. : ill. ; 23 cm.
Series	SUNY series, studies in the long nineteenth century
Subject(s)	English literature — 19th century — History and criticism.

Subject(s)	Nature in literature.
	Literature and science — Great Britain — History — 19th century.
	Natural history in literature.

Source: University of Denver, Penrose Library catalog

The Library of Congress Subject Headings (LCSH) are in the shaded area and reveal new terms which can be searched as keywords: *britain*, *natural history*, and *19th century*. The most relevant of these subject headings is *Literature and science—Great Britain—History—19th century*. If the library catalog is Web-based, a link may be provided to other records with the same subject heading. If not, do a subject field search using this subject heading. The remaining three subject headings, however, are too broad for our topic, but they do provide us with additional keywords to consider searching.

Databases other than library catalogs also use controlled vocabulary, but many of these create their own thesauri to use when assigning subjects to an item. Whenever a relevant citation is located, look at the subject heading or descriptor fields to find which words are used to describe the materials relevant to your topic. You may, if the subject heading is accurate enough, do a subject field search and focus your search on that section of the record. Otherwise, add the relevant words to your list of keywords, and try using them in keyword searches.

Relevancy Searching

Some search engines display results using relevancy ranking. In relevancy searches, a formula is used to rank results based upon selected criteria, which varies by search engine. Essentially, results are ranked and displayed, with the most "relevant" results listed first, employing some of the following types of criteria:

- the presence of all or some of the keywords in the record
- the number of occurrences of the words searched (the more times the words are used the higher the result is ranked)
- the proximity of the search terms to each other (the closer the words are to each other, the higher the result is ranked in the display order)
- the location of the terms within the record (present in an important field such as the title or subject/descriptor, or abstract, or located in the first paragraph or near the beginning of the document)

Some subscription-based search engines offer the ability to activate or deactivate relevancy searching. Check the help screens to see if the option is the default in the database you are using. If relevancy searching is not the default in the database, and if you would like to use it, look at the help screens to see if the option is available and how to activate it. The authors of this book don't find relevancy ranking helpful because we find we retrieve too many irrelevant results, especially results with only one of the keywords searched, but this type of searching has its advocates.

Limiting/Modifying

Limiting, or modifying, is an important feature which allows a set of search results to be narrowed down by specific characteristics such as language, material type (e.g., book, serial, video, dissertation, journal article, book chapter), year (or range of years), publisher, or place of publication. Even *Google* allows limiting to a specific domain, such as *.edu*, *.com*, or *.gov*.

Step 5: Databases versus Search Engines

Once you have brainstormed terms and have mastered Boolean logic and truncation, you are ready to develop a search strategy to use online. You must tailor the search to the search engine you are using. As stated above, content is provided by the database, and the interface used to access the database provides the search engine. For example, the content of *MLAIB*, discussed in Chapter 4, is created by the Modern Language Association (or MLA). But a variety of search engines can be used to access the content of the database: *SilverPlatter*, *EbscoHost*, *Gale*, and *FirstSearch*, to name a few. Each search engine operates differently. Table 1.3 illustrates the above.

Table 1.3. List of databases and search engines used to access the databases

DATABASE Content	SEARCH ENGINE Access to Content
MLAIB	EbscoHost
	FirstSearch (OCLC)
	Ovid
	SilverPlatter

WorldCat	FirstSearch (OCLC)
English Short Title Catalogue	Eureka (RLG)
RLG Union Catalog	Eureka (RLG)
Poole's Index to Periodical Literature	Paratext
Eighteenth Century Collection Online	InfoTrac (Gale)
ABELL	Chadwyck-Healy/ProQuest
The Times Digital Archive	InfoTrac (Gale)

To understand how the database is being searched by the search engine, you must read the help screens provided. Whenever you approach a new database, look for the *Help* or *Frequently Asked Questions* section. Questions to ask yourself as you read through the documentation:

- Does the database require the use of the Boolean *and* to connect separate concepts?
- If *and* is required, does it need to be all upper case?
- Is truncation allowed? If so, what is the truncation symbol?
- What is the internal wildcard symbol?
- Are quotation marks required for phrase searching? Or are proximity operators required?
- Does the search engine allow limiting by date, type of publication, language, material type, etc.?
- How are results displayed? By author? Title? Date?
- Does the database display records based upon a relevancy formula? If so, what are the criteria used for ranking?

It is advisable to review periodically the help screens within databases you use frequently because search engines do change. When the authors of this book first started using *WorldCat*, *FirstSearch* didn't allow quotation marks to indicate phrase searching, so we never used them. It wasn't until a student pointed out to us that this feature was added that we went back and reviewed how to search this database and discovered this change had been made.

In the following chapters, we provided the URLs for the vendors of the online subscription databases instead of URLs for the databases. Unless your library subscribes to the database, you cannot get access through a direct link. If possible, we linked to the vendor description of the database, but more often we linked to the main Web page. To find the database description within the vendors' website: if a search box is available, search for the title of the database; use the alphabetic list of titles if available; look for a link to information about electronic or digital product; or look for a link for academic products. For a complete list of vendors which provide access to *MLAIB*, consult the MLA website at www.mla.org/bib_electronic.

Step 6: Understanding Google Searches

Google is one of the most popular, powerful search engines for surfing the World Wide Web. A website is retrieved based upon certain criteria: popularity and importance in terms of the amount of traffic it receives and the quality of the links to the site, and word proximity within the results. *Google* employs many of the search features described above, but not all. Although there is a general directory to the websites through *Google*, no subject headings are assigned. Boolean operators, *OR* and *AND*, in upper case, and phrase searching using quotation marks are allowed. Technically, truncation is not available; instead, "stemming" allows relevant words to be retrieved: *roman* will retrieve records with *rome, roman, romans,* but not *romantic*, and *romantics* will retrieve *romantic*, but not *roman*. *Google* prevents *stop words* (e.g., a, an, the, at, etc.), which are so common they slow down the retrieval process, from being searched unless you tell it to search those terms. To ensure a stop word is included, either include it in a phrase search or precede the word with the "+" symbol: +to +be +or +not +to +be will retrieve records with all the terms present, but not necessarily in that order, while "to be or not to be" will retrieve the phrase. If looking for websites with the Shakespearean quotation, the latter search will be the most effective.

The University of California, Berkeley, maintains an excellent website, *Internet Guides* <www.lib.berkeley.edu/TeachingLib/Guides/Internet/> which provides useful information about Web search engines, effective search strategies, and general challenges you might encounter when searching the Internet.

Most academic resources available online through individual library catalogs or subscription services, such as *MLA International Bibliography*, are not searchable using any of the general Web search engines, including *Google*. There are exceptions to this, such as

RedLightGreen, which will be covered in Chapter 3. Therefore, at present, the vast majority of scholarly sources a Romantic researcher will need cannot be found on what is called the "visible Web"—what can be found using a tool such as *Google*—and therefore *Google* is a supplementary part of the search process. However, in the case of manuscripts and archives, *Google* may prove to be very useful.

Conclusion

The search techniques and strategies described above are applicable across the online world, whether searching library catalogs, subscription databases such as *MLA International Bibliography*, or the World Wide Web using *Google*. The information in this chapter will serve as part of the foundation for the book as a whole. We may refer back to specific parts of this chapter, or we may assume a level of knowledge about search strategies based upon the information provided here. Practice the techniques covered in this chapter, including Boolean operators, truncation, keyword searching, subject/descriptor searching, and proximity searching. Make sure you understand the differences between a database and a search engine, and why it is important to understand the difference. In the twenty-first century, the stronger the online search skills, the more effective and efficient the researcher. This chapter provides the foundation for online searching and the best practices to follow for more efficient techniques and effective results.

Chapter 2
General Literary Reference Resources

General literary reference resources, such as research guides, encyclopedias, dictionaries, companions, and biographical sources, can serve as the initial foundation for your research project. The reference sources described in this chapter provide an introduction to the authors, works, and themes of the Romantic period, or, in the case of research guides, describe the basic resources necessary for investigating a literary topic. Consider these sources springboards for initiating your research, or tools for filling in background information. These annotations will give you an idea of the kind of information to be found in these resources, and how best to use them for furthering your research goals.

Research Guides

Harner, James L. *Literary Research Guide: An Annotated Listing of Reference Sources in English Literary Studies*. 4th ed. New York: Modern Language Association, 2002.

Harner, James L. *Literary Research Guide*, 28 September 2004, at www-english.tamu.edu/pubs/lrg/ (accessed 3 December 2004).

Marcuse, Michael J. *A Reference Guide for English Studies*. Berkeley, CA: University of California Press, 1990.

Graduate students in English literature may be familiar with the following two research guides. Harner's *Literary Research Guide* and Marcuse's *A Reference Guide for English Studies* both describe the principal sources used in literary research. You will want to consult these guides for their annotations of pertinent resources not covered in *The British Romantic Era: A Guide to Literary Research and Resources*.

The ***Literary Research Guide*** is the principal handbook to research in literary studies for advanced undergraduates, graduate students, and scholars in the United States. Often referred to simply as "Harner," this source is excellent for introducing the main resources for conducting literary research and should be used as both a starting point for your project and as a guide to identifying and using additional resources. Since the book's range is so extensive, however, Harner only covers selected period-specific reference tools, and does not describe sources for the study of individual authors like those addressed in *A Reference Guide for English Studies*. Harner provides, for the most part, evaluative annotations for more than 1,200 selected print and electronic reference sources organized into chapters by type of general literary resource (e.g., dictionaries, bibliographies, indexes, library catalogs, manuscripts, dissertations, Internet resources, biographical sources, periodicals), genres, national literatures (e.g., English, Irish, Scottish, Welsh, American), other literatures in English, foreign-language literatures, comparative literature, and literature-related topics and sources.

Students of British Romantic-era literature will want to review the English literature sections on "Restoration and Eighteenth-Century Literature" and "Nineteenth-Century Literature" which cover the following period-specific resources: histories and surveys; handbooks, dictionaries, and encyclopedias; bibliographies of bibliographies; guides to primary works; guides to scholarship and criticism; biographical dictionaries; periodicals; background reading; and genres (e.g., fiction, drama and theater, poetry, and prose). Although many of the sources discussed in these sections are also addressed in this research guide, Harner features supplementary sources for projects concerned with the earlier eighteenth century and later nineteenth century, as well as period surveys of British drama, literature, and history. Depending on your research topic, you may also want to use Harner to identify relevant sources in other sections, such as those for Irish, Scottish, and Welsh literatures, or for guidance with general literary sources not covered in this book.

Each entry begins with a complete citation that frequently notes existing reprints and supplements, as well as Library of Congress and Dewey call numbers. The main body of the annotation outlines the source's scope and organization, discusses its strengths and limitations as a research tool, compares the source with similar works, notes indexing, lists selected reviews, and concludes with "see also" references to other relevant sections and works within the *Guide*. The *Literary Research Guide* contains three indexes: names of people responsible for works in the citations or annotations (including authors, editors, compilers, translators, and revisers but excluding literary authors); titles (including current, former, and variant titles for books, essays, and periodicals); and subjects. Harner provides a working copy of his revisions for the fifth edition at his *Literary Research Guide* website.

A useful complementary resource to Harner, *A Reference Guide for English Studies* by Michael J. Marcuse, also describes English language and literature reference works published primarily through 1985, with limited coverage to 1990. These resources are arranged in the following twenty-four sections: general works; libraries; retrospective and current national bibliography; serial publications; miscellany (e.g., dissertations, microforms, reprints, reviews); history and ancillae to historical study; biography and biographical references; archives and manuscripts; language, linguistics, and philology; literary materials and contexts (e.g., folklore, mythology, the Bible); literature (e.g., classical studies, foreign literatures, children's literature, women's studies, women and literature); English literature (Scottish, Anglo-Irish, Anglo-Welsh, commonwealth literatures); medieval literature; Renaissance and early seventeenth century; Restoration and eighteenth century; nineteenth century; twentieth century; American literature; poetry and versification; theater, drama, and film; prose fiction and nonfictional prose; theory, rhetoric, and composition; bibliography; and the profession of English. Marcuse cautions in the preface that users of the guide should begin with the subject index rather than the table of contents, in order not to miss works relevant to their area of interest that may not be listed in obvious sections.

In general, these sections cover research guides and research reviews, bibliographies, encyclopedias, dictionaries, companions, standard histories, and in some cases, scholarly journals and recommended works for particular fields of specialization which are not annotated. With an intended goal of indicating a reference work's utility, the entries provide a citation and Library of Congress call number, describe the work's history, purpose, scope, arrangement, strengths and weaknesses, and sometimes feature cross-references to related works. A subsection on the Romantic Movement is found within the "Literature of the Nineteenth Century" section and includes a bibliography of forty-eight recommended works on Romanticism, but scholars of this period will want to review the "Restoration and Eighteenth Century" section as well. Also be sure to read section "M-60 Guides to Individual Authors." This section presents unannotated reference works for canonical authors, including Austen, Blake, Byron, Coleridge, Keats, Scott, Shelley, and Wordsworth, and covers journals and newsletters devoted to the author, bibliographies, handbooks, editions, concordances, and biographies. The *Reference Guide for English Studies* concludes with three indexes of subjects, authors/compilers/editors, and titles.

Marcuse's strengths are the inclusion of reference works concerned with specific authors and the recommended works bibliographies. One needs to be aware that since the guide only covers resources published before 1990, a supplementary source, such as O'Neill's *Literature of the Romantic Period: A Bibliographical Guide* (described in Chapter 4), should be used to identify more current resources.

Romantic Period Encyclopedias and Companions

Bloom, Abigail Burnham, ed. *Nineteenth-Century British Women Writers: A Bio-Bibliographical Critical Sourcebook.* Westport, CT: Greenwood Press, 2000.

Curran, Stuart, ed. *The Cambridge Companion to British Romanticism.* Cambridge: Cambridge University Press, 1993.

Krueger, Christine L., general ed. *Encyclopedia of British Writers.* Vol. 1: 19th Century. New York: Facts on File, 2003.

McCalman, Iain, general ed. *An Oxford Companion to the Romantic Age: British Culture 1776–1832.* New York: Oxford University Press, 1999.

Murray, Christopher John, ed. *Encyclopedia of the Romantic Era, 1760–1850.* 2 vols. New York: Fitzroy Dearborn, 2004.

Richetti, John, ed. *The Cambridge Companion to the Eighteenth-Century Novel.* New York: Cambridge University Press, 1996.

Sitter, John, ed. *The Cambridge Companion to Eighteenth-Century Poetry.* New York: Cambridge University Press, 2001.

Wu, Duncan, ed. *A Companion to Romanticism.* Malden, MA: Blackwell Publishers, 1998.

Although the terms companion and encyclopedia may be used interchangeably, the sources profiled in this section either adopt a broad scope illustrated by numerous brief entries that cover a wide range of related topics, or provide detailed, critical essays to examine the period through a more focused lens. In general, encyclopedias present signed entries arranged in alphabetical order that range in length from a paragraph to several pages. Designed for ready reference, these entries feature factual information about important figures, works, and concepts. Cross-references are provided to related entries, and the entries typically conclude with a bibliography of selected secondary sources. Most encyclopedias also contain an index, and some also include supplementary material, such as subject bibliographies, chronologies, illustrations, and thematic lists of entries. Companions to numerous disciplines published by Oxford University Press represent this particular type of encyclopedic resource (e.g., *Oxford Companion to English Literature*, *Oxford Companion to Philosophy*). In contrast, the other kind of companion resource usually offers a more in-depth treatment of the subject with fewer but longer scholarly essays that can range from ten to twenty-five pages. These essays frequently are arranged thematically, and end with a reference list, as well as suggested sources for further reading. Typically called companions, handbooks, or guides, these resources also can feature supplementary bibliographies, chronologies, and thematic lists, in addition to one or more indexes. Reference books such as *The Cambridge Companion to Romanticism* fall within this category. Regardless of approach or format, the resources described in this section present information about the authors, works, themes, and historical and social context for the Romantic period.

Recipient of an ALA Outstanding Reference Source award in 2004, the ***Encyclopedia of the Romantic Era, 1760–1850*** offers an interdisciplinary approach to the longer Romantic period in Britain, continental Europe, and the Americas. The 770 entries cover people; individual works of literature, music, and art; cultural and historical national surveys; and essays addressing particular themes, concepts, critical approaches (e.g., deconstruction, feminist and gay approaches), and events. The encyclopedia provides survey essays not only for Britain, France, Germany, and the United States but also for countries and regions as diverse as Switzerland, Portugal, the Ukraine, Spanish America and Brazil, Denmark, and the Balkans, in addition to essays on Jews and Jewish culture. Most of the essays are concerned with writers, artists, composers, and philosophers. The essays devoted to British literature address fifty-three authors, in addition to British poetry, fiction, drama, folk literature, letters, travel writing, and literary criticism, but not periodicals. The signed essays can be accessed by subject lists (e.g., architecture, art, dance, general surveys and themes, literature and thought, music, and science) or by national development lists. Be sure to check the comprehensive list of entries, however, since the thematic lists are sometimes incomplete. For example, the entry "Drama: Britain" is omitted from the "Literature and Thought" category in the list of entries by subject, as well as from the list of entries by national development. Despite these inconsistencies, this is a good source for comparing the British Romantic period with contemporary cultural developments in other European countries, the United States, and to a lesser extent, countries in Latin America.

Following a historical overview of Romantic-era encyclopedias, the two-part ***An Oxford Companion to the Romantic Age: British Culture 1776–1832*** begins with forty-one major essays organized in the following thematic headings: "Transforming Polity and Nation" (e.g., revolution, war, democracy, women, empire, slavery); "Reordering Social and Private Worlds" (e.g., religion, sensibility, poverty, industrialization, class, education); "Culture, Consumption, and the Arts" (e.g., consumerism, publishing, popular culture, theatre, poetry, prose, novels); and "Emerging Knowledges" (e.g., enlightenment, political economy, antiquarianism, exploration, language, literary theory). The second part of the encyclopedia features brief entries on individuals, movements, events, ideas, and terms relevant to the period's cultural history. Take note that titles of works do not have individual entries but are discussed within the author's entry. More than one hundred black and white illustrations enhance the entries and include reproductions of engravings, paintings, prints, portraits, texts, and artifacts. A single index serves the essays in Part 1 only and should be used in conjunction with the alphabetical arrangement of Part 2. This encyclopedia is valuable for its treatment of historical and cultural topics relevant to study of the period, the complementary descriptive entries of people, events, topics, and for its emphasis on British culture.

Designed as an introduction to the range of contemporary theoretical approaches to British literature of the Romantic period, **A *Companion to Romanticism*** features fifty-two scholarly essays arranged in four parts. Part 1, "Contexts and Perspectives, 1790–1830," provides historical and cultural background information in essays that address, for example, the concept of Romanticism, Britain at war, literature and religion, and the Romantic reader. Part 2, "Readings," features critical introductions to twenty-three individual authors of the period with essays on specific works, such as Blake's *Songs of Innocence and Experience*, Baillie's plays, Smith's *Beachy Head*, Hazlitt's the *Spirit of the Age*, and Hemans's *Records of Women*, in addition to an essay about anti-Jacobin poetry. "Genres and Modes" forms the focus for discussions in Part 3 about drama, the novel, Gothic fiction, parody and imitation, travel writing, and Romantic literary criticism. Part 4, titled "Issues and Debates," presents specific critical approaches to the period, including gender studies, feminism, new historicism, ecocriticism, psychological approaches, dialogic approaches, and performative language and speech-act theory. Other essays in this section cover slavery and Romantic writing, the Romantic imagination, England and Germany, Romantic responses to science, and Romantic authors' relationships to Shakespeare and Milton.

The Cambridge Companion to British Romanticism offers eleven original essays by scholars from the United States, Canada, and the United Kingdom that survey the "historical roots, intellectual ferment, and the cultural range of the Romantic age" (xiv) in Britain. The essays discuss the following topics: Romanticism, criticism and theory; Romanticism and the Enlightenment; poetry in the age of revolution; German Romantic idealism; Romanticism and language; the role of contemporary reviews; Romantic Hellenism; women readers and authors; Romantic fiction; poetry; and Romantic literature and the visual arts. An appended bibliography complements the essays and covers standard editions for canonical authors, as well as related works on philosophy, criticism and theory, language, history, the periodical press, women authors, Romantic Hellenism, fiction, poetry, and the culture of Romanticism. A chronology features primarily published texts and selected historical events for the years 1749 to 1830.

For scholars working with figures traditionally associated with the eighteenth century, *The Cambridge Companion to the Eighteenth-Century Novel* and *The Cambridge Companion to Eighteenth-Century Poetry* provide scholarly essays on individual authors, themes, genres, and social and historical contexts for the period. The companion to the novel features chapters primarily on individual authors, but also addresses women writers and the eighteenth-century novel, sentimental novels, and the Enlightenment, popular culture, and Gothic fiction. More thematic in approach, the companion to poetry presents chapters on publishing and reading poetry, "Nature" poetry, women poets and readers, the poetry of sensibility, and "Pre-Romanticism" and the ends of eighteenth-century poetry.

Focused entirely on authors, the *Encyclopedia of British Writers, 19th Century* spans the century from Burke through Shaw, and includes entries for many early nineteenth-century figures. The entries provide biographical and literary career overviews; some also present a separate "critical analysis" of specific works or prevailing themes, and most include representative texts by and about the author. An authors' timeline lists the profiled authors in order of birth date and a bibliography of critical studies, anthologies, and reference books concludes the encyclopedia.

Originally conceived as an aid to professors of Victorian literature who wanted to expand their syllabi beyond the familiar canonical authors and texts, the *Nineteenth-Century British Women Writers: A Bio-Bibliographical Critical Sourcebook* features entries for 113 British women poets, novelists, journalists, travel writers, letter writers, authors of self-help books, and biographers who produced their work primarily during the nineteenth century. Each of the signed entries consists of four parts: a biographical profile; a discussion of the author's major works and themes; an overview of the author's critical reception from contemporary reviews through the present; and a bibliography of works by the author and works about her with notes on texts that were

in print at the time of the sourcebook's publication. In the case of pro-
lific authors, the bibliography is limited to major works only. The entries vary in detail and length, ranging from three to four pages for authors such as Landon and Hemans to eight to ten pages for Austen, the
Brontës, and Martineau. Although the selection is weighted towards
Victorian figures, several authors of the Romantic period are covered.
A concluding bibliography lists additional sources by category and
includes recommended general, poetry, and prose anthologies, in addition to works about women authors of the period and a selection of
electronic resources.

Genre and General British Literary
Encyclopedias and Companions

Drabble, Margaret, ed. *The Oxford Companion to English Literature*.
6th ed. New York: Oxford University Press, 2000.

Edwards, Hywel Teifi, ed. *A Guide to Welsh Literature*. Vol. V (c.
1800–1900). Cardiff: University of Wales Press, 2000.

Hogle, Jerrold E., ed. *The Cambridge Companion to Gothic Fiction*.
New York: Cambridge University Press, 2002.

Jarvis, Branwen, ed. *A Guide to Welsh Literature*. Vol. IV (c. 1700–
1800). Cardiff: University of Wales Press, 2000.

Mulvey-Roberts, Marie, ed. *The Handbook to Gothic Literature*. New
York: New York University Press, 1998.

Ousby, Ian, ed. *The Cambridge Guide to Literature in English*. Rev. ed.
New York: Cambridge University Press, 1993.

Royle, Trevor. *The Mainstream Companion to Scottish Literature*. Edinburgh: Mainstream Publishing, 1993.

Schlueter, Paul and June Schlueter, eds. *An Encyclopedia of British
Women Writers*. Rev. and expanded ed. New Brunswick, NJ: Rut-
gers University Press, 1998.

Serafin, Steven R. and Valerie Grosvenor Myer, eds. *The Continuum
Encyclopedia of British Literature*. New York: Continuum, 2003.

Stephens, Meic, comp. and ed. *The New Companion to the Literature
of Wales*. Cardiff: University of Wales Press, 1998.

Welch, Robert, ed. *The Oxford Companion to Irish Literature*. New
York: Oxford University Press, 1996.

The reference sources in this section are similar in format to the encyclopedias and companions described above, but instead of focusing on
one literary period, they concentrate on either a genre (e.g., Gothic literature), or the history of a national literature (e.g., British, Scottish,

Irish, Welsh). Although their coverage is broader than the traditional Romantic era, they may prove to be useful resources for finding information about authors and topics not addressed in the Romantic period sources.

Covering 250 years of the Gothic tradition, *The Cambridge Companion to Gothic Fiction* seeks to explain "the historical, cultural, and aesthetic forces" (17) that shaped British, European, and American Gothic prose, poetry, drama, and film from the eighteenth to the twenty-first century. The *Companion* presents fourteen scholarly essays that address the following topics: the beginnings of Gothic fiction; the Gothic and British Romantic writing; Scottish and Irish Gothic; English Gothic theatre; the height of Gothic in the 1790s; French and German Gothic; colonial and postcolonial Gothic in the Caribbean, and contemporary Gothic. Additional features include a chronology of literary, dramatic, and selected historical events from 1750 to 2001, a bibliography organized by major Gothic texts, anthologies, critical studies, and bibliographies, and a filmography.

The Handbook to Gothic Literature also covers primarily British, European, and American Gothic literature from the eighteenth to the twentieth century, as well as the Gothic in related disciplines of art, architecture, film, music, and photography. The 123 signed entries are arranged in two sections, "Gothic Writers and Key Terms" and "Gothic Specialisms." The first section features longer essays (one to thirteen pages) on thirty-five individual authors, national movements (e.g., American, Australian, English-Canadian, German, Irish, Russian, Scottish, Welsh), genres (e.g., drama, film, novel, romance, ghost stories), schools (e.g., Frenétique, graveyard), and topics, such as Romanticism, female Gothic, sublime, terror, madness, death, orientalism, and imagination. The second section, "Gothic Specialisms," offers brief entries (one to three paragraphs) on peripheral topics, including the fantastic, doppelgänger, *Northanger* novels, sensation fiction, sensibility, and transgression. The handbook concludes with a bibliography of selected books and journal articles for further reading, including general works, the female Gothic, and authors Mary Shelley, Radcliffe, and Walpole. Unfortunately, the *Handbook* does not provide selected bibliographies for all the authors and key terms; nor is there an index. These weaknesses detract from an otherwise useful resource.

If you are looking for biographical information about a female author not included in *Nineteenth-Century British Women Writers*, *An Encyclopedia of British Women Writers* features profiles for six hundred authors who were either born or lived in Great Britain primarily from the eighteenth century through the twentieth century, although selective figures from earlier centuries are also included. The entries begin by noting known place and date of birth and death, parents, spouse(s) and date of marriage(s), and pseudonyms, if applicable. The main content of the entry provides an overview of the author's literary career, discusses plot and reception of specific works, and provides a brief assessment of the author's current critical stature. Each essay then concludes with a list of the author's primary works in book form and a bibliography of selected books, critical essays, and relevant reference works published through 1997. Alternative names, such as pseudonyms, married names, titles, etc., are cross-referenced within the encyclopedia's alphabetical arrangement. *An Encyclopedia of British Women Writers* covers many authors from the Romantic period, including Eliza Acton, Caroline Lamb, Charlotte Bury, and Clara Reeve.

Although *The Mainstream Companion to Scottish Literature* broadly covers Scottish literature from its beginnings through the twentieth century, you may find authors here neglected by the other sources described in the preceding section. The *Companion* features primarily biographical entries for Scottish poets, novelists, dramatists, and critics who wrote in English, Scots, or Gaelic, in addition to entries for other prose writers (e.g., historians, philosophers, diarists), individual works, literary movements, institutions, historical events, and people. These individuals either were born in Scotland, had Scottish parentage, or resided in Scotland long enough to contribute to its literary heritage. The author entries provide biographical information, discuss principal works, and conclude with brief bibliographies of the author's works and selected critical and biographical studies.

If you are interested in Irish or Welsh authors, works, and topics, be sure to consult *The Oxford Companion to Irish Literature*, *The New Companion to the Literature of Wales* (originally published as *The Oxford Companion to the Literature of Wales*. Oxford: Oxford University Press, 1986) and *A Guide to Welsh Literature*, Volume IV (c. 1700–1800) and Volume V (c. 1800–1900). The first two sources are similar to other Oxford companion reference works in their encyclopedic format and scope. *A Guide to Welsh Literature*, in contrast, features the in-depth treatment and thematic essays typical of companion reference sources.

In addition to these sources, you may want or need to consult other general British literature encyclopedias. *The Continuum Encyclopedia of British Literature* offers more than 1,200 entries on authors and individual works, as well as topical essays on the Gothic novel, Romanticism, sentiment, and nature and landscape. The author entries feature biographical information, a critical overview of the author's work, and a brief bibliography of books and journal articles. The encyclopedia also includes an outline of monarchs of Great Britain, a historical-literary timeline (up to 2002), literary awards and prizes, and one index. *The Oxford Companion to English Literature* and *The Cambridge Guide to Literature in English* both feature brief entries for writers, individual works, literary groups and movements, genres, and related literary topics and events.

Biographical Sources

Dictionary of Literary Biography. Detroit: Gale, 1978–.
Matthew, Henry C. G. and Brian Harrison, eds. *Oxford Dictionary of National Biography* (in association with The British Academy: From the earliest times to the year 2000). 61 vols. Rev. ed. New York: Oxford University Press, 2004.

Many of the encyclopedias discussed above provide biographical information for authors and figures of the Romantic period. The *Oxford Dictionary of National Biography* and the *Dictionary of Literary Biography* are wide-ranging sources that focus specifically on biographical profiles. You should check these sources to supplement the encyclopedia entries, or to find information for figures not covered in the preceding sources.

The *Oxford Dictionary of National Biography* (*ODNB*) provides more than fifty thousand articles about influential people who were born or lived in the British Isles or its territories from the fourth century B.C. through the twentieth century. A compilation and revision of the prominent *Dictionary of National Biography*, the Oxford version features rewritten or revised entries for all 38,807 subjects covered in the original *DNB* (1885–1900) and its supplements (1901–1996), in addition to new articles for a total coverage of 54,922 people. An effort was made not only to extend the coverage in all periods and professions, but also to strengthen previously neglected areas, particularly of women, people in business and labor, Britain's Roman rulers, pre-independence Americans, and twentieth-century subjects (viii). As with its predecessor, all figures in the *ODNB* are dead, and must have died by December 31, 2000 in order to be included. Although most of the entries concern individuals, 408 entries address significant families or groups.

The alphabetically arranged entries focus on the subject's life and work with factual information about birth, education, marriage, death, burial, parents and spouses, and places of residence. The primary focus of the entry is to provide an overview and assessment of the person's "activities, character, and significance" (v) and sometimes indicate the person's posthumous reputation. The entries range from a few paragraphs to well-developed essays arranged by chronological and topical headings. For example, the Wordsworth essay illustrates the typical range of coverage for canonical figures with the following headings: "Childhood and schooling"; "Cambridge and the Alps, 1787–1790"; "London, 1791, and France"; "London to Racedown, 1793–1795"; "Racedown and Alfoxden, 1795–1798"; "Alfoxden to Grasmere, 1797–1799"; "Grasmere, 1800–1806"; "Writings, 1798–1807"; "From Dove Cottage to Rydal Mount"; "Writings, 1807–1815"; "Travel and revision, 1815–1832"; "Later writings"; "Personal characteristics"; "Friendships"; "Final years, 1833–1850"; "Aftermath"; and "The poet." Other figures receive a more condensed treatment, such as John Clare: "Early life"; "Love, marriage, and poetry"; and "Decline." Be aware that only significant publications by subject authors are discussed within the context of the essay, rather than appended in a comprehensive bibliography. All the essays are signed by the contributor, the original author is noted in the case of revised essays, and the essays conclude with a list of sources used to write the profile. In addition, archival repositories for manuscripts and papers, resources for likenesses of the subject, and the person's wealth at death are noted. More than ten thousand black and white images organized by the National Portrait Gallery provide visual references for the *ODNB*'s subjects and include portraits, coins, effigies, and iconographic material. A separately published volume, the *Index of Contributors*, lists the authors who either wrote new material or revised previous essays, and indicates the articles for which they were responsible.

The *Oxford Dictionary of National Biography* is also available online as a subscription database from Oxford University Press. The advanced "People" search option permits field searching by name, areas of interest (e.g., literature, theatre, travel and exploration), sex, life dates, events (e.g., birth, baptism, education, burial), religious affiliation, and by keyword within all or specific parts of the essay. One strange quirk exists in both the quick and advanced name search; if you type the subject's name in the reverse order typically used by library catalogs (e.g., Baillie, Joanna), be sure to separate the name with a comma or you will retrieve no results. Unlike a library catalog, you can also type the subject's name in regular order (e.g., Joanna Baillie). Other search options include keyword and phrase searching within the article text or the reference material appended to the articles, by contributor, or an image search by artist and date.

The essays in the online database are the same as those in the print volumes. They are enhanced, however, by hyperlinks to other relevant essays, such as those for related or affiliated figures (e.g., Mary Shelley, Clara Clairmont, Mary Jane Godwin, William Godwin, Mary

Wollstonecraft, William Godwin (1803–1832), and Percy Shelley), as well as links to original *Dictionary of National Biography* essays in the *DNB* archive (for example, the one for Mary Shelley was written in 1897). Some essays also possess links to additional online resources, including entries for the subject in the *National Register of Archives*. The online *ODNB* also provides thematic lists of biographical subjects (e.g., poets laureate, 1668–2000, masters of the king's and queen's music, 1626–2000) or historical events, such as Trevithick's locomotive of 1804 and the development of steam technology, or women and religion in the *ODNB*.

The *ODNB* is an excellent place to gather introductory biographical information about British Romantic-era authors and figures. The list of secondary sources, archival repositories, and image resources may prove to be especially useful for figures not accorded their own bibliography in other Romantic or literary reference sources. For those people who only have access to the original *Dictionary of National Biography*, read Harner's description in the *Literary Research Guide* for an overview of the *DNB*'s strengths and weaknesses.

Each volume in the multi-volume series, **Dictionary of Literary Biography** (*DLB*) (currently at three hundred volumes) focuses on writers of a specific genre, national literature, and/or literary period. Although the *DLB* covers writers from antiquity to the present and from countries around the world, there is a decided emphasis on British and American authors. Students of the Romantic era will be concerned with volumes that address this period. Relevant examples published in the last ten years include: *British Children's Writers, 1800–1880*; *British Short-Fiction Writers, 1800–1880*; *British Reform Writers, 1789–1832*; *British Literary Book Trade, 1700–1820*; and *Nineteenth-Century British Literary Biographers*. Older titles cover British Romantic prose writers, poets, and novelists, as well as prose writers from 1660 to 1800 and British literary publishing houses from 1820 to 1880.

Within each volume, the signed author profiles begin with the author's birth and death dates, note cross-references to entries in other volumes, and list the author's books, including editions and collections. The main body of the essay discusses the author's life and literary career by highlighting selected works that fit the volume's thematic focus. An assessment of the author's influence and current reputation are also noted. The essays are illustrated with portraits, photographs, or sample manuscript and/or text pages. A concluding bibliography frequently lists some or all of the following categories: published letters, bibliographies, biographies, selected critical studies, and manuscript/archival repositories. In addition, some volumes feature special appendices. For example *British Romantic Prose Writers, 1789–1832* contains an appendix on literary reviewing, with individual chapters about *La Belle Assemblée, Blackwood's Edinburgh Magazine, British Critic*, the *British Review and London Critical Journal, Eclectic Review, Edinburgh Review, Examiner, Literary Chronicle and Weekly Review, London Magazine, Monthly Review, New Monthly Magazine, Quarterly Review, Spectator, Tait's Edinburgh Magazine*, and the *Westminster Review*. For further information about these periodicals and best practices for conducting periodical review research, see Chapter 6, "Contemporary Reviews." All volumes also include a list of books for further reading on the designated topic. Since authors often are covered in more than one volume, the researcher should consult the cumulative index in the latest volume in order to identify all relevant entries in the preceding volumes.

The *Dictionary of Literary Biography* is also offered online as a subscription database from Gale, either separately or as part of the *Literature Resource Center* <http://www.gale.com/LitRC/>, and provides access to over ten thousand essays that comprise the print volumes. Field searches may be conducted by subject author, title of work, birth year, death year, nationality, subject or genre, and essay topic, or you can search by keyword in the full text of the essay. Additional search fields include ethnicity, gender, and *DLB* volume title (which can also be browsed). The online essays are almost identical to those in the printed volumes with a few noted exceptions; the essay bibliographies are sometimes slightly rearranged and there aren't any reproductions of photographs, paintings, or manuscript pages. Advantages to the database include hyperlinks to other *DLB* essays about the author, hyperlinks within the essay to other subject authors, and a greater range of access points, such as the ability to search for topics or authors mentioned within the full text of all the essays.

Chronologies

Cox, Michael, ed. *The Oxford Chronology of English Literature*. 2 vols. New York: Oxford University Press, 2002.

Even though this section describes only one English literary chronology, take note that the website, *Romantic Chronology* (described in Chapter 10), provides a detailed listing of literary, cultural, and historical events for the years 1785 to 1851, with selective coverage of the seventeenth and eighteenth centuries. The *Cambridge Companion to British Romanticism* and the *Cambridge Companion to Gothic Fiction* include period chronologies, as do many reference works devoted to individual authors.

Spanning the years from 1474 to 2000, *The Oxford Chronology of English Literature* provides a list of printed books arranged by their year of imprint (or actual year of publication) that the editors considered "significant *and* representative works" (xiii). The *Chronology* covers over four thousand authors and almost thirty thousand works, with an emphasis on poetry, novels, drama, and short stories but also including non-fiction (e.g., biographies, letters, criticism), historical and literary scholarship, and reference works, such as the *Encyclopaedia Britannica*. An attempt was made to represent a wide range of authors from canonical figures to lesser-known writers, to illustrate the contributions of women authors, and to include works from popular and high culture. For each year, the entries are arranged alphabetically by the author's last name and include title of the work, title-page matter, imprint details, and notes, including information such as serialization details, illustrator, dates of succeeding editions, contextual information, and cross-references to related titles. The *Chronology* is a good source for comparing which authors and works were being published simultaneously. Since its focus is only on printed literature, however, you need to consult another chronology in order to place these works within their historical context, such as the chronologies described above. Three indexes, author, title, and translated authors, comprise the entire second volume.

Individual Author Sources

Becker, Michael G., Robert J. Dilligan, and Todd K. Bender, eds. *A Concordance to the Poems of John Keats*. New York: Garland Publishing, 1981.

Bold, Alan. *A Burns Companion*. New York: St. Martin's Press, 1991.

Damon, S. Foster. *A Blake Dictionary: The Ideas and Symbols of William Blake*. Rev. ed. Hanover, NH: for Brown University Press by University Press of New England, 1988. New foreword and annotated bibliography by Morris Eaves.

Garrett, Martin. *A Mary Shelley Chronology*. New York: Palgrave, 2002.

Poplawski, Paul. *A Jane Austen Encyclopedia*. Westport, CT: Greenwood Press, 1998.

General reference works devoted to a specific author exist in many forms, including dictionaries, encyclopedias, chronologies, companions, handbooks, and concordances. Typically, canonical figures are better represented by these sources than lesser-known figures. If you want to identify this type of resource for a particular author, you can consult the appropriate author entry in the print reference source, the *Cambridge Bibliography of English Literature*, or you can search your local library catalog or a union catalog such as *WorldCat*. To conduct this kind of inquiry, do a keyword search with your author's name and the type of resource. For example, type in the search string *blake and concordance** or *austen and encyclopedia**. You will discover that there are Library of Congress subject headings for some types of reference sources but not for others (e.g., companions), and that some headings use the plural form (e.g., dictionaries) while others use the singular (e.g., chronology). Since companions usually have a "Criticism and interpretation" subject heading, you can retrieve these types of resources with a keyword search that will usually pick up the terms *companion or companions* in the title or series title, such as in the series *Cambridge Companions to Literature*. In fact, this series features companions to Wollstonecraft, Coleridge, Keats, Austen, Wordsworth, Blake, Byron, and Mary Shelley. If you are not able to find a separately published chronology for your author, keep in mind that author bibliographies, anthologies, or critical studies may include a chronology as supplemental material. Sometimes this can be determined by a keyword search in the library catalog or *WorldCat* if the book's contents are indexed. The *Cambridge Companions to Literature* series frequently includes a chronology in their publications. Sample subject headings follow to illustrate the range and format typical for general author reference sources:

> Blake, William, 1757–1827—Concordances
> Austen, Jane, 1775–1817—Encyclopedias
> Wordsworth, William, 1770–1850—Chronology
> Keats, John, 1795–1821—Criticism and interpretation—Handbooks, manuals, etc.

This section will provide a representative selection of general author resources.

*A **Jane Austen Encyclopedia*** serves as several reference books in one source. The three-part encyclopedia begins with the following chronologies: one of Austen's life and writing career from her father's birth in 1731 to the 1996 publication of *Jane Austen: Collected Poems and Verse of the Austen Family*; a narrative overview of historical events from 1750 to 1820; and a literary timeline from 1749 to 1820 that aims to place Austen's works within their literary context, as well as to indicate by an asterisk which works and/or authors Austen read or was familiar with from evidence in her letters, novels, or biographical information (e.g., Mary Brunton's *Self-Control, a Novel*). These chronologies are enhanced with the following contextual material: a map of places associated with Austen; a genealogical family chart; portraits of her father and brothers; fashion sketches from 1790–1820; a sketch of carriage types, circa 1800; and photographs of Bath, Chawton Cottage, Lyme Regis, and Winchester.

The main body of the encyclopedia consists of alphabetically arranged entries for all of Austen's works, including her juvenilia, entries for almost every character from these works, and biographical profiles for Austen and her immediate family. The entries range from one to two sentences for minor characters to several page essays on Austen "Criticism" and "Themes and Concerns." The novels also receive a longer treatment, including an extensive plot summary, lists of major and minor characters, and references to works in the concluding bibliographies. These bibliographies consist of works by Austen, a list of critical and biographical books and pamphlets on Austen published through 1996 with a chronological summary of these works, and a bibliography of selected critical essays from the nineteenth century through 1996, emphasizing works published after 1983. The encyclopedia concludes with an index; the "themes and concerns" heading leads to entries for keywords, such as affectation, courtship, duplicity, income, prudence, sense, travel and journeying, and wit and wittiness. More than just an encyclopedia, a *Jane Austen Encyclopedia* is an author reference work that fulfills a range of research needs.

Part of Palgrave's *Author Chronologies* series, **A Mary Shelley Chronology** presents a narrative account of Shelley's life and literary career from her birth, August 30, 1797, to her death on February 1, 1851. The chronology is arranged by year; events are noted by month and also by day, when known. In entries that range from a sentence to a paragraph, Mary Shelley's publications, travels, reading, collaborations with other writers, activities, relevant activities and publications of her family and friends, and historical events are described. References are provided for some entries and for all quotations, so that the reader can consult the original text. The main sources used to compile the chronology are appended in a bibliography and include works by Mary Shelley, critical studies and journal articles, and William Godwin's, Claire Clairmont's, and Percy Shelley's letters and journals.

Using Stillinger's *The Poems of John Keats* (Harvard, 1978) as its text source, **A Concordance to the Poems of John Keats** provides an alphabetical list of the English words used by Keats in all of his poems, the play *Otho the Great*, the fragment of the play *King Stephen*, the

Morgan Library fragment associated with the *Eve of St. Mark*, all headings, subtitles, and substantive variants, including Keats's notes and dedications, and provides the context lines for these words. Epigraphs and end notes that consist of proverbs, song titles, and lines of verse and prose from classical and modern authors are excluded. In the word entry, the following information is outlined for each context line: the poem's full or abbreviated title; the copy text date; book, part, canto, act and scene or stanza, and the line number; and notes, such as variant readings, deletions, and alterations, if any, and the manuscript(s) that contain the variants. In the introductory note, the editors advise users to consult Stillinger's edition in conjunction with the *Concordance* for the "fullest understanding of all substantive variants, emendations, and alternations in the collated texts" (vii). The *Concordance* features three supplemental tables: word frequencies in alphabetical order, word frequencies in rank order, and type/token ratios which can be used together to determine the frequency distribution of each word, or type, and occurrence of a word, or token (x). Two additional indexes cover omitted words, and poem titles included in the *Concordance* and their corresponding page numbers in *The Poems of John Keats*.

Described by Eaves in the introduction as "a digest of Damon's ideas that had become common property over the years" (x), *A Blake Dictionary: The Ideas and Symbols of William Blake* describes words, places, and concepts of symbolic significance found in Blake's writing, including Biblical characters and place names. Originally published in 1965, this revised edition features a forward, an annotated bibliography, and an index written by the well-known Blake scholar Morris Eaves; otherwise the content is essentially the same as Damon's original text. The entries are arranged from "Abarim" to "Zoa," and feature textual references to support the explanation. For example, the entry for "Horses" states that horses represent Reason, they are associated with tigers, and they are animals of Urizen, with supporting quotations from *The Marriage of Heaven and Hell*, *The Four Zoas*, *Jerusalem*, and *Milton*. All textual references are to *The Complete Writings of William Blake* (1957), edited by Geoffrey Keynes, unless otherwise noted. Eaves's index provides important cross-references to subjects addressed by the *Dictionary* that are not given their own entry, especially to subjects that may be discussed in places not obvious to the novice reader. He cites, for example, the "Druids" entry that contains eighteenth-century theories on the idea of Britain as the seat of Biblical history (463). The annotated bibliography presents works cited in the preface, works about S. Foster Damon, selected Blake biographies, Erdman's standard edition of Blake's works, facsimiles, study aids, works about Blake's painting and printmaking, and criticism of the

Illuminated Books since Damon's *Dictionary*, published through 1986. The *Dictionary* also includes ten black and white illustrations from selected works, and two maps of London and its neighboring villages in Blake's time.

Designed as a "biographical and critical guide to Burns" (xi), *A Burns Companion* offers a wide range of contextual and critical material about the author. Arranged in six parts, the first part, "Burns in Context," features a narrative chronology of events from the poet's life and literary career from 1757 to 1796, biographical sketches of people associated with the Burns circle, and a topography of places from his life and works. Several of the biographical sketches contain direct quotations from the profiled figure about Burns, or quotations from Burns about the subject. In these cases, references are provided for the source texts. The next two sections, "Aspects of Burns," and "An Approach to Burns," present essays on dialect and diction, as well as Burns and religion, politics, philosophy, alcohol, the theatre, sex, and his literary reputation. The main body of the companion offers critical discussions of selected poems, verse epistles, songs, election ballads, epitaphs and epigrams, letters, and the common place books. For the twenty-five poems represented, Bold notes the date of composition, publication information, and reception, as well as thematic content. A bibliography covers Burns bibliographies, reference books, manuscripts, editions of verse and prose, biographies, critical studies, topography, related studies, fictional accounts, and journals. The companion concludes with appended textual material, a glossary of Scots words used by Burns and their English equivalent, an index of poem titles, and a general index.

Conclusion

General reference sources, such as those described in this chapter, are initial and supplementary tools for research. Depending on the individual source, they can outline selected resources for investigating a literary topic, provide specific factual information (e.g., birth, death, and publication dates), or serve as introductions to the authors, texts, genres, prevailing themes, and historical background of the Romantic period. By understanding the typical layout and kinds of information to be found in the different general reference source categories, you will have a better idea of which source to consult for specific research problems or needs.

Chapter 3
Library Catalogs

A major resource for your research will be library catalogs, covered by this chapter. Included here are library catalogs themselves, as you would find in a typical academic library, as well as related items such as national union catalogs, the catalogs of national libraries, and union catalogs maintained by cooperatives, specifically OCLC and Research Library Group.

Library catalogs have changed radically in the past twenty years, from card catalogs to online public access catalogs (OPACs). Even though most undergraduate and perhaps many graduate students may not have used a traditional card catalog before, it is important to keep in mind that online catalogs are a relatively recent phenomenon. As a consequence, even though many libraries now feature their catalogs in an electronic format, not every item in a library's collection may be included in the online catalog, especially in the case of older materials. Although most research will be conducted using online catalogs, you may still need to rely on printed catalogs or finding aids to identify relevant materials, or to ensure a comprehensive search.

Library catalogs will be essential to your literary research, whether using your local university's catalog to find books by a specific author or on a subject, or searching an international union catalog such as *WorldCat* to identify which libraries possess a particular edition of an author's work or a Romantic-era periodical. Searching an online catalog entails using the same general access points as a traditional catalog, that is, searching by author, title, or subject. The main difference and advantage of an online catalog, however, is that it usually permits keyword searching of the title, subject heading, and sometimes author, publisher, series, contents, and notes fields, as discussed in Chapter 1. Other search options often include periodical title, ISBN/ISSN, Library of Congress call number, or government document number. In addition, online catalog searches frequently can be limited by publication date, language, and format. Many catalogs also feature opportunities to print, download, and e-mail records, as well as format search results in specific citation formats, such as MLA and APA.

Although online library catalogs will vary according to the way the catalog database is structured and the type of software used to search the catalog, each library nevertheless follows certain standards when constructing records for items in their collection. These standards include cataloging items by the Anglo-American cataloging rules, using controlled vocabulary, and placing records in MARC (**Ma**chine **R**eadable **C**ataloging) format. Followed in most English-speaking countries, the *Anglo-American Cataloguing Rules* (*AACR2R*) provides guidelines for describing an item's publication and physical information in a consistent format. The cataloging process also entails using controlled vocabulary, words and phrases selected by an organization to impose standard language on bibliographic and content description. Controlled vocabulary includes subject headings, standardized phrases that are used to describe an item's content, and authority headings that provide a designated phrase for an author's name or a serial title. In the United States, Library of Congress subject and authority headings are the standards used by most academic and public libraries, while more specialized libraries may use other headings such as Sears (general headings created by Minnie E. Sears and used primarily in school and small public libraries) and MeSH (National Library of Medicine medical subject headings). After an item is cataloged and subject headings are assigned, this standardized bibliographic information is then placed into specific fields within a MARC record so that the information can be read and exchanged electronically. The development of MARC bibliographic records and computer-generated catalogs has contributed to the sharing of bibliographic information between libraries, and has increased access to library holdings worldwide.

The standards outlined above enable the researcher to find some consistency across the range of library catalogs he or she will encounter, especially since the primary access points—author, title, and subject headings—will be cataloged similarly in the United States and Britain. You will discover that author names generally are cataloged with the same authority heading (although there are many exceptions in the case of older materials), and subject headings are fairly consistent for items cataloged in the United States. Despite these similarities, however, keep in mind that each library can structure its catalog database differently. The savvy researcher will identify which fields a particular database indexes by consulting the catalog's help screen for sample searches, or by requesting assistance from a reference librarian. And, although author, title, and subject heading searches are often consistent for library catalogs in the United States, researchers will discover that keyword searches can vary tremendously. You will need to review an individual catalog's help screen to identify which fields are searched by a keyword search, and also to determine if the catalog software executes Boolean, phrase, or proximity keyword searching. Be sure to review Chapter 1, "Basics of Online Searching," for an overview of search components and techniques.

The search strategies described in this chapter are tailored to reflect best practices for particular types of library catalogs at the time the resources were reviewed. Use the information in these examples as general guidelines that may need to be modified depending on the indexing and search capabilities of the particular catalog you are searching.

Author Searches and Evaluation of Results

To find works by a Romantic-era author, you will want to begin with an author field search in your library catalog. In the context of this volume, works can be defined as the writings created by an individual or several authors that may or may not have been published. A work can be a novel, essay, poem, play, letter, or a collection of these endeavors. For canonical authors, an author field search will be a straightforward process of putting in the author's last name, followed by first name (e.g., *keats, john*, or *austen, jane*).

To make certain that you have the correct author, use the authoritative name heading which includes the author's birth and death dates (e.g., "Keats, John, 1795–1821"). If you don't know this information, scan the list of results after conducting the simple name search until you find the authoritative heading. An alternative way to find the correct author heading is to do a title search of one of their works. The title search *mansfield park* will retrieve the author heading "Austen, Jane, 1775–1817." Sometimes additional information is included in the heading, as in the official entry for Lord Byron, who is given the lengthy assignment, "Byron, George Gordon Byron, Baron, 1788–1824."

Keep in mind, however, that not every work by your author will have been cataloged with an authoritative Library of Congress heading; you will find many exceptions, especially in the case of older editions. Works by women authors of the Romantic period, in particular, may be cataloged with a variety of names (e.g., Mrs. Smith, pseudonyms, etc.). If you are searching for a comprehensive list of your author's titles held by a library, you will want to try both the more specific and general name search strategies.

Finding works by less well-known authors will entail the same author search techniques. If you have trouble finding works by your author, especially if his or her works are not widely published in separate editions, you may have more luck searching for an anthology that contains works by many authors. For example, a keyword search using *anthology* **and** *women* **and** *Romantic** will identify collected works by women authors and poets of the period. You can also try other keywords such as *literary collections*, or *sources*. The texts, *Slavery, Abolition, and Emancipation: Writings in the British Romantic Period*, *Romantic Period Writings, 1798–1832: An Anthology*, and *From Enlightenment to Romanticism: Anthology* are culled from the list of results retrieved by the keyword search *Romantic** **and** *sources*.

Using the author's name as a keyword search may also retrieve anthologies or other sources that include a work by the author, but only if the author is credited in the contents field or listed in a subject heading. For example, in some catalogs the keyword search *anna seward* retrieves the collection, *Bluestocking Feminism: Writings of the Bluestocking Circle, 1738–1785*, in which the fourth volume is composed entirely of her writings (see Figure 3.1). An author search with her name will not retrieve this text, since she is listed only in the contents.

Figure 3.1. Modified catalog record for *Bluestocking Feminism*

Title	Bluestocking feminism : writings of the Bluestocking Circle, 1738–1785 / general editor, Gary Kelly ; volume editors, Elizabeth Eger ... [et al.].
Publ info	London ; Brookfield, Vt. : Pickering & Chatto, 1999.

LOCATION	CALL #	STATUS
Books Upper Level	PR1111.F45 B59 1999	AVAILABLE

Description	6 v. ; 25 cm.
Note(s)	Includes bibliographical references.
Contents	v. 1. Elizabeth Montagu / edited by Elizabeth Eger—v. 2. Elizabeth Carter / edited by Judith Hawley—v. 3. Catherine Talbot & Hester Chapone / edited by Rhoda Zuk—*v. 4. Anna Seward* / edited by Jennifer Kelly—v. 5. Sarah Scott / edited by Gary Kelly—v. 6. Sarah Scott & Clara Reeve / edited by Gary Kelly.
Subject(s)	Feminism—England—Literary collections.
	Feminism—England—History—18th century—Sources.
	Women—England—History—18th century—Sources.

Women—England—Literary collections.
English literature—Women authors.
English literature—18th century.
ISBN   1851965149 (set : alk. paper)

Source: University of Denver, Penrose Library catalog

The keyword search *tighe mary* picks up the inverted phrase in a subject heading to retrieve an 1893 edition of the translated works of Apuleius to which is added Mrs. Tighe's poem "Psyche." The keyword search *mary tighe* retrieves different results, including collected works by Romantic-era British women poets and the Ladies of Llangollen. None of these sources include Mary Tighe in the author field. If the library system software searches on keyword phrases, try both regular and inverted searches of the author's name, since they may retrieve different results depending on how the author is listed in the contents or, occasionally, in the subject heading fields. Although using the author's name as a keyword search will inevitably retrieve irrelevant titles, it still can be used as a broad approach to find texts that have been included in thematic anthologies or literary collections.

Once you have conducted your author search, you will evaluate the results to determine which sources are going to be the best choices for your research project. An author search will retrieve works that are available in the library, and depending on the size or range of the collection, these works will be published in a variety of editions, reprints, and formats. Each type of edition or format will have its own characteristics and strengths. Works by Romantic-era authors may exist in manuscript facsimiles, be reproduced on microfilm, be offered in a modern edition which may include a critical introduction and/or contextual documents, be an original edition published in the eighteenth or nineteenth century, or even take the form of an electronic text. You will need to decide what type of format and edition best suits your research needs and choose accordingly. Altick advises students in *The Art of Literary Research* to "use the latest scholarly edition" since the quality and reliability of editions can vary tremendously; however, he cautions that even authoritative texts "may well be flawed to a greater or lesser degree."[1] Standard editions of Romantic-era literary works for primarily canonical authors are noted in Marcuse and in O'Neill (see Chapters 2 and 4 respectively).

If you do not require a standard edition, or if one is not recommended for your author, you should consider the following elements when evaluating a text: the authority of the publisher and editors, the currency or relevancy of the publication date, and the place of publication. If you are interested in using primary documents, keep in mind that these sources are likely to be available only in special collections at major research libraries, often with restricted access. Chapter 9 features best practices for working with manuscripts and other archival materials. Microform reproductions of original materials are more widely available and now, of course, digital versions of primary documents are becoming more common on the Web and through subscription databases. These types of resources are discussed in Chapter 8, "Microform and Digital Collections."

Title Searches

A title field search will retrieve all copies of a particular title that your library owns and consequently, will require the same assessment of edition, publisher, and format. Take note that titles of the same work, as previously defined, can exist in several variants, especially in the case of older materials. Canonical works, in particular, can be published in facsimiles, scholarly editions, and anthologies—all of which might have different titles. Mary Shelley's novel *Frankenstein* serves as a telling example. If you type *frankenstein* in the title field, your initial results may show several works entitled *Frankenstein*. Only some of these titles were actually written by Mary Shelley, however, whereas others are adaptations of her work. And unless you are persistent and browse through all of the alphabetically arranged title index results, you may miss copies of the edited edition, *Frankenstein: Complete, authoritative text with biographical, historical, and cultural contexts, critical history, and essays from contemporary critical perspectives*, the facsimile edition entitled, *The Frankenstein notebooks: a facsimile edition of Mary Shelley's manuscript novel, 1816–17 (with alterations in the hand of Percy Bysshe Shelley) as it survives in draft and fair copy deposited by Lord Abinger in the Bodleian Library, Oxford*, or the important alternative title, *Frankenstein: or, The Modern Prometheus* (see Figure 3.2). We chose these sample texts specifically to emphasize the different titles by which a single work may be represented, but also to underscore the types of scholarly editions available. Depending on your research project, these particular editions may prove to be critical resources that you would not have wanted to overlook. This example also illustrates the importance of corroborating a title search with an author search in order to ensure that no important editions of the work are missed.

Figure 3.2. Modified catalog record for title field search *Frankenstein*

Num	Mark	Title (1–12 of 22)	Year
		Frankenstein	
		Reserve; VIDEO CASSETTE 2995	c1999
1	☐	Book Stacks; PR5397 .F7 1994	c1994
		Book Stacks; PS3552.I47 F72 1973x	c1973
		Internet; PR5397.F3 .S54	1996
		10 additional entries	
2	☐	Frankenstein (1973)	
		Book Stacks; PS3552.I47 F72 1973x	c1973
3	☐	Frankenstein, A Play In Two Acts	
		Book Stacks; PS3557.I12 F7 1982	c1982
4	☐	Frankenstein Catalog	
		Book Stacks; PR5397.F73 G487 1984	c1984
5	☐	***Frankenstein: Complete, Authoritative Text With Biographical, Historical, And Cultural Contexts, Critical***	
		Book Stacks; PR5397 .F7 2000	c2000
6	☐	Frankenstein, Creation And Monstrosity	
		Book Stacks; PR5397.F73 F736 1994	1994
7	☐	Frankenstein Files	
		Reserve; PN1995.9.H6 F735 1999 DVD	1999
8	☐	Frankenstein In Love	
		Book Stacks; PR6052.A6475 I49 1995	1995
9	☐	Frankenstein, Incorporated	
		Book Stacks; HD2731.W6	1931
10	☐	Frankenstein Legend: A Tribute To Mary Shelley And Boris Karloff	
		Book Stacks; PR5397.F73 G4	1973
11	☐	Frankenstein (Motion Picture)	
		Reserve; VIDEO CASSETTE 3008	1999

12	☐	*Frankenstein Notebooks: A Facsimile Edition Of Mary Shelley's Manuscript Novel, 1816–17, With Alteration*	
		Book Stacks; PR5397.F73 S54 1996	1996
13	☐	Frankenstein, Or, The Man And The Monster!: An Original Melo Drama In Two Acts	
		Microforms; CARD B 5675 ENGLISH	
14	☐	*Frankenstein, Or, The Modern Prometheus*	
		Book Stacks; PR5397 .F7 1994	

Source: University of Denver, Penrose Library catalog

Not only can a distinctive work be published with variant titles; it can also have the same title but be different in content. In some cases, identical titles can be drawn from different source texts. The *Oxford English Novels* series edition of *Frankenstein*, for example, uses the 1831 edition, whereas the *Broadview Literary Text* series prefers the 1818 version (see Figure 3.3). Be sure to look in the note(s) field of the catalog record to identify which edition or source a publication is based on, if this information isn't indicated in the bibliographic citation. You also will want to evaluate each edition of a work based on the criteria outlined above in the evaluating author results section to be sure to choose the appropriate texts for your research.

Figure 3.3. Modified catalog record for *Frankenstein, or, The Modern Prometheus*

Author	Shelley, Mary Wollstonecraft, 1797–1851.
Unif title	Frankenstein
Title	Frankenstein, or, The modern Prometheus / Mary Wollstonecraft Shelley ; edited by D.L. Macdonald & Kathleen Scherf.
Publ info	Peterborough, Ont. : Broadview Press, c1994.

LOCATION	CALL #	STATUS
Books Upper Level	PR5397 .F7 1994	AVAILABLE

Description	371 p. : port. ; 22 cm.
Series	Broadview literary texts

Note(s)	*"The 1818 version."*
	Includes bibliographical references (p. 367–371).
Subject(s)	Frankenstein (Fictitious character)—Fiction.
	Monsters—Fiction.
ISBN	1551110385 :

Source: University of Denver, Penrose Library catalog

If you do not find the title of the work you are seeking published separately, try searching for it as a keyword, especially if it is a shorter work that may be included in an anthology. The keyword search *shelley and Frankenstein* retrieves two Oxford University Press publications: the collection *Four Gothic Novels*, which reproduces the entire text of *Frankenstein*; and *Literature and Science in the Nineteenth Century: An Anthology* that features selections from Shelley's novel, in addition to works and selections by Austen, De Quincey, Bentham, and Malthus, among many other British and American nineteenth-century literary figures. As with author keyword searches, this strategy will work only if the title keywords are listed in the contents field and are indexed by the library's database.

In addition to books, title searches can be used to identify journals and series titles held in the library's collection. Use a title search to discover if your library subscribes to the journal *European Romantic Review*, for example, or if it has either print or microfilm access to issues of *The Quarterly Review*. Individual titles from a series such as *Manuscripts of the Younger Romantics* or *Cambridge Studies in Romanticism* can also be identified with a title field search. As discussed in Chapter 1, some library catalogs feature specific indexes for periodical title and series title searches, which should be used if available. If you do not find your item in these indexes, however, be sure to try again with the title field search. Keep in mind that title searches can also be employed to find other items, including: videos, DVDs, Web resources, databases, music, maps, government documents, and archival materials.

Subject Searches

Subject searches facilitate finding items about an author, particular work, genre, historical period, or theoretical approach, etc. Subject searches can be conducted usually in two ways: as a keyword search, or as a subject heading search. As previously discussed and depending on the search engine, a keyword search may look for your topic words in the author, title, publisher, series title, subject heading, and sometimes contents or notes fields. Keyword searches can be effective for broad searches, since they will retrieve items that contain your words anywhere in the indicated fields. Check to see if the library catalog permits keyword phrase searching, and if the default search places an *and* or an *or* between terms. The way a keyword search is executed, as well as the specific fields in which the terms are searched, will affect significantly the type of results you retrieve. Keeping these search parameters in mind, keyword searches can be a useful way to identify the authoritative subject headings for your topic if you don't know them already, since you can check your keyword search results for relevant subject headings. If you want to find criticism, bibliographies, biographies, or correspondence for a particular author, you can conduct a keyword search using your author's name and the appropriate term. Sample searches include: *hazlitt **and** correspondence*, *austen **and** emma **and** criticism*, or *blake **and** bibliograph**.

Subject searches scan the catalog's index of Library of Congress or other subject headings. When an author is referred to as a subject, the heading includes birth and death dates, just as in the author headings illustrated below. Keep in mind that subject headings have changed over time; older works may not even have an assigned subject heading, or may have been cataloged with simple headings such as "Criticism," "Romanticism," "Women authors," or "Poets, English." Moreover, works of fiction typically do not have assigned subject headings. Below is a representative selection of Library of Congress subject headings for Romantic literature:

> Romanticism — England
> Romanticism — Great Britain — Sources
> English fiction — 18th century — History and criticism
> English poetry — 19th century — Book reviews
> English prose literature — 19th century — History and criticism
> English drama — Women authors — Bibliography
> Horror tales, English — History and criticism — Theory, etc.
> Gothic revival (Literature) — Great Britain
> Women and literature — Great Britain — Historiography
> Periodicals — Publishing — Great Britain — History — 19th century
> Theater — England — History — 18th century
> Austen, Jane, 1775–1817 — Political and social views
> Baillie, Joanna, 1762–1851 — Knowledge — Performing arts
> Coleridge, Samuel Taylor, 1772–1834 — Religion

Scott, Walter, Sir, 1771–1832 — Technique

Shelley, Mary Wollstonecraft, 1797–1851 — Manuscripts — Facsimiles

Smith, Charlotte Turner, 1749–1806 — Criticism and interpretation

Once you are familiar with the typical elements and format of subject headings, you can use that knowledge to refine your searches both in your university and other library catalogs. Also take the time to browse through the library catalog subject index entries for your author if you are researching a particular figure. You would do this by searching for the author's name in the subject field. For example, the subject search *byron* reveals multiple subject headings for this author, as demonstrated in Figure 3.4. This strategy will enable you to identify not only what types of resources your library owns about your author but also to ascertain the principal areas of research investigating your author's works.

Figure 3.4. Modified catalog record for Byron as the Library of Congress subject heading

Num	LC Subject Headings (13–24 of 95)
13	Byron, George Gordon Byron, Baron, 1788–1824—Biography
14	Byron, George Gordon Byron, Baron, 1788–1824—Biography—Last Years
15	Byron, George Gordon Byron, Baron, 1788–1824—Books And Reading
16	Byron, George Gordon Byron, Baron, 1788–1824. Byron's Don Juan—See—Byron, George Gordon Byron, Baron, 1788–1824. Don Juan
17	Byron, George Gordon Byron, Baron, 1788–1824. Cain
18	Byron, George Gordon Byron, Baron, 1788–1824—Censorship
19	Byron, George Gordon Byron, Baron, 1788–1824—Characters—Devil
20	Byron, George Gordon Byron, Baron, 1788–1824—Characters—Heroines
21	Byron, George Gordon Byron, Baron, 1788–1824. Childe Harold—See—Byron, George Gordon Byron, Baron, 1788–1824. Childe Harold's Pilgrimage

22	Byron, George Gordon Byron, Baron, 1788–1824. Childe Harold's Pilgrimage
23	Byron, George Gordon Byron, Baron, 1788–1824—Childhood And Youth
24	Byron, George Gordon Byron, Baron, 1788–1824—Congresses

Source: University of Denver, Penrose Library catalog

Union Catalogs

Copac, at www.copac.ac.uk (accessed 5 December 2004).

Library of Congress and the National Union Catalog Subcommittee of the Resources Committee of the Resources and Technical Services Division, American Library Association. *National Union Catalog, Pre-1956 Imprints: a Cumulative Author List Representing Library of Congress Printed Cards and Titles Reported by Other American Libraries*. 754 vols. London: Mansell, 1968–1981.

RedLightGreen.com, at www.redlightgreen.com (accessed 5 December 2004).

RLG Union Catalog. Mountain View, CA: RLG. www.rlg.org.

WorldCat. Dublin, OH: OCLC. www.oclc.org/firstsearch.

Open WorldCat, at www.oclc.org/worldcat/open/default.htm (accessed 5 December 2004).

After you have exhausted your local library's resources, the next step is to search a union catalog. Union catalogs combine the individual holdings of participating libraries to form one cohesive print catalog or database. A union catalog can be the product of local university and/or public libraries, a state or regional consortium, or national and even international library alliances. The strength of the union catalog is that it provides a greater number of bibliographic records that may be reviewed simultaneously, or even may be searched online if produced in an electronic format. Large union catalogs, such as *WorldCat*, *Copac*, *RLG Union Catalog*, and the *National Union Catalog* are particularly useful for finding and locating extant editions of an author's works.

WorldCat, the OCLC (Online Computer Library Center) union catalog, is an immense subscription database that presents bibliographic information for more than 52,000,000 items cataloged by its member libraries. As the largest union catalog, *WorldCat* currently represents the reported holdings of 45,000 libraries in eighty-four countries and territories around the world. Despite this extensive coverage, you will discover that most searches regarding Romantic-era literature will retrieve items from libraries in the United States, the United Kingdom, and Canada. The database includes books, journals, newspapers, manuscripts, websites, musical scores, maps, sound and video recordings, and computer programs. Even though *WorldCat* covers over fifty million items, it is important to remember that it does not contain each member library's entire holdings, only items that have been reported.

In addition to its size, *WorldCat* is notable for its detailed search features; the database can be searched by keyword, author, title, series title, subject, ISBN, ISSN, publisher, publisher location, material type, and individual components within each of these categories. Furthermore, a search may be limited by date, language, number of holding libraries, and format. Search results are ranked in descending order by the number of libraries that hold the item, unless you select other ranking options (e.g., relevance, date). Such capabilities enable the researcher, for example, to construct a search for London as the publisher location, set a publication date range of 1780 to 1830, and limit the search to serials, in order to retrieve a partial list of British serials published during the Romantic period. This particular search can be used as a starting point for identifying relevant journals, but it must be followed by consulting the periodical finding aids discussed in Chapter 7, "Eighteenth- and Nineteenth-Century Journals."

Due to its impressive size and dynamic search features, *WorldCat* is a powerful tool for finding publications written by a particular author, or items about an author or subject, and then for identifying which libraries cataloged those works. Keep in mind, however, that since it was designed for cataloging purposes, author searches and subject searches work most effectively once you determine the authoritative heading. After you have conducted your initial search, try exploring the "Find Related" options from each record. These links will retrieve sources with the same author and title, which is good for finding variant editions and formats, and items about the author, which carries out an *author as subject* search. The sample below illustrates these options using the *WorldCat* record for a modern edition of Charlotte Smith's novel, *Desmond* (see Figure 3.5).

Figure 3.5. Modified WorldCat record for *Desmond*

Desmond /
Charlotte Turner Smith; Janet M Todd; Antje Blank
2001
English Book : Fiction 488 p. ; 22 cm.

Peterborough, Ont. : Broadview Press, ; ISBN: 1551112744
(pbk.) :

GET THIS ITEM	
Availability:	Check the catalogs in your library. Libraries worldwide that own item: 89 Search the catalog at Penrose Library
External Resources:	Click to make ILL request

FIND RELATED	
Find Items About:	**Desmond / (1); Smith, Charlotte Turner, (max: 91)**

Title:	**Desmond /**
Author(s):	Smith, Charlotte Turner, 1749–1806. ; Todd, Janet M.,; 1942– ; Blank, Antje,; 1965–
Publication:	Peterborough, Ont. : Broadview Press,
Year:	2001
Language:	English
Series:	Broadview literary texts;
Standard No:	**ISBN:** 1551112744 (pbk.) :; **National Library:** 009328777
Note(s):	Includes bibliographical references.
Class Descriptors:	**LC:** PR3688.S4; **Dewey:** 823/.6; **NLC:** PR3688 S4; PR3688; PR3688 S4
Responsibility:	Charlotte Smith ; edited by Antje Blank and Janet Todd.
Material Type:	Fiction (fic)
Document Type:	Book
Entry:	20001107
Update:	20041111
Accession No:	**OCLC:** 45486616
Database:	WorldCat

Source: *WorldCat*, via *FirstSearch*

The bibliographic information for each title in *WorldCat* contains a link to the number of libraries that report holding the item worldwide, and a list of those holding libraries. Be forewarned, however, that it is very important to understand the difference between reported and actual holdings. Always check the holding library's catalog directly to confirm that the library does indeed have, or still have, the item you are seeking. You can use the *WorldCat* holding libraries list to identify these libraries, or to make an interlibrary loan request through your own institution. If your institution utilizes the *WorldCat* interlibrary loan feature, you can use the database to make the loan request directly.

Through the **Open WorldCat** program, OCLC has made most of *WorldCat*'s records available in abridged form to *Google, Yahoo! Search*, and non-search engine sites, such as bibliographic and bookselling sites. When a Web user types a title that matches an open *WorldCat* record in a search engine such as *Google*, the search results list will include a *WorldCat* link. This link, called "Find in a Library," will provide brief bibliographic information and a means to search for holding libraries by postal code, state, province, or country. After the geographic library search is conducted, a list of matching local libraries is retrieved that includes distance and contact information, as well as links to online catalogs if available. These catalogs then should be checked to ascertain if the library does indeed own the item desired. After July 1, 2005, only libraries that maintain a subscription to the *WorldCat* database will have their holdings available through the *Open WorldCat* program, as long as they agree to participate. You can learn more about the *Open WorldCat* program, how it works, and future plans for the project at the OCLC *Open WorldCat* website.

Another important union catalog for Romantic scholars is the British Web catalog, **Copac**, which provides unified access at no charge to twenty-six of the twenty-seven online catalogs of Consortium of University Research Libraries (CURL) in the United Kingdom and Ireland, including the British Library, National Library of Scotland, Cambridge University, Oxford University, Trinity College Dublin Library, and the University of Edinburgh. The National Library of Wales online catalog will be added to the database in the near future. *Copac* contains over thirty million records, most of which are books, although journals, conferences, printed and recorded music, videos, and electronic resources are also represented. Materials range in date from 1200 A.D. to the present, with more than a third of the items published after 1980. As with *WorldCat*, it is important to note that *Copac* offers access only to its member libraries' online catalogs, not their entire holdings. To determine what items are covered by each library's online catalog, you will need to check each individual library's website. *Copac* also includes selected non-member library records that were updated and created for three projects which may be of interest to the Romantic scholar: the *Revelation Project* of nineteenth- and twentieth-century church history and Christian theology texts; the *19th Century Pamphlets Project* which includes pamphlets published between 1801 and 1914; and *Pamphlets and Polemic: Pamphlets as a guide to the controversies of the 17th to 19th century.*

Possessing more limited search capabilities than *WorldCat*, the *Copac* database may be searched by author/title, or subject, with options to search only periodicals or maps. Within the author and subject searches, some of the following fields can be selected: title, organization, publisher, ISBN/ISSN, keyword, and subject, with limits of publication date, language, and specific libraries. A few features make the *Copac* search engine more flexible than it initially appears. The *Copac* subject search option does not require the authoritative subject heading to retrieve relevant results. For example, entering *William Wordsworth* as a subject retrieves the same number of items as the inverted *Wordsworth William.* An author search that uses first name initials will find the relevant full name author entries as well. Although entries in *Copac* for the most part use Library of Congress subject headings, you will find some entries with alternative subject headings. Keeping in mind that subject headings have changed over time, these examples could have been created, perhaps, before the standardized use of Library of Congress headings, or they could represent original cataloging endeavors:

> English literature, 1745–1837
> English literature, 1745–1837, Romanticism, Critical studies
> English literature, 1745–1837, Sentimentalism — Critical studies
> English literature, Romanticism. History, 1745–1837
> Sensibility — Sentimentalism — English — 18th century — Literary Criticism

Copac searches will retrieve a list of brief citations in alphabetical order by title and then date for author/title searches, or rank results by relevancy for title only searches. The "full record details" option displays features typical to most union catalogs, including: edition, publisher, physical description, notes, subject headings, additional names, and links to holding libraries if they are available. Particular to *Copac*, an asterisk by the holding library's name indicates that current information about the book's call number or classmark, branch library holdings, and circulation status are retrieved from the library's catalog and displayed. The sample *Copac* record (Figure 3.6) highlights the differences between a *WorldCat* and *Copac* record for the same resource.

Figure 3.6. Modified Copac record for *Desmond*

3.		
	Main Author:	Smith, Charlotte Turner, 1749–1806
	Title Details:	Desmond / Charlotte Smith ; edited by Antje Blank and Janet Todd
	Series:	Broadview literary texts
	Publisher:	Peterborough, Ont. : Broadview Press, c2001
	ISBN/ISSN:	1551112744
	Note:	Includes bibliographical references
	Subject:	Sex role - Great Britain - History - 18th century - Fiction France - History - Revolution, 1789-1799 - Fiction Great Britain - Social life and customs - 18th century - Fiction
	Other Names:	Blank, Antje, 1965- Todd, Janet M., 1942-
	Document Type:	Fiction

For holdings information select a library from those below. Those marked with an asterisk give current availability. ***Held by: Birmingham* ; Edinburgh* ; Manchester* ; Oxford* ; ULL* ; Warwick****

Source: *Copac*

Searching *Copac* is straightforward; however, it doesn't offer as many options as *WorldCat* for refining and controlling your search. Nevertheless, with its unique coverage *Copac* can be used to identify potentially useful sources for your research that may be held only by British libraries. If you do find relevant items through *Copac* that are not available in *WorldCat*, contact your institution to see if an interlibrary loan request is possible. You can also check with your reference librarian to see if the item is available through a digitization project. For items that are not available to loan, in digital format, or that are under restricted access, you can contact the holding library directly to inquire as to what other options might be permitted.

Like *WorldCat*, the Research Libraries Group *RLG Union Catalog*, is a subscription database that features the holdings of member research libraries worldwide, including academic, public, museum, archival, and historical society libraries. This database covers books, serials, manuscripts, archival collections, maps, sound recordings, electronic resources, and other items that number in the millions. The basic search interface, *Eureka*, permits searching by author, title, subject, and keyword. The advanced search offers additional options, including: title, author, and subject word; Web link; related title; form and genre; ISBN; and ISSN; in addition to limits by date, language, or type of material. Previous searches are saved and can be combined to execute new searches.

If you are searching for items by a particular author, we recommend that you use the "Advanced search" option, and select "author word" from the menu. This choice will retrieve all variant author entries, including those headings that do and do not separate the name with a comma, and those that contain birth and death dates. See the search results in Table 3.1, which illustrates the variant entries for Charlotte Smith. If you conduct an author search (not an author word search) without a comma in either the basic or advanced search, however, you will retrieve an incomplete list, as demonstrated by the author search *smith charlotte* which shows no matches in the author index since, in this case, all of the Charlotte Smith variants employ a comma after her surname.

Table 3.1. Records retrieved from Charlotte Smith "author word" search in *RLG Union Catalog*

Count	Author
0	Smith Charlotte
113	Smith, Charlotte
22	Smith, Charlotte Mrs.
251	Smith, Charlotte Turner
12	Smith, Charlotte Turner Mrs
8	Smith, Charlotte Turner 1749 1806
1	Smith, Charlotte Turner, 1749 1806
2	Smith, Mrs Charlotte Turner

The same strategy also applies to "author as subject" searches. Use the advanced "subject word" option in order to retrieve all variant subject headings. You will need to browse through the subject index to find all relevant variants, since inevitably there will be subject headings that do not use a comma, those that do separate the author's name, and those that add birth and death dates.

After a search is conducted, you can select records from the results list and display them in either a brief or full format. In addition to the typical components found in most union catalog records, the *RLG Union Catalog* records also include genre or form headings (e.g., bildungsroman, humorous fiction) and a location feature that enables you to display each institution's version of a particular record by selecting the institution's name from the location list. You can then use this information when making an interlibrary loan request through your own institution.

In an effort to make bibliographic information about their holdings available to a wider audience, the Research Libraries Group now offers free searching of the *RLG Union Catalog* at the website **RedLight-Green.com**. Since the project is still in its pilot stage, check the information page to determine which bibliographic records from the *RLG Union Catalog* are actually included in the Web catalog. Designed initially to meet the needs of undergraduates, the database features a "user friendly" interface with basic keyword searching, or the option to search by author, title, subject, or standard numbers and limit the search by language. Search results are ranked by relevance to search terms and related subject headings are displayed to the left of the screen. Each record lists the number of available editions and the date range of their publication, and notes the primary subject heading for the title. After selecting a title from the results page, users may view the brief or full bibliographic record, display additional editions, locate the nearest library that owns the title, check their library catalog directly to see if the title is available, link to an electronic version of the text or related Web resources (e.g., tables of contents, publishers' descriptions) if provided, connect to an online bookstore to purchase the title, or obtain a citation for the title in MLA, Chicago, Turabian, or APA style formats to paste to their research papers.

If your intention is to search for every work and/or edition by a particular Romantic-era author, then you will want to consult the **National Union Catalog, Pre-1956 Imprints** (*NUC*), in addition to your searches of *WorldCat* and the *RLG Union Catalog*. Composed of 754 volumes, the *NUC Pre-1956 Imprints* reproduces Library of Congress printed catalog cards, as well as catalog cards for titles from other libraries in the United States and Canada. The entries are arranged by author, by title for anonymous works only, and occasionally by editor for anthologies and collections. If a major author has several works, those entries may be arranged by category, instead of being listed only alphabetically by title. For example, entries for Jane Austen are arranged in the following manner: collected works; two or more works; letters; individual titles; minor works; and selections; with each group further arranged by language and imprint date. Information for each title entry varies from detailed descriptions to very brief citations. Each entry also indicates by code which library cataloged a copy of that title. Because the *NUC Pre-1956 Imprints* was compiled from the records of many libraries, a title record with any variation was listed as if it were a separate edition. Due to this practice, you need to be aware that a listed card may not, in fact, represent a distinct work. The *NUC* remains valuable for identifying older works in a library's collection that may not yet be recorded in that institution's online catalog.

National Library Catalogs

British Library Integrated Catalogue, at catalogue.bl.uk (accessed 6 December 2004).
British Library Manuscripts Catalogue, at www.bl.uk/catalogues/ manuscripts/INDEX.asp (accessed 5 December 2004).
British Library Newspapers Catalogue, at www.bl.uk/catalogues/ newspapers.html (accessed 5 December 2004).
Library of Congress Online Catalog, 29 June 2004, at catalog.loc.gov (accessed 5 December 2004).

National libraries are important resources for research. Since they usually serve as a depository library, they receive a copy of every work published in that country. Both the Library of Congress and the British Library possess significant collections, a great part of which can be searched online through the library catalogs at no cost.

One of the largest libraries in the world, the Library of Congress (LOC) is composed of almost 128 million items, including books and other printed materials, recordings, photographs, maps, and manuscripts. More than twelve million items may be searched in the *Library of Congress Online Catalog*; two additional online catalogs search the print and photograph and sound recording collections. The *Library of Congress Online Catalog* features both basic and guided search interfaces. The basic search enables the user to search by title, author/creator, subject, keyword, LC call number, ISSN/ISBN, series title, and author/creator sorted by title. Only the title, keyword, and standard number searches can be limited by date, language, material type, location within the Library of Congress, and place of publication. The guided search option enables the searcher to construct keyword searches of specific fields and set the limits noted above (e.g., *blake, william* in the personal name field and *visions of the daughters of albion* in the title field, or search for *blake, william* in the personal name field and limit your results to items located in Rare Books and Special Collections). As the library of "last resort," any request that you make for an item in the Library of Congress collections will be filled by another library unless there is no other copy available to loan. Search the *LOC Online Catalog* to complement your searches of *WorldCat* and the *RLG Union Catalog*, or if you do not have access to these subscription databases, use the *Library of Congress Online Catalog* as a free way to identify materials from one of the most impressive library research collections in the world.

The British Library is the depository library for the United Kingdom and Ireland; currently it holds more than one hundred and fifty million items, including 310,000 manuscript volumes. For those researching authors of the Romantic era, the British Library stands as a literary mecca. The **British Library Integrated Catalogue** covers twelve million items from the Reference and Document Supply catalogs, in addition to the Serials and Periodicals, Newspapers, Cartographic, Printed Music, and Asia, Pacific and Africa Collections catalogs. The basic search interface enables you to search by single or phrase keywords in the author, title, LC and other subject headings, publisher, publication year, ISBN/ISSN, or shelfmark number fields. The advanced search facilitates constructing a search from multiple fields and also presents the option to limit by language, year, or format. In order to search one or more individual catalogs within the *Integrated Catalogue*, select the "Catalogue Subset" search that includes every catalog except the Newspapers collection which must still be searched separately as described below. If you are interested in requesting a copy of an item, the library's "Information and Research Services" page describes its range of services and fees, as well as its loan policies and procedures.

Separate online catalogs permit you to search the newspaper and manuscript collections. The **British Library Newspapers Catalogue** contains 52,000 newspaper and periodical titles, including United Kingdom national daily and Sunday newspapers from 1801 to the present, as well as many British and Irish provincial papers from the eighteenth century onwards. Basic keyword searches may be sorted by title, place of publication, or date. Chapter 7, "Eighteenth- and Nineteenth-Century Journals and Newspapers," describes the *Newspapers Catalogue* at greater length. The main **Manuscripts Catalogue** searches the indexes and descriptions of holdings in the Department of Manuscripts that were acquired from 1753 to the present. As the electronic

Manuscripts Catalogue is an ongoing project, note that not every index and descriptive catalog is available to be searched online yet (you can read the *Manuscripts Catalogue* overview to determine which catalogs are currently available). The "Index" search features searching by name, additional name, descriptive adjunct, index entry, language, state of the manuscript, start and end year, or manuscript number. The "Search Tips" section provides a helpful guide to these individual categories with illustrative searches. The "Descriptive" search permits searching by keyword or manuscript number. Click on the highlighted manuscript number from your search results list conducted in either search option for a brief or full description of the manuscript. Chapter 9, "Manuscripts and Archives," gives a fuller description and outlines best practices for searching the various components of the *Manuscripts Catalogue*.

Conclusion

Thanks to the development of online catalogs and the Internet, researchers today have unprecedented access to library holdings around the world. Access to the holdings of all libraries has been increased not only by the ability to conduct standard author, title, and subject searches in an online format, but also to search for items in multiple fields with keyword searches. Even though not every item in a library's collection may be included in their online catalog, these online sources make the researcher's task much easier. Union catalogs further increase the researcher's access to potentially relevant items, as projects such as *WorldCat*, *RLG Union Catalog*, and *Copac* provide researchers with a substantial body of materials from which to conduct their research. National library catalogs can also assist the scholar with free searching of their impressive collections. With the advent of online catalogs, the scholar of Romantic-era literature now has numerous options for identifying relevant books, journals, manuscripts, and source materials—access which hopefully will enhance the researcher's endeavors to make exciting new contributions to the field.

Note

1. Altick, Richard D. and John J. Fenstermaker. *The Art of Literary Research.* 4th ed. (New York: W. W. Norton, 1993), 32.

Chapter 4
Print and Electronic Bibliographies, Indexes, and Annual Reviews

Bibliographies, in their most typical form, are lists of resources. The bibliographies described in this chapter concern sources for literary studies, especially those compiled for studying the Romantic period of British literature. Although bibliographies can take different forms and be presented in different mediums, at their most basic they all provide bibliographic information for materials that fall within the scope determined by the bibliography's compilers. These items can be distinguished as primary materials (e.g., manuscripts, first editions, letters) or secondary critical materials (e.g., scholarly monographs, journals and journal articles, dissertations, book reviews); bibliographies can include either one or both types of resources.

Some bibliographies serve to record the existence of items, usually but not exclusively the existence of primary materials. In this case, the bibliography's governing principles are to be as comprehensive as possible, to supply bibliographic descriptions of the items, and potentially to indicate the location of the items. These types of bibliographies are represented here by the *English Short Title Catalogue* and the *Nineteenth Century Short Title Catalogue*, both of which aim to list all materials printed within the British Isles and their colonies during a specified time and by *Romantic Poetry by Women: A Bibliography, 1770–1835* which has a similar goal for poetry published by women during the Romantic period.

In contrast, other bibliographies are purposefully selective in nature, compiled to assist scholars in identifying important, relevant, or recommended works within a particular subject area. Many such bibliographies are thematically focused and emphasize literary periods, national literatures, literary movements, genres, authors, or any combination thereof. The bibliographies of this type range from large endeavors like the *Modern Language Association International Bibliography*

(*MLAIB*) which addresses all modern languages and literatures to narrowly specified bibliographies such as those dedicated to individual Romantic-era authors.

One specific type of bibliography discussed in this chapter is the annual review that provides an overview of secondary literature (e.g., criticism, reviews, critical editions, anthologies, relevant reference works) published within a year. Although some annual reviews aim for comprehensiveness, more often the compilers select works for their importance to the field and assess these works in descriptive and/or evaluative annotations. Annual reviews include *Year's Work in English Studies* and *Eighteenth Century: A Current Bibliography*, as well as reviews in journals such as *SEL: Studies in English Literature* and the *Wordsworth Circle*. It is important to be aware of the time lag that is common to book-length annual reviews. By the time they are published, the items they review were typically published a few years ago. Annual reviews published in journals, however, tend to be more current and review the previous year's work.

Another type of resource discussed in this chapter is the index. The index provides access to the contents of a single book, journal, or to multiple items, typically by author, title, and subject access points. *MLAIB* and *ABELL* are considered both bibliographies and indexes, since they serve as finding aids to language and literature resources by listing books, book chapters, journal articles, dissertations, and book reviews published each year that fall within the bibliography's scope and by providing access to these items through indexing of the authors/editors, titles, and assigned, controlled vocabulary subject headings. Full-text databases, such as *Project Muse* and *JSTOR* provide this same function, but also offer the full text of each source the database indexes.

The advent of electronic media and the Web have dramatically changed access to the standard literary bibliographies. Now that *MLAIB*, *ABELL*, and the short title catalogs are available in online versions, the resources within these bibliographies can be retrieved by numerous fields beyond the printed bibliography's standard author, title, and subject index access points. For example, a typical record in the online *MLAIB* can be searched by author, title, all text, dissertation information, ISBN/ISSN, journal title, publication date, publisher, series title, subject, and keyword and limited by date, publication type, and language. Depending on the database and vendor, it may be possible to link to full-text versions of the indexed resources in another database, or search for the item in your institution's library catalog. *ABELL* is offered as part of *Literature Online*, a multi-use literary database of full-text English and American poetry, drama, and prose texts, as well as 136 full-text literature journals and reference works. In this resource, *ABELL* features links from the bibliographic entries to full-text sources if available.

Another advantage to the online bibliography is its currency, which is especially useful when using bibliographies of secondary materials. Unlike the print bibliographies that are published each year at best, records are added to the online databases usually on a monthly basis, thereby providing access to recent criticism without a lengthy delay. Not only do these databases provide access to recent scholarship, they make it much easier to identify earlier works of criticism. With the print indexes of *MLAIB* and *ABELL*, you need to search through each year's index to find relevant items. The online version of *MLAIB* permits comprehensive searching of its yearly bibliographies from 1963 to the present. *ABELL* online provides cumulative access to records from 1920 to 2003 with selective coverage of items published from 1892 to 1919. Although currency is not as relevant for databases of primary materials, scholars using the *ESTC* and *NSTC* benefit from the online format as it increases their access points to the material. In contrast to a print bibliography that is a relatively finite resource (apart from supplements), the online short title catalogs are ongoing projects that will continue to add relevant materials to the databases.

The major drawback to online databases, however, is that only subscribers may use them. Even so, most university libraries will subscribe to *MLAIB* or a similar full-text literature resource like *Literature Online* or *Project Muse*. Even general databases that offer multidisciplinary coverage, such as *Academic Search Premier* <www.ebsco.com> or *Expanded Academic ASAP* <www.gale.com>, will index selected literary criticism. The Web can also be a pertinent medium for publishing bibliographies. For example, the *Romantic Circles* website now offers the well-known "*Keats-Shelley Journal* Bibliography" as part of its *Romantic Circles Bibliography* which features recent tables of contents for selected Romantic studies journals, in addition to an annual list of relevant books. Chapter 10, "Web Resources," discusses several online bibliographies both of primary and secondary materials.

The first major bibliography dedicated specifically to British Romantic literature was the "Romantic Movement: A Selective and Critical Bibliography" which was published annually first in the journal *ELH* from 1936 to 1948, then *Philological Quarterly* from 1949 to 1963, followed by *English Language Notes* from 1964 to 1979, and finally as a separate book published by Garland until 1999. The annual *Eighteenth Century: A Current Bibliography* was first published in *Philological Quarterly* from 1926 to 1975. Many literary and author journals feature an annual bibliography, only some of which are mentioned here. Be sure to check for these annual bibliographies in journals relevant to your particular area of study.

Regardless of whether you consult a print or an electronic bibliography, there are some general best practices that will help you use these resources more effectively. Although it seems obvious, read the front matter, introduction, or "About" link to the bibliography since this is where the compilers will outline the scope of the resource. By taking the time to familiarize yourself with the resource, you should be able to determine the purpose of the bibliography, identify how items were selected, get a sense of what is included and excluded, learn how the bibliography is arranged, and note how frequently, if at all, the bibliography is updated. The elements for each bibliographic record should be explained and the introduction might also point out suggestions for using the bibliography and indexes, including any known quirks or inconsistencies.

Many print bibliographies are arranged by subject categories. Although it is a good idea to begin looking for items in the categories that seem relevant, you should also consult the indexes in order not to miss a potentially valuable resource that may be listed in an unlikely place. With online bibliographies, it is important to become familiar with the controlled vocabulary particular to that database, so that you can choose appropriate subject headings. You will also need to learn how to search the database—the help screen will give you examples of search strategies. Specific strategies for the literary databases covered in this chapter are discussed in the appropriate annotations.

Finally, choose the bibliography and medium to suit your purpose. For instance, if you are trying to identify first editions by a canonical author, use a source like *Cambridge Bibliography of English Literature* which lists an author's works. If you want an overview of the critical response to their work, however, a source such as *Literature of the Romantic Period* provides an assessment of the critical tradition; bibliographies dedicated to an author typically offer the same type of information. For authors associated with a particular genre, you will want to consult genre-specific bibliographies. The short title catalogs are good for finding primary material published in the eighteenth or early nineteenth centuries. If you need to conduct a comprehensive search for criticism or need to find the latest articles about a Romantic-era figure or topic use the online versions of *ABELL* and *MLAIB* to cover the years 1920 to the present. But if you want evaluations of recent scholarship, turn to a source like *Year's Work in English Studies (YWES)* that assesses the important works published in the field. Each bibliography has its own strengths and weaknesses; familiarizing yourself with the different types will enable you to make the most of each resource.

This chapter describes the general literary and Romantic-era literature bibliographies that will be integral to your research and, by doing so, aims to help you determine which ones will be most useful for your particular project.

General Literature Bibliographies

Annual Bibliography of English Language and Literature (*ABELL*). Leeds: Maney Publishing for the Modern Humanities Research Association, 1921–. Annual. Available online via www.chadwyck.com.

Bateson, F.W., ed. *Cambridge Bibliography of English Literature*. 4 vols. Cambridge: Cambridge University Press, 1940. Watson, George, ed. *Supplement*. 1957.

JSTOR: The Scholarly Journal Archive. New York: JSTOR, 1995–. www.jstor.org/

Modern Language Association International Bibliography of Books and Articles on the Modern Languages and Literatures. New York: Modern Language Association of America, 1922 –. Annual. Available online through various vendors. Check www.mla.org/bib_electronic for list of online vendors.

Project Muse. Baltimore, MD: Johns Hopkins University, 1993–. muse.jhu.edu.

Shattock, Joanne, ed. *The Cambridge Bibliography of English Literature*. 3rd ed. Vol. 4: 1800–1900. New York: Cambridge University Press, 1999.

Watson, George, ed. *The New Cambridge Bibliography of English Literature*. 2nd ed. Vol. 2: 1660–1800. Cambridge: Cambridge University Press, 1971.

Year's Work in English Studies. Oxford: Published for the English Association by Oxford University Press, 1921–. Annual. www3.oup.co.uk/ywes.

Most students are probably familiar with the online versions of at least one, if not more, of the main literature bibliographies discussed in this section. Well known both to scholars and students alike, the ***Modern Language Association International Bibliography*** (*MLAIB*) is the primary bibliographic source used for literary studies in the United States. Originally titled *American Bibliography* from 1921 to 1955, the bibliography was published annually in *PMLA* (*Publications of the Modern Language Association of America*) to 1968. Most libraries will have the reprints of these bibliographies (published as separate vol-

umes). In 1969, the bibliography became a separate four-volume publication with each volume dedicated to the following subject areas: 1)
General, English, American, Medieval and Neo-Latin, and Celtic literatures; 2) European, Asian, African, and Latin-American literatures; 3)
linguistics; and 4) pedagogy in foreign languages compiled by the
American Council on the Teaching of Foreign Languages (ACTFL).
Each of these volumes contains its own table of contents and au-
thor/editor/compiler index. A fifth volume was added to the bibliography in 1981 to cover folklore. In that same year, the author and subject
indexes were compiled for the entire bibliography and published in a
separate volume. Reflecting its original title *American Bibliography*,
the bibliography covered scholarship that was generally but not exclusively from the United States until 1956, when it changed its scope
from a national to an international focus.

Currently *MLAIB* covers books, articles, and dissertations that address modern languages, literatures, folklore, and linguistics published
during the year reviewed. The bibliography is still presented in five
volumes arranged now in the following manner: 1) British and Irish,
Commonwealth, English Caribbean, and American literatures; 2) European, Asian, African, and Latin American literatures; 3) Linguistics;
4) General literature, humanities, teaching of literature, and rhetoric
and composition; and 5) Folklore. The comprehensive subject index for
all five volumes is published separately. Scholars of British Romantic-
era literature will need to consult Volume 1 of the current print bibliography for the sections on "English literature/1700–1799" and "English
literature/1800–1899," as well as Irish, Scottish, and Welsh literatures
with the same period divisions. Within each of these sections, entries
are organized alphabetically by general studies, genre (e.g., theater,
autobiography, criticism, drama, letters, novel, opera, periodicals, poetry, prose, translation, travel literature), and by literary author. Each
item or entry is assigned descriptors to indicate that work's subject content.

The Modern Language Association provides the standardized descriptors that are assigned to works included in the bibliography. Sample descriptors include "English literature. Novel: Gothic Novel. 1800–
1899: Romantic period" and "Scottish literature. Drama by women
dramatists. 1800–1899: Romantic period." The subject index presents
headings for "persons, languages, groups, genres, stylistic and struc-
tural features, themes, sources, influences, processes, theories and related topics." Sample headings related to Romantic literature include:
"Gothic Fiction," "Gothic Literature," "Gothic Novel," "Gothic Tradition," "Romantic Period," "Romantic Poetry," "Romantic Poets,"
"Romantic Women Writers," and "Romanticism." The subject index

provides cross-references to items in all volumes, as well as "see also" references for narrower, preferred, and related terms. Since sources are listed only once in the bibliography, it is important to check the pertinent classified sections for your topic or author and the subject index to prevent overlooking a relevant work that may have been listed in another section.

MLA International Bibliography is available online from 1963 to the present from various vendors. The description offered here is based on the *EBSCO* version. The advanced search interface permits searching by keyword in the default fields or in any of twenty-eight individual fields, including distinct fields such as: dissertation information, folklore topic, genre/classification, linguistics topic, literature topic, primary subject author, subject literature, and table of contents. Searches can be limited by publication date, publication type (e.g., book, book collection, dissertation abstract, and journal article), language, genre, and period. These numerous options illustrate the degree of detailed indexing featured by *MLAIB*, certainly one of its strengths, and the potential control it entails upon the researcher for conducting refined searches. The online thesaurus provides authoritative subject headings for the bibliography, with cross-references to relevant terms. Selected headings can then be pasted to your search. Each entry in the database is assigned general subject areas including: subject literature, period, primary subject author, and genre, in addition to subject terms (see Figure 4.1). Results are listed as brief citations in reverse chronological order by publication date. The full records include the general subject areas and subject terms but no abstract.

Figure 4.1. Modified *MLAIB* record for "Interracial Sexual Desire in Charlotte Dacre's *Zofloya*"

Record: 1

Title:	Interracial Sexual Desire in Charlotte Dacre's Zofloya
Author(s):	Mellor, Anne K.
Source:	European Romantic Review (ERR) 2002 June; 13 (2): 169–73.[Journal Detail]
Peer Reviewed:	Yes

ISSN:	1050-9585
General Subject Areas:	Subject Literature: English literature; Period: 1800–1899; Primary Subject Author: Dacre, Charlotte (b. 1782); Primary Subject Work: Zofloya, or the Moor (1806); Genre: novel; gothic novel;
Subject Terms:	treatment of female sexual desire; interracial love
Document Information:	Publication Type: journal article Language of Publication: English Update Code: 200201 Sequence Numbers: 2002–1–6274
Accession Number:	2002297358
Database:	MLA International Bibliography

Source: *MLAIB*, via *EBSCO*

The British equivalent to the *MLAIB*, the **Annual Bibliography of English Language and Literature** (*ABELL*) has been published since 1921 for the British Modern Humanities Research Association. This extensive bibliography covers books, journal articles, critical editions, essay collections, reviews, and doctoral dissertations (the latter in the online database only from 1920–1999) concerned with English language and literatures in English from Britain, the United States, Canada, Australia, Africa, and Asia and includes scholarship published worldwide and in any language. Recent print volumes are organized in the following categories: festschriften and other collections; bibliography; scholarly method; language, literature, and the computer; newspapers and other periodicals; English language; traditional culture, folklore, and folklife; and English literature. The English literature section is subdivided by general studies, old English, Middle English and the fifteenth century, and by centuries thereafter, with additional divisions for genres, children's literature, related studies, literary theory, and authors. Within each category, the works are assigned reference numbers and are arranged alphabetically by critic. Some entries cite reviews or include cross-references. Because of the broad literary period arrangement, scholars of Romantic-era literature will need to consult both the eighteenth- and nineteenth-century sections. Since no attempt is made to organize works by nationality (e.g., nineteenth-century British

literature), you will need to look through all works in each appropriate
section to find those items relevant to British Romantic-era authors and
topics. The authors and subjects index will assist in this endeavor but
works best for authors, as there aren't subject entries for Romanticism
or Gothic and only very general subject entries. Another index lists
critics.

ABELL is offered cumulatively on CD-ROM and online through
Chadwyck-Healey for the years 1920 to 2003, with selective coverage
of items published between 1892 and 1919 that were indexed retrospec-
tively. The online version is offered both as a separate database and as
part of *Literature Online* which includes links from the bibliographic
entries to full-text sources when available. The online bibliography
posts forthcoming records on a monthly basis, so it is more current than
the print version. The *ABELL* interface features searching by keyword,
title keyword, subject, author/reviewer, publication details, journal title,
and publication year, with the option to limit the search to articles,
books, or reviews. The main search fields include a browse function so
that you can look for indexed terms to paste to or to help refine your
search. The subject headings are very basic and follow these formulas:
English Literature: Eighteenth Century: Authors: (specific authors);
biography and autobiography; drama and the theatre; fiction; general
literary; general; literary theory; literature for children; poetry; prose;
and related studies. The same divisions are provided for nineteenth-
century literature (see Figure 4.2). Subject headings for authors are
cross-referenced so that if you type in *wordsworth william* you will
retrieve all entries with the authoritative heading "English Literature:
Nineteenth Century: Authors: Wordsworth, William." (Note that in the
subject heading English literature does not mean British literature.)
Although there are no subject headings for the concepts Romanticism
or Gothic, these terms are listed in the keyword index (romanticism,
4824 entries; Gothic, 1743 entries). Search results are arranged by the
most recent publications first in reverse chronological order.

**Figure 4.2. Modified *ABELL* record for "Interracial Sexual Desire
in Charlotte Dacre's *Zofloya*"**

```
ABELL
Author: Mellor, Anne K.
Title: Interracial sexual desire in Charlotte
Dacre's Zofloya.
Publication Details: European Romantic Re-
view(13:2)2002, 169-73.
Publication Year: 2002
```

Subject: English Literature: Nineteenth Century: Authors: Dacre, Charlotte (Rosa Matilda)

Subject: English Literature: Nineteenth Century: Authors: Matilda, Rosa (Charlotte Dacre)

Reference Number: 2002:10186
Source: Literature Online
_____
Source: *ABELL*, via *Literature Online*

    Although *ABELL* and *MLAIB* possess many records in common, they have enough difference in coverage to make it worthwhile to search both bibliographies in order to conduct as comprehensive a search as possible. Harner points out that *ABELL* is particularly strong for its indexing of books published only in Britain, as well for providing access to articles in small British periodicals. Also note that only *ABELL* indexes book reviews. Moreover, *ABELL* offers easier access to scholarship published before 1963 than *MLAIB* since its online coverage extends back to 1920. For scholarship published after 1980, however, Harner recommends starting with *MLAIB* since it provides more detailed subject indexing and greater online searching flexibility. *MLAIB* also features more current scholarship; at this time, online *ABELL* includes records only through 2003.

    The sample records from *MLAIB* and *ABELL* for the journal article "Interracial Sexual Desire in Charlotte Dacre's *Zofloya*" illustrate the different indexing between the databases, particularly in regard to subject access. Instead of incorporating the subject content into a single heading as done in the *ABELL* heading, "English Literature: Nineteenth Century: Authors: Dacre, Charlotte (Rosa Matilda)," the *MLAIB* record breaks the content into separate headings for subject literature, period, primary subject author, primary work, genre, and then distinctive subject terms, "interracial love" and "treatment of female sexual desire." Consequently, these numerous subject access points mean that a keyword search of *gothic and sexual desire* would retrieve this record in *MLAIB* but not in *ABELL*. The *ABELL* record, however, provides Charlotte Dacre's pseudonym, Rosa Matilda, which *MLAIB* does not include. A keyword search in *MLAIB* of *matilda rosa* yields zero hits and *rosa matilda* only four, whereas the same searches in *ABELL* retrieves nine and fifteen records respectively. These discrepancies emphasize the need to search both databases, not only for their potentially unique records but also for the way that their distinct indexing can produce different search results.

Large online bibliographies such as *MLAIB* and *ABELL* are best to use for comprehensive literature reviews. Sometimes getting access to the articles identified by your searches can be frustrating, however, since these bibliographies index many more sources than are typically owned by many university libraries. *MLAIB* and *ABELL* do provide limited access to some linked full-text sources, but not to every item indexed. Although interlibrary loan is always an option in these cases, for those students who want to find recent criticism on a particular topic, a full-text database is frequently a more expeditious alternative. *Project Muse* is a subscription database that offers full-text articles from approximately 250 scholarly journals in the arts, humanities, and social sciences. Journals in literary studies are well-represented and currently cover fifty-five titles, including *ELH, SEL: Studies in English Literature, 1500–1900*, and *Eighteenth-Century Studies* which frequently address Romantic-era authors. Even though coverage for each individual title varies, the database usually features access to the last five years or so of a journal's run. The advanced search interface permits searching the entire database, a subject collection such as literature, or an individual journal by keyword in the following fields: all text, all fields except text, article text, article author, article title, Library of Congress subject heading, or journal, with limit capabilities by document type (e.g., article, review, poetry, fiction, drama), date, and journals by subject or institutional subscription. Search results are listed as bibliographic citations usually but not always with subject headings; clicking on the title links to the full-text article in HTML or occasionally PDF. Alternatively, you can go directly to each journal's individual page, and browse through the tables of contents for each volume provided.

Literature searches in *Project Muse* are complemented by **JSTOR: The Scholarly Journal Archive**. This subscription database, like *Project Muse*, features full-text articles from scholarly journals, except with a collection emphasis on older rather than relatively recent issues. In fact, some journal runs are digitized back to the nineteenth century. *Project Muse* and *JSTOR* have established a reciprocal linking project, so that (currently) twenty-five selected titles in common link to each other to offer searching of complete digital journal runs, including the literary journals *Eighteenth Century Studies, ELH, MLN, Modern Language Notes, New Literary History*, and *Studies in English Literature*. The Language and Literature collection, which is split between Arts and Sciences I and Arts and Sciences III collections, includes forty-six titles identified as core resources for the field. Currently researchers will find the following titles relevant to Romantic literary studies: *ELH* (1934–1994); *MLN* (1962–1994) and *Modern Language Notes* (1886–

1961); *Modern Philology* (1903–1998); *Nineteenth-Century Literature* (1986–1999) and *Nineteenth-Century Fiction* (1949–1986); *New Literary History* (1969–1994); PMLA (1889–1990), *Transactions and Proceedings of the Modern Language Association of America* (1886–1887), *Modern Language Association of America Proceedings* (1884–1885), and *Transactions of the Modern Language Association of America* (1884–1885); *Review of English Studies* (1925–1998); and *SEL: Studies in English Literature, 1500–1900* (1961–1998). Depending on your institution's subscription coverage, you will be able to search all or only some of these journals.

If you are focusing on interdisciplinary work, you may also want to search one of the other subject collections, such as history, classical studies, philosophy, economics, or history of science. The basic search screen permits searching by keyword in the full-text, author, title, abstract, or caption fields and then selecting one or more subject journal collections or individual titles. Searches may then be limited by date or publication type (e.g., articles, reviews, opinion pieces, other including bibliographies). Results are listed as bibliographic citations with links to the citation/abstract, to print or download in PDF, or to save the citation. Clicking on the article title will let you browse through the article by page, link to the preceding or next article in that issue of the journal, or link to the table of contents.

Designed more for selective guidance rather than comprehensive coverage, *The Cambridge Bibliography of English Literature* (CBEL) has been a standard print reference source for identifying primary and selected secondary works by and about British literary authors since the first edition was published in 1940. Covering all periods of English literature (the most recent edition will continue through the entire twentieth century), *CBEL* is currently in the process of publishing its third edition. Luckily for scholars of Romantic-era literature, the first and only volume published so far is Volume 4 which covers the years 1800 to 1900. This volume differs from the earlier editions by eliminating the distinction between principal and minor authors, by covering many new authors previously excluded, especially poets who published in the later Romantic period (1800–1835), and by featuring more women authors across all genres. The bibliography presents primary material and selected secondary criticism and reference sources for authors native to or resident of England, Scotland, Wales, and Ireland who were born between 1760 and 1865, and whose major works were published before 1900. Romantic-era figures born before 1760, such as Blake and Godwin, will be covered in Volume 3. Entries are arranged into the following topical categories: book production and distribution; literary relations with the Continent; poetry; the novel and children's books;

drama; prose; history; political economy; philosophy and science; religion; English studies; travel; household books; sport; education; and newspapers and magazines. Following a general section, the poetry, novel, drama, and non-fictional prose categories are further arranged into three chronological periods, 1800–1835, 1835–1870, and 1870–1900; authors are assigned to each period by their date of birth. The poetry section also contains a selection of general histories and surveys of the Romantic movement, as well as essays and studies on the ideals and poetic theories of the Romantic school published between 1800 and 1920.

The author entries are organized alphabetically within the genre or subject section in which the majority of their work was published or with which they are most closely identified (with cross-references to the main entry from other relevant sections). Although there is no longer an official distinction between major and minor authors, it becomes apparent by the length of a bibliographic entry just who is considered an important figure and who is not. As Shattock notes in the preface, bibliographic detail for each entry varies "according to the state of knowledge of the subject, and sometimes according to the emphasis chosen by the contributor" (viii). Taking this fact into consideration, the entries present a range of primary and secondary materials. In the primary material section, the entry provides a chronological list of the author's individual works by date of first publication; these works can also include contributions to periodicals and collaborative works, letters, diaries, journals, notebooks, translations, prefaces or introductions by the author, works written under a pseudonym, and misattributed or spurious works. Users should be aware that full titles are sometimes abbreviated and that periodical article citations include volume and year but no page numbers. For some authors, the entry begins with locations of major manuscript collections, a list of bibliographies and reference works, details of collections and selections, contemporary reviews of individual works, and translations into other languages. The secondary material section features any of the following: a selective list of criticism published primarily but not exclusively before 1920 that "contributed signally to the establishment or revaluation of the writer concerned" (viii), textual and bibliographical criticism of the author's works, and authoritative biographies. Major author entries may also include obituaries, periodicals devoted to the author, as well as film, television, and radio adaptations. The main index will be published in Volume 6 but this volume concludes with a provisional index of names and selected subjects.

Scholars working with Romantic-era authors born before 1760 will need to consult the *New Cambridge Bibliography of English Litera-*

ture, Volume 2: 1660–1800. This second edition is structured similarly to the third, in that it contains primary and secondary works for British and Irish native or resident authors whose major works were published during the noted period, but there are a few significant differences. Poetry, the novel, and drama sections separate authors into major and minor categories; Scottish literature has its own section which covers poetry, drama, and prose (Irish and Welsh authors are integrated into the main bibliography); and criticism isn't capped at 1920 but includes works published through 1969. Another important difference is that critical studies written by an individual scholar are grouped together rather than listed in standard chronological sequence by publication date. The bibliography is arranged in the following sections: introduction (including general works, literary theory, literary relations with the Continent, medieval influences, book production and distribution); poetry; drama; the novel; prose (which includes essayists and pamphleteers, periodical publications, travel, translations into English, sport, letters, diaries, autobiographies and memoirs, religion, history, literary studies, classical and oriental studies, philosophy, science, law, and education); and Scottish literature. Within these sections, entries for individual authors are presented in a similar format to the third edition with any of the following possible subdivisions: notes on manuscript locations, bibliographies, collections, primary works, translations, letters and diaries, and secondary materials. Volume 5 contains the cumulative index for the previous four volumes. Scholars may still want to consult the second edition of *New Cambridge Bibliography of English Literature, Volume 3: 1800–1900* to identify potentially relevant criticism published between 1920 and 1969. Keep in mind that the first edition, *Cambridge Bibliography of English Literature* (1940) features sections on social life and political background that were excluded from the second and third editions. If you are interested in this information, see Volume 2: 1660–1800 and Volume 3: 1800–1900.

Also designed for selective guidance, the well-respected *Year's Work in English Studies* (YWES) provides evaluative descriptions of the year's significant scholarship in English language and literatures written in English. The narrative bibliography currently is arranged in the following chapters: English language; Old English literature; Middle English excluding Chaucer; Chaucer; the sixteenth century excluding drama after 1550; Shakespeare; Renaissance drama excluding Shakespeare; earlier seventeenth century covering general works, prose, and women's writing; Milton and poetry 1603–1660; the later seventeenth century; the eighteenth century; the Romantic period; the Victorian period; modern literature; American literature to 1900; twentieth-century American literature; literatures of Africa, Australia, Canada, Caribbean, India, New Zealand, and the South Pacific; and bibliography and textual criticism. Each chapter is written by scholars who discuss the significant contributions to the field for the year, including books, essays/book chapters, journal articles, critical editions, and sometimes reference works primarily published in Britain, the United States, and Canada. In Volume 81 (covering work published in 2000), the Romantic period chapter is divided into sections devoted to general works, prose fiction, non-fictional prose, poetry, Blake, Wordsworth and Coleridge, women Romantic poets, and drama and concludes with a list of books reviewed. The bibliography offers two indexes: critics and; authors and subjects.

Although there is a time lag of several years between the scholarship covered and the bibliography's publication, nevertheless, *YWES* provides an important, if delayed, assessment and overview of scholarship and critical trends in literary studies. Take note, however, that *YWES* is selective in its coverage. Use *YWES* as an initial tool for your research and then consult other review bibliographies to make sure not to miss any additional relevant works. For those with either an individual or institution subscription, *YWES* is available online at the Oxford University Press website. Here subscribers can access the full-text bibliography in HTML or PDF from Volume 80 (covering work published in 1999) to installment chapters submitted for the most recent volume.

Period Bibliographies

The Eighteenth Century: A Current Bibliography. New York: AMS Press, 1978–. Annual. The bibliography was published in *Philological Quarterly* 1926–1975 for the years 1925–1974 with different titles: English Literature of the Restoration and Eighteenth Century: A Current Bibliography (1925–1926); English Literature, 1660–1800: A Current Bibliography (1927–1969); The Eighteenth Century: A Current Bibliography (1970–1974).

English Literature, 1660–1800: A Bibliography of Modern Studies. 6 vols. Princeton, NJ: Princeton University Press, 1950–1972.

English Short Title Catalogue, 1473–1800 (ESTC). CD-ROM. 3rd ed. Farmington Hills, MI: Gale, 2003. Available online via www.rlg.org.

Nineteenth Century Short Title Catalogue (NSTC). Newcastle-upon-Tyne, England: Avero, 1984–. *Series I, Phase I, 1801–1815.* 6 vols. 1984–1986. CD-ROM. *Series II, Phase I, 1816–1870.* 56 vols. 1986–1995. CD-ROM. *Series III, 1871–1919.* 1996–2002. CD-ROM. Available online via nstc.chadwyck.com.

The bibliographies described in this section emphasize a particular period in the history of English literature. The first two sources, the *English Short Title Catalogue* and the *Nineteenth Century Short Title Catalogue*, are concerned exclusively with primary sources.

A joint endeavor of the American Antiquarian Society, the British Library, and the Center for Bibliographical Studies and Research at UC Riverside, the **English Short Title Catalogue** (*ESTC*) is an impressive bibliographic database currently featuring more than 465,000 records of letterpress works from the British Isles, colonial America, the United States, and Canada printed between 1473 and 1800, in addition to works printed entirely or partly in English or British vernacular from anywhere in the world during the same time period. These records represent books, newspapers, periodicals, broadsides, songs, advertisements, and some categories of engraved material but exclude trade and visiting cards, labels, tickets, invitations, playbills, theatre programs, playing cards, games, and puzzles. The *ESTC* incorporates every record from the (revised) Pollard and Redgrave's *A Short-title Catalogue of Books Printed in England, Scotland, & Ireland and of English Books Printed Abroad, 1475–1640* (*STC*) and Wing's *Short-title Catalogue of Books Printed in England, Scotland, Ireland, Wales, and British America, and of English Books Printed in Other Countries, 1641–1700*, as well as other works from the North American Imprints Program <http://www.americanantiquarian.org/naip.htm>. Formerly available on microfilm as the *Eighteenth Century Short Title Catalogue*, the database is offered online from the Research Libraries Group and on CD-ROM from Gale. It should be noted that the *ESTC* is not a completed project and users will encounter a range of records from full bibliographic records with subject headings for pre-1701 monographs, serials, and newspapers to unedited records and placeholder records for some items from *STC* and Wing. In fact, monograph records dating from 1701 to 1800 that were created for the original *Eighteenth Century Short Title Catalogue* were cataloged with truncated title and imprint information and were not assigned subject headings. Consequently, it is not possible to search for these monographs with a subject search but you can still achieve limited subject access with a keyword search in the title field.

The *ESTC* is distinguished by its detailed indexing which allows for searches in many parts of the record and opens the bibliographic records to previously unparalleled access. Although the online and CD-ROM versions differ slightly in their search forms, both facilitate this increased accessibility. The Research Libraries Group (RLG) features online access by subscription to the *ESTC*. This online version is updated daily. The advanced search option permits searching by keyword, author, author word, title, title word, subject, subject word, imprint or imprint year, word, or place; publication year; record ID; country of publication; genre; language; words from general notes; exact citation to a standard bibliography; words from citations; location words; and shelfmark or call number. Limits may then be set for date ranges and language. Unlike the CD-ROM version, the indexes in the RLG version cannot be browsed in order to find authoritative terms or paste terms to your search. Take note author and author word searches must separate the last and first name with a comma in order to work. Search results may be displayed in either brief or full citation form. The full record includes physical details, location(s), shelfmark(s), notes, references, and record ID.

The CD-ROM version also offers a detailed search form with drop down menus that permit searching by keyword; keyword in title, corporate author, publisher, imprint, general notes, references, microform notes, and subject heading fields; personal or corporate author; title; country, place, date, or language of publication; genre; library (e.g., British, North America, other, all); personal or corporate name or title as subject; subject heading; *ESTC* record number; and key phrase. Searches can also be limited by date range. By selecting a field from the drop down menu and then clicking on the Browse button, you can review terms from the appropriate index and then paste desired terms to the search form. After the search is executed, the number of hits is displayed next to the search query in the Current Search section. By clicking on the search query, the titles will be displayed in brief format or you can select the full format option from the tool bar. These full records typically include the *ESTC* record number, author, title, imprint, date, physical description, genre, notes, microform editions, country, language, primary location of item used to create the record, and either verified or unverified additional locations. The *ESTC*, in either version, is an excellent tool for identifying and locating texts published before 1800. And even though authoritative subject access is not provided at this point in time, researchers can still search by keyword in the titles, notes, and imprint fields to retrieve texts on particular topics.

The ***Nineteenth Century Short Title Catalogue*** (*NSTC*) is an ongoing project that seeks to provide a comprehensive list of books and terpress materials published in Great Britain, its colonies, and the United States between 1801 and 1919, in addition to books published in English throughout the world and translations from English for the same time period. This list is compiled from the in-house and printed catalogs of the Bodleian Library at Oxford University, Cambridge University Library, the British Library, Trinity College in Dublin, the National Library of Scotland, and Newcastle University Library, as well as the Harvard University Library and the Library of Congress for books published between 1816 and 1919. The print *NSTC* is available in two series, *Series I, Phase I* which covers the years 1801 to 1815 and *Series II, Phase I* which covers 1816 to 1870; both are also offered in CD-ROM format. *Series III* is available on CD-ROM only and completes the set from 1871 to 1919. All three series may be searched through the *ABC-CLIO* database which contains more than one million records. The online version features searching by keyword, author, subject, epithet, title, life span, publication date, place of publication, language, location, series ID, and entry number. Browsing features are available for all but the keyword, title, publication date, and entry number indexes. Each record contains series ID, author, title, epithet, life span, subject, entry number, publication date, place, and location(s) of copies in the participating libraries (occasionally with shelfmark number). Note that only the year and place of publication, but not the publisher, are included in each record for items published between 1801 and 1870. Also be aware that subject headings are very general (e.g., English poetry, English letters, biography, literary history and criticism) and are based on Dewey Decimal classification. Some records in *Series III* do not have subject headings at all in the online version.

Similar for its focus on a particular literary period, ***The Eighteenth Century: A Current Bibliography*** (*ECCB*) is concerned with the secondary literature about authors of the Restoration and eighteenth century. Originally published in *Philological Quarterly* during the years 1926 to 1975 and addressing critical works published from 1925 to 1974, the bibliography assumed the following titles: "English Literature of the Restoration and Eighteenth Century: A Current Bibliography" (1925–1926); "English Literature, 1660–1800: A Current Bibliography" (1927–1969); and "The Eighteenth Century: A Current Bibliography" (1970–1974). In 1970, the bibliography changed from its emphasis on English literature to a more interdisciplinary focus. Since 1978, *The Eighteenth Century: A Current Bibliography* has been a separate annual publication offered by AMS Press. Although the *ECCB* has suffered significant publication delays since the 1990s (Volume 25 is the latest published which covers scholarship from 1999 and initiates a single volume format again), you may find the *Eighteenth Century* bibliography's multidisciplinary scope, international coverage, and selective detailed annotations worth perusing as a complement to other standard bibliographies.

Until Volume 25, the entries were arranged alphabetically by author in six categories: printing and bibliographical studies; historical, social, and economic studies; philosophy, science, and religion; fine arts; literary studies; and individual authors. The latest volume restructures the bibliography by replacing literary studies and individual author categories with "v. foreign literatures and languages" and "vi: British and American literatures." The editors of Volume 25 also state in their preface that the *ECCB* will discontinue its "long-term bibliographical flirtation with the Romantic poets" and Romantic topics (x), however, the bibliography will "continue to monitor scholarship on so-called 'pre-Romantic' writers like John Clare or Mary Wollstonecraft"(xi). In fact, a survey of the British and American literature category reveals numerous entries about Austen, as well as Burney, Blake, Inchbald, Radcliffe, Scott, Smith, Wollstonecraft, Gothic literature, and general works such as *Landscape, Liberty and Authority: Poetry, Criticism, and Politics from Thomson to Wordsworth*, *Unnatural Affections: Women and Fiction in the Later Eighteenth Century*, and *Women's Reading in Britain, 1750–1835: A Dangerous Recreation*. In an effort to catch up, Volumes 20–21 (1994–1995) and 22–24 (1996–1998) were published as combined volumes, the 22–24 issue at more than 600 pages.

The current bibliography continues to selectively cover books, journal articles, and reviews and exclude dissertations. Many of the entries are descriptively annotated and reviews are listed for the source, some of which indicate the nature of the review (e.g., favorably, mixed). Selected works receive signed, in-depth reviews by scholars in the field that range from one to three pages. The "Literary Studies" section in Volumes 22–24 is arranged by language: English literature including American literature, French literature, German literature, and Spanish literature. Individual authors represented in Volumes 22–24 include Blake, Burney, Burns, Clare, Cowper, Edgeworth, Godwin, Lewis, Smith, Williams, and Wollstonecraft. This is a good source if you are interested in topics that cover other disciplines of the eighteenth century and if you want selective in-depth annotations. Use the single name index to find entries for authors not listed in the individual author section for volumes previous to Volume 25, and to find references within the new British and American literatures section. For example, books about Ann Radcliffe are also in the "Printing and Bibliography" section, and an edition of Elizabeth Inchbald's *Nature and Art* is discussed in the "Literary Studies" section—none of which are referenced in the "Individual authors" section in Volumes 22–24.

English Literature, 1660–1800: A Bibliography of Modern Studies is a compilation of reprinted "The Eighteenth Century" bibliographies originally published in *Philological Quarterly* from 1926 to 1970. Each bibliography selectively covers books, journal articles, and reviews published during the previous year that concerned British literature during the years 1660 to 1800. Although the arrangement varies over time, the bibliographies are generally organized with the following categories: bibliographies and bibliographical studies; topical studies (e.g., language, political and social studies, philosophy, science and religion, literary history and criticism); individual author studies; and Continental background. Many of the entries are annotated; selected items receive signed, detailed, evaluative annotations, sometimes several pages in length. Reviews are also noted. Although the bibliographies cover works primarily in English, French, and German, studies in other languages are occasionally featured. Romantic-era authors that are addressed in the bibliographies include: Austen, Blake, Burke, Burney, Burns, Crabbe, Edgeworth, Godwin, Inchbald, Lewis, Radcliffe, and Seward. The bibliography contains cumulative indexes in Volumes 2, 4, and 6 that cover authors, editors, reviewers, and selected subjects for the preceding two volumes.

Romantic-Era Bibliographies

Elkins, Aubrey C., Jr. and Lorne J. Forstner, eds. *The Romantic Movement Bibliography, 1936–1970: A Master Cumulation from ELH, Philological Quarterly and English Language Notes.* 7 vols. Ann Arbor, MI: Pierian Press in association with R. R. Bowker, 1973.

Frank, Frederick S. *The First Gothics: A Critical Guide to the English Gothic Novel.* New York: Garland, 1987.

———. *Guide to the Gothic: An Annotated Bibliography of Criticism.* Metuchen, NJ: Scarecrow Press, 1984.

———. *Guide to the Gothic II: An Annotated Bibliography of Criticism, 1983–1993.* Lanham, MD: Scarecrow Press, 1995.

Garside, Peter, James Raven, and Rainer Schöwerling, general eds. *The English Novel 1770–1829: A Bibliographical Survey of Prose Fiction Published in the British Isles.* 2 vols. New York: Oxford University Press, 2000.

Jackson, J. R. de J. *Romantic Poetry by Women: A Bibliography, 1770–1835.* New York: Oxford University Press, 1993.

Jordan, Frank, ed. *The English Romantic Poets: A Review of Research and Criticism.* 4th ed. New York: Modern Language Association of America, 1985.

O'Neill, Michael, ed. *Literature of the Romantic Period: A Bibliographical Guide.* New York: Oxford University Press, 1998.

The Romantic Movement: A Selective and Critical Bibliography for the Year. New York: Garland, 1980–1999. Annual. ISSN: 0557-2738.

Thomson, Douglass H., Jack G. Voller, and Frederick S. Frank, eds. *Gothic Writers: A Critical and Bibliographical Guide.* Westport, CT: Greenwood Press, 2002.

Bibliographies dedicated specifically to the Romantic era of British literature comprise both works that address the period in general and those bibliographies that are organized around a particular genre, such as the novel, poetry, or Gothic literature. The principal and longstanding bibliography for Romantic literature was the "Romantic Movement: A Selective and Critical Bibliography" which was published annually in the journals *ELH* from 1936 to 1948, *Philological Quarterly* from 1949 to 1963, and *English Language Notes* from 1964 to 1979. Garland continued the bibliography as *The Romantic Movement: A Selective and Critical Bibliography for the Year*, in its *Reference Library of the Humanities* series from 1980 until 1999. A separately published bibliography, entitled *The Romantic Movement Bibliography, 1936–1970: A Master Cumulation from ELH, Philological Quarterly and English Language Notes* reprints the original journal bibliographies for the noted years. In the introduction to this compilation, Elkins explains that even though the "Romantic Movement" was selective, it still attempted to cover "the more significant books, articles and reviews dealing with the literature of romanticism, in England and other countries" (1), mainly continental Europe. Erdman cautions in the foreword to the compilation, however, that despite inconsistent coverage throughout the bibliography's history, significant works have been included, in addition to works of "'minor but scholarly interest'" not listed in the *MLA Bibliography* (vii).

The *Romantic Movement* bibliography maintained a fairly consistent arrangement through the years of a general section and the following national literature divisions: English, French, German, Italian, and Spanish, with sections at times for Scandinavian, Slavonic, Danish, and Portuguese languages. Within these divisions, the entries are arranged by types of resources, including bibliographies, critical works, and studies of individual authors, with occasionally a section devoted to relevant works on art, society, politics, and religion listed under the heading "Environment." Many of the entries are annotated and reviews are noted. The *Romantic Movement Bibliography, 1936–1970* offers the advantage of three cumulative indexes: author/main entry/reviewer, subject by personal name, and subject by categorical headings and subheadings. Recent volumes of the bibliography only contain an index of critics. Now that *The Romantic Movement* is no longer published, scholars will need to consult the "*Keats-Shelley Journal* Bibliography," the *Romantic Circles Bibliography, MLAIB, ABELL*, and the other relevant bibliographies described in this chapter to stay abreast of current publications in Romantic-era literature.

One of the most recent general bibliographies of criticism to be published about British Romantic-era literature, O'Neill's *Literature of the Romantic Period: A Bibliographical Guide* features bibliographic essays on "the best and the typical in scholarship and criticism" (v) addressing the Romantic period from 1785 to 1830. Eleven chapters are devoted to individual canonical authors (e.g., Blake, Wordsworth, Coleridge, Byron, Shelley, Keats, Clare, Scott, Austen, Peacock, and Mary Shelley) and seven other chapters address general studies, women poets, male poets, fiction, Romantic Gothic, essayists, and political prose. Written by scholars primarily from British universities, the signed essays all follow a similar format. Most begin with a brief introduction to the figure or genre, then progress to discuss the author's texts, including publication history, standard and recommended recent editions, and any pertinent issues surrounding textual scholarship. The main part of the essay provides an overview and analysis of the criticism about the author(s) from contemporary reception through late twentieth-century trends and concerns. All the works cited in the chapter are noted in a concluding list of references. Students will find this bibliography a useful resource for identifying the standard editions for their author and for its introduction both to the historical critical tradition and recent trends in scholarship.

Several journals dedicated to Romantic-era literature feature annual reviews of scholarship. The *Keats-Shelley Journal* offers an annual bibliography, *SEL: Studies in English Literature* covers recent studies in nineteenth-century literature in the autumn issue, and *Wordsworth Circle* provides reviews in the fall issue. The *Romantic Circles* website also features a bibliography of selected journal tables of contents and an annual listing of books relevant to the study of Romantic literature, which now incorporates the online *Keats-Shelley Journal Bibliography*. Please refer to Chapter 5 for more complete descriptions of these journal bibliographies and Chapter 10 for the *Romantic Circles Bibliography*.

Scholars working with Romantic literary texts associated with specific genres may want to consult a genre bibliography, which can provide guidance to primary works and/or criticism, as well as sometimes an introduction to or critical overview of the genre during the period addressed. The bibliographies described below are representative selections of this type of resource.

Lauded by Harner as "an invaluable and trustworthy guide to six decades of English fiction,"[1] *The English Novel 1770–1829: A Bibliographical Survey of Prose Fiction Published in the British Isles* attempts to comprehensively list all known first edition English-language novels published in the British Isles from 1770 to 1829, as well as first English translations of novels published originally in Europe and first British editions of novels published in North America during the same period. The works included in the bibliography were actually consulted; for those titles with no extant first edition, information is provided based on printing and publishing records, contemporary reviews, or advertisements and circulating library catalogs. Selections for inclusion were based on each title's categorization as a novel in contemporary periodical reviews and under circulating library catalog headings. Religious tracts, chapbooks, children's literature and short, separately published tales are excluded, but collections of tales are not. The bibliography is published in two volumes which cover the years 1770 to 1799 and 1800 to 1829.

Following an introductory essay in each volume entitled, "The Novel Comes of Age" (Volume 1) and "The English Novel in the Romantic Era: Consolidation and Dispersal" (Volume 2), the entries are arranged by year of imprint, then alphabetically first by title of anonymous works, and then by known authors, translators, or pseudonym when the actual author has not been identified. Entries for each source are detailed and include: author's name; full title taken from the title page; place of publication and imprint information; pagination, format and price; contemporary review references from the major periodicals; location and shelfmark of copy consulted and selected additional holding libraries; and notes which record details such as dedications, subscription lists, advertisements, past incorrect attributions of authorship, and subsequent editions through 1850. In the first volume only, extracts from the original reviews are also reproduced. Appendices provide a selection of novels for children and non-fiction (Volume 1) and children's novels, shorter tales and miscellanies, didactic fiction, historical memoirs, reissues/reprints and later translations, and uncertain reconstituted/unseen titles (Volume 2). Both volumes feature three indexes: authors/translators, titles, booksellers and printers, and in Volume 1, an additional notes index. The *English Novel* is an excellent source for identifying specific works, as well as for assessing the state of the novel during the Romantic period.

Poetry, of course, is the genre most typically associated with the Romantic period, especially the poetry of the canonical male figures. Jackson seeks to balance the scales with *Romantic Poetry by Women: A Bibliography, 1770 –1835*. Based on an earlier project called *Annals of English Verse 1770–1835: A Preliminary Survey of Volumes Published* (1985), this bibliography aims to comprehensively list all volumes of verse published in English by women authors during the years 1770 to 1835. Verse translations into English from other languages are also included. Entries for approximately nine hundred authors are arranged alphabetically by the author's most commonly used surname during this period, with individual works listed in order of publication and edition. Anonymous authors are found under entries for "Anonymous," "A Lady," and "A Young Lady" with cross-references to attributed authors. Biographical information is noted when known, and sometimes includes birth and death dates, parents, record of marriage, children, and non-poetical activities. For many authors, however, nothing is known beyond their name; other entries range from such cryptic statements as "She probably lived in Brighton" for Mary Dash, to full paragraphs for more well-known figures such as Letitia Elizabeth Landon. Sources that were consulted for the biographical information are listed in parentheses. Each entry concludes with a reference to the library in which the work was consulted with its shelfmark or call number. The bibliography also includes an appendix of books written by men using a female pseudonym and a note on the annual rate of publication for first and all editions published by year from 1770 to 1835, in addition to indexes of authors' names, titles, and publishers by place of publication. This will be a good source for identifying poetry by more obscure authors and the locations of these texts, and in some instances, serve as a starting place for biographical information.

Although superseded by more recent compilations of research, scholars focusing on the history of critical reception may still find *The English Romantic Poets: A Review of Research and Criticism* useful. The bibliography is arranged in seven chapters; one devoted to the Romantic movement in England and the rest to the big six: Blake, Wordsworth, Coleridge, Byron, Shelley, and Keats. It should be noted that this fourth edition adds Blake for the first time—moving him from the companion volume on the minor Romantic poets and essayists to the major league (Houtchens, Carolyn Washburn, and Lawrence Huston Houtchens, eds. *The English Romantic Poets and Essayists: A Review of Research and Criticism*. Rev. ed. New York University Press for MLA, 1966). Written by scholars in the field, each chapter provides a narrative bibliographic essay with an emphasis on recent criticism (at that time in the mid-1980s) but also with the goal of placing this scholarship within its historical context. Although the author chapters vary in their organization and emphasis, they each tend to cover similar types of sources, including: bibliographies and other reference works, editions, biographical resources, and criticism (e.g., general studies, individual works, and thematic approaches) with occasional discussions of either trends or reputation and influence, such as for Keats, Shelley, and Byron. "The Romantic Movement in England" chapter discusses bibliographies, histories, general studies, and then groups criticism by topic, such as "Romanticism and Science," "Romantic Images and Themes," and "English Romanticism Abroad." The bibliography concludes with one index of authors/critics, titles, and selected subjects.

Gothic literature has been the subject of recent critical attention and several bibliographies serve as guides both to primary and secondary sources for the genre. Covering the period from 1753 to 1832, *The First Gothics: A Critical Guide to the English Gothic Novel* provides publication information and critical synopses for five hundred titles selected to be a representative cross-section of the English Gothic. Frank chose the featured novels based on contemporary availability of the title; artistic merit, historical importance, and popularity with their original audience as well as with scholars; and the title's role in the development of the Gothic movement. The entries are arranged alphabetically by author, with bibliographic information about the first edition, and a note on any modern editions. The entries also include a "Gothic Type" classification for each title, such as doppelgänger, pure or high Gothic, chapbook Gothic, or monastic shocker, and provide a select list of secondary sources about the author and text, if available. This bibliography is distinguished by the critical plot synopses, ranging in length from one paragraph to two pages, that typically conclude with a brief analysis of the title's influence and role within the genre. Additional appendices enhance the usefulness of the bibliography: the "Glossary of Gothic Terms" offers definitions for the types referred to in the bibliographic entry, as well as related terms such as algolagnia, Graveyard poetry, and toweromania; a bibliography of secondary sources presents the "best and most pertinent" twentieth-century criticism on the Gothic; and a chronology lists the five hundred titles by year of publication. This source also includes an introductory historical overview of the Gothic in the eighteenth and nineteenth centuries, fourteen black and white reproductions of the original engravings and woodcuts from selected works, and three indexes of Gothic authors, titles, and critics.

Frank has written two other complementary bibliographies of criticism, *Guide to the Gothic: An Annotated Bibliography of Criticism* and *Guide to the Gothic II: An Annotated Bibliography of Criticism,*

1983–1993. The first bibliography attempts to comprehensively cover criticism published on the Gothic between 1900 and 1982, arranged by the following categories: previous Gothic bibliographies; nationality, including English, Canadian, American, French, German, and other nationalities, that is further divided chronologically by authors from the eighteenth to the twentieth century; and special subject areas (e.g., Gothicism of the Romantic poets, parodies of the Gothic, death by spontaneous combustion, Gothic films). The work concludes with a list of journals cited, an index of critics, and an index of authors, artists, and actors. *Guide to the Gothic II: An Annotated Bibliography of Criticism, 1983–1993* is arranged in a similar format (e.g., general guides, nationalities, special subjects) and offers more entries than the first volume but covers fewer and sometimes different authors, as well as slightly different subject areas, such as "Vampirism and Werewolfery," and "Recent Anthologies of Gothic Fiction." The author index also incorporates titles. *Guide to the Gothic III* is scheduled to be published in 2005 and will cover criticism from 1994 to 2003.

A more recent response to the late twentieth-century heightened academic and general interest in Gothic literature, **Gothic Writers: A Critical and Bibliographical Guide** provides critical overviews and bibliographies of primary and secondary works for Gothic authors primarily from Britain and the United States. The editors have taken a wider interpretation of the Gothic by including authors not traditionally associated with the Gothic canon, and as such, include a few non-Western figures. Students of Romantic-era literature will find many authors from the late eighteenth and early nineteenth centuries. Following a historical overview of the critical response to the genre, the fifty-four entries are arranged alphabetically by author rather than chronologically. All but three of the entries are concerned with individual or related authors (e.g., John Aikin and Anna Laetitia Aikin Barbauld, Charlotte and Emily Brontë); the others address Gothic chapbooks, bluebooks, and short stories in magazines from 1790 to 1820, Gothic drama, and Jane Austen and the *Northanger* novelists (e.g., Flammenberg, Grosse, Lathom, Parsons, Roche, and Sleath).

Written by various contributors from the United States, Canada and Britain (most of the entries are by the American editors), each of the signed entries begins by listing the author's principal Gothic works, as well as modern reprints and editions. The main body of the entry presents a critical discussion of the author's literary career and his/her role within the Gothic tradition which ranges in length from two to ten pages. Finally, the entry concludes with a concisely annotated bibliography of selected recent criticism. Additional resources are listed in the "General Bibliography of Critical Sources and Resources" at the end of the guide, which covers primary and secondary bibliographies of the Gothic, works that treat the term Gothic in history and literature, reference works, general histories and studies in definition and theory, journals and special journal issues, and Web resources. The guide also concludes with a timeline of Gothic authors and their works from 1762 to 1999, an author/title index, and an index of critics, editors, and translators. This source is a good place to begin research on a particular figure from the Gothic tradition since it compiles pertinent information about the author's major works, as well as modern reprints, and editions, features a summary of the author's literary career, and presents descriptions of recent critical works about the author.

Romantic-Era Author Bibliographies

Corson, James Clarkson. *A Bibliography of Sir Walter Scott. A Classified and Annotated List of Books and Articles Relating to His Life and Works, 1797–1940.* Edinburgh, London: Oliver and Boyd Ltd., 1943. Reprinted New York: Burt Franklin, 1968.

Goode, Clement Tyson. *George Gordon, Lord Byron: A Comprehensive, Annotated Research Bibliography of Secondary Materials in English, 1973–1994.* Lanham, MD: Scarecrow Press, 1997.

Lyles, William H. *Mary Shelley: An Annotated Bibliography.* New York: Garland Publishing, 1975.

Santucho, Oscar José. *George Gordon, Lord Byron: A Comprehensive Bibliography of Secondary Materials in English, 1807–1974.* With a critical review of research by Clement Tyson Goode, Jr. Metuchen, NJ: Scarecrow Press, 1977.

Scholars working on individual authors will want to look for bibliographies dedicated specifically to their figure. Resources such as the *Cambridge Bibliography of English Literature* and O'Neill's *Literature of the Romantic Period* are good starting points for identifying recommended author bibliographies. You can also check the other relevant bibliographies discussed in this chapter, or search in a union catalog such as *WorldCat* (strategies for finding author bibliographies in a library catalog are outlined in Chapter 3). Author bibliographies can focus on primary or secondary sources and be published in a book, journal, or on the Web. The bibliographies discussed below are selective representations of monograph bibliographies you may encounter. Take note that bibliographies published many years ago may still be recommended, usually for their thorough or insightful assessment of the early criticism, or for other reasons. These older sources can be updated by using *MLAIB*, *ABELL*, or *YWES* to identify more recent criticism.

Still considered a standard guide to earlier criticism ("guides readers deftly through the Scott craze at its peak"[2]), Corson's *A Bibliography of Sir Walter Scott. A Classified and Annotated List of Books and Articles Relating to His Life and Works, 1797–1940* (1943, reprinted 1968) covers books and articles devoted exclusively to Scott and his works that were published from 1797 to 1940, however, it does not include editions of Scott's works. The entries are arranged in four parts: bibliographical material, biographical sources, literary, and those that combine both literary and biographical material. The biographical section is subdivided by specialized subjects, including: original sources, biographies, special periods (e.g., boyhood and early manhood, Continental tours, funeral), character, portraits, finance and business relationships, family, servants, and contemporaries. The literary section is organized by literary histories, poems, dramas, Waverley novels, prose works, translations, edited works and prefaces, and literary relations. The last section covers sources on special subjects (e.g., animals, law, religion, topography). Most of the entries contain brief, often evaluative annotations, and excerpts are frequently provided for reviews. The bibliography concludes with one index for authors, selected titles, and subjects.

George Gordon, Lord Byron: A Comprehensive Bibliography of Secondary Materials in English, 1807–1974 is a two-part bibliography that begins with a substantial overview of Byron scholarship from 1807 to 1974 that traces the "critical fortunes of the poet" (3) and places the works cited in the bibliography in their historical and critical context. The second part of the bibliography lists more than five thousand secondary, printed materials about Byron written in English covering the same time frame. Both sections are arranged chronologically in ten periods that reflect trends in scholarship from "Byron's Lifetime, 1807–1824" to "Balance Restored: Renaissance in Biography and Criticism, 1957–1972." The bibliographical entries are grouped by year and contain a brief, descriptive annotation only if the content is not apparent from the title. Several appendices cover the following specific sources: doctoral dissertations; notes on sales, library acquisitions, and holdings; places associated with Byron; poetical tributes, attacks, satires, epistles, and admonitions; imitations, continuations, dramatizations, adaptations, parodies, satires, and poems occasioned by the works of Byron; and Byron in drama, fiction, and poetry. The bibliography concludes with one author index, but no title or subject access.

Goode has updated this bibliography with a new publication, *George Gordon, Lord Byron: A Comprehensive, Annotated Research*

Bibliography of Secondary Materials in English, 1973–1994 which illustrates by its length of seven hundred pages the surge in Byron scholarship during the last part of the twentieth century. This source omits the critical overview but maintains the scope and chronological arrangement of the original. Entries are grouped alphabetically by year and except for reviews and articles concerning Byron Society activities, every entry in the bibliography includes a concise, descriptive annotation. The appendices cover the same types of thematic sources as noted above, however, this volume features indexes by author, subject, and Byron's works.

Recommended in both the *Cambridge Bibliography of English Literature* (3rd ed.) and O'Neill's *Literature of the Romantic Period*, Lyle's *Mary Shelley: An Annotated Bibliography* remains a standard source despite its publication date of 1975. Unlike the other author bibliographies described in this chapter, this bibliography covers both primary and secondary sources. Part one of the bibliography chronologically lists known editions of Shelley's works in the following categories: journals and letters, novels, dramas, stories, poems, travel writing, biographies, articles and reviews, and edited works. Each citation includes notes about the text, references to reviews, and notes on reprints or reissues. The second part of the bibliography is concerned with criticism or works about Mary Shelley published from 1817 to the early 1970s. This section is organized alphabetically by author and grouped by source type, including books, periodicals, reviews, Ph.D. dissertations and M.A. theses, non-English-language materials, and fictional works about Mary Shelley. Each entry is described with an annotation ranging from one sentence to a paragraph and is frequently illustrated with an extract from the original source; cross-references are provided to reprints and related entries. Several appendices enhance the bibliography, including: a chronological list of Mary Shelley's works; the legend of George of Frankenstein; theatrical, film, and television versions of *Frankenstein*; and selling prices for selected works by and about Mary Shelley. The index covers authors and titles from the main entries, except those from Part II, sections A and B, and all titles, periodicals, and persons from the annotations.

Conclusion

Scholars of Romantic-era literature are fortunate that several bibliographies exist for their literary period. Although bibliographic efforts concentrated on the canonical poets through most of the twentieth century, recent bibliographies reflect the period's changing definition and broader critical interest. In addition, scholars now have the advantage of being able to search standard bibliographies online with a greater range of access points, thereby significantly increasing their ability to identify both primary materials from the eighteenth and nineteenth centuries, as well as criticism from the early twentieth century through the present. Using a combination of traditional print and online bibliographies will enable the scholar to research literature of the Romantic period in an unprecedented way.

Notes

1. Harner, James L. *Literary Research Guide: An Annotated Listing of Reference Sources in English Literary Studies.* 4th ed. (New York: Modern Language Association, 2002), 274.

2. O'Neill, Michael, ed. *Literature of the Romantic Period: A Bibliographical Guide* (New York: Oxford University Press, 1998), 224.

Chapter 5
Romantic Literature:
Scholarly Journals

Academic journals provide one of the principal forums for presenting literary research. Scholars use journals to identify articles relevant to their own research projects, to keep informed of recent findings and trends in the field both through articles and reviews of newly published books, and to select appropriate venues for their own work. This chapter lists and describes the major journals that cover Romantic- and Regency-era authors, works, and topics, as well as a selection of British eighteenth-century literature, nineteenth-century literature, and general literature journals that address authors of the Romantic period on a regular basis. The journals are grouped in five main categories: the Romantic period, eighteenth century, nineteenth century, the Victorian period, and general British literature (e.g., journals that cover more than one literary period). Each description outlines the journal's scope, indicates how many and the average length of essays published per issue, and provides a few examples of current article topics. Keep in mind that with only a few exceptions, most of these journals are indexed in *MLA International Bibliography* and *ABELL: Annual Bibliography of English Language and Literature*. Many are also offered full-text in other subscription databases such as *Project Muse*, *Academic Search Premier*, *JSTOR*, and *Ingenta*. If the journal has a Web component from which it offers tables of contents or article abstracts, that information is noted in the journal description and the Web address is listed in the bibliography at the beginning of each section.

The first journals devoted solely to the Romantics were not firmly established until the mid-twentieth century, with the *C.L.S. Bulletin* in 1935 (which was not included in "The Romantic Movement: A Selective and Critical Bibliography"), the regular publication of the *Keats-Shelley Memorial Bulletin* in 1950, and the *Keats-Shelley Journal* in 1952. Before that time, articles about Romantic-era authors appeared in the standard literary and philological journals of the early twentieth century. Several of these early venues for Romantic scholarship continue to be important sources for articles on Romantic literature.

A survey of "The Romantic Movement: A Selective and Critical Bibliography," which was compiled yearly from 1937 to 1979 by the journals *ELH* (1936–1948), *Philological Quarterly* (1949–1963), and *English Language Notes* (1964–1979) and covers literature published between 1936 and 1978, gives a representative overview of the principal journals that published articles on Romantic-era authors and topics during that period. *The Romantic Movement: A Selective and Critical Bibliography for the Year* was a separate publication from 1980 to 1999. Although this bibliography was selective in nature, it still attempted to include "all books and articles of substantial interest to scholars of English and Continental Romanticism."[1] The English literature "Critical" and "Studies of Authors" sections of "The Romantic Movement" reveal that throughout the late 1930s and 1940s, articles relevant to British Romantic studies were frequently published in *ELH*, *Explicator*, *Huntington Library Quarterly*, *Journal of English and Germanic Philology*, *Modern Language Notes*, *Modern Language Quarterly*, *Modern Language Review*, *Modern Philology*, *Notes and Queries*, *Philological Quarterly*, *PMLA*, *Review of English Studies*, *Studies in Philology*, *Times Literary Supplement*, and the *University of Toronto Quarterly*. Articles also appeared in the *Dalhousie Review*, *Kenyon Review*, and the *Sewanee Review*. During the 1950s, these journals continued to publish articles regularly on the Romantics and were joined by the *Keats-Shelley* journals noted above, *Bulletin of the New York Public Library*, *Comparative Literature*, *Essays in Criticism*, *Harvard Library Bulletin*, *Journal of the History of Ideas*, and *Nineteenth-Century Fiction*.

A new journal devoted to the Romantics, *Studies in Romanticism*, made its appearance in 1961; other journals that began publishing on the Romantics in the 1960s include, *English Language Notes*, *Review of English Literature*, *Studies in English Literature*, *Studies in Scottish Literature*, and *Texas Studies in Language and Literature*. Reflecting the emergent interest in William Blake in the late 1960s, the *Blake Newsletter* (1967–1977, continued by *Blake*, 1977–present) and *Blake Studies* (1968–1980) were introduced. Other journals dedicated primarily to individual authors also appeared in the 1970s and 1980s, including: *Wordsworth Circle* (1970), *Byron Journal* (1973), *Charles Lamb Bulletin* (1973, preceded by the *C.L.S. Bulletin* 1935–1972), *Persuasions* (1980), *John Clare Society Journal* (1982), and the *Coleridge Bulletin* (1988). During this period, *Milton and the Romantics* was initiated in 1975, became *Romanticism: Past and Present* in 1980, and settled on *Nineteenth-Century Contexts* in 1987. The *Keats-Shelley Memorial Bulletin* also changed its title in 1986 to the *Keats-Shelley Review*.

The 1990s witnessed the establishment of four more Romantic literature journals: *Romanticism* (1995) which is concerned primarily with British Romantic authors; the interdisciplinary journals *European Romantic Review* (1990) and *Prism(s)* (1993); and the first electronic Romantic studies journal, *Romanticism on the Net* (1996). Apart from *Blake Studies* which ceased in 1980, all of the journals concerned specifically with Romantic-era authors are still in existence and currently provide scholars with an arena of fourteen core journals dedicated to publishing scholarship in the field.

Because articles relevant to Romantic studies continue to be published in numerous journals, the most effective way to find articles for your research will be to search an online literary bibliography, such as *MLA International Bibliography*, or *ABELL: Annual Bibliography of English Language and Literature* (discussed in Chapter 4) in order to conduct a comprehensive literature review. These resources index a wide variety of journals relevant to English literary studies and are subscribed to by most academic libraries. If you want to review the latest contents of the main Romantic journals, however, you can link directly to each journal's website or peruse the *Romantic Circles Bibliographies* page or *Romanticism on the Net* "Journals" section, both of which present tables of contents for selected Romantic studies journals (described in Chapter 10). Most academic journals post their current tables of contents online. In addition to highlighting the latest scholarship in the field, these contents also can be used to ascertain which theoretical approaches the journal supports, as well as which authors and topics are currently in vogue. If you are looking for an appropriate forum for your own work, a journal's website frequently provides submission guidelines, posts calls for papers for upcoming issues, and relays relevant conference announcements.

Romantic Era

Blake. "An Illustrated Quarterly." (Blake) University of Rochester, 1977–. Quarterly. ISSN: 0160-628X. Former title: Blake Newsletter (1967–1977) 0006–453X. www.rochester.edu/college/eng/blake/.

Byron Journal (*ByronJ*). The Byron Society Journal Ltd., 1973–. Annual. ISSN: 0301-7257. www.raindog.pwp.blueyonder.co.uk/byronjourn.

Charles Lamb Bulletin (ChLB). Charles Lamb Society, 1973–. Quarterly. ISSN: 0308-0951. Former titles: C.L.S. Bulletin: Organ of the Charles Lamb Society (1941–1972); Monthly Bulletin (1935–1941). users.ox.ac.uk/~scat0385/clbulletin.html.

Coleridge Bulletin (ColeridgeB). Friends of Coleridge in Somerset, 1988–. 2/yr. ISSN: 0968-0551. www.friendsofcoleridge.com/Coleridge-Bulletin.htm.

European Romantic Review (ERR). Routledge, 1990–. Quarterly (spring 1997–); formerly semiannual (1990–1997). ISSN: 1050-9585. www.tandf.co.uk/journals/titles/10509585.html.

John Clare Society Journal (JCSJ). The John Clare Society, 1982–. Annual. No ISSN. human.ntu.ac.uk/clare/jcsjindex.html and human.ntu.ac.uk/clare.

Keats-Shelley Journal: Keats, Shelley, Byron, Hunt, and Their Circles (KSJ). Keats-Shelley Association of America, 1952–. Annual. ISSN: 0453-4387. naples.cc.sunysb.edu/CAS/ksj.nsf.

Keats-Shelley Review (KSMB). The Keats-Shelley Memorial Association, 1986–. Annual. ISSN: 0952-4142. Former titles: Keats-Shelley Memorial Bulletin (1950–1985); Bulletin and Review of the Keats-Shelley Memorial, Rome (1913); Keats-Shelley Memorial, Rome. Bulletin of the Keats-Shelley Memorial, Rome (1910). www.rc.umd.edu/bibliographies/andusers.ox.ac.uk/~scat0385/ksmr.html.

Persuasions (Persuasions). Jane Austen Society of North America, 1980–. Annual. ISSN: 0821-0314. Former title: Persuasion (Victoria, B.C.).

Persuasions: The Jane Austen Journal On-line, at www.jasna.org/persuas.html (accessed 10 December 2004).

Prism(s): Essays in Romanticism (Prism(s)). American Conference on Romanticism, 1993–. Annual. ISSN: 1096-651X. www.marquette.edu/acr/prismcontent.htm.

Romanticism: The Journal of Romantic Culture and Criticism (Romanticism). Edinburgh University Press, 1995–. 2/yr. ISSN: 1354-991X. www.ron.umontreal.ca/journals_romanticism.shtml and www.eup.ed.ac.uk/journals/Romanticism.

Romanticism on the Net: An Electronic Journal Devoted to Romantic Studies (RoN). 1996–. Quarterly. ISSN: 1467-1255. www.ron.umontreal.ca (accessed 10 December 2004).

Studies in Romanticism (SIR). Graduate School, Boston University, 1961–. Quarterly. ISSN: 0039-3762. www.rc.umd.edu/bibliographies.

The Wordsworth Circle (WC). Department of English, Temple University, 1970–. Quarterly. ISSN: 0043-8006. www.nyu.edu/gsas/dept/english/journal/wordsworth/   and   www.rc.umd.edu/bibliographies.

The journals concerned with Romantic-era literature range from more traditional sources that address primarily canonical British authors, to those that also treat European and American Romantic figures and take an interdisciplinary approach. Most of these journals roughly cover the standard period from the late eighteenth century through the early/mid–nineteenth century. Fairly similar in format, these journals typically offer several essays, book reviews, lists of books received, and occasionally, overviews of recent publications in the field. Falling within the traditional camp, *Studies in Romanticism* publishes four to six articles each issue that examine Romantic literature and culture with an emphasis on studies of canonical British authors. Many issues are devoted to special topics, including issues on Godwin, Blake, psychoanalytic articles, and Scott, Scotland, and Romantic nationalism. Essays range from sixteen to thirty-six pages in length, and are followed typically by four to six book reviews. You'll find articles such as, "Blake's Material Sublime," "Figuring Disfiguration: Reading Shelley After De Man," and "Relations of Scarcity: Ecology and Eschatology in *The Ruined Cottage.*" A list of books received and notes on the contributors are also frequently included. Tables of contents for the journal, excluding reviews (2000–2002), are posted on the *Romantic Circles Bibliographies* page.

Despite its title, *The Wordsworth Circle* is actually concerned with English Romantic literature, culture, and society from 1760 to 1850, and addresses major figures as well as minor and popular authors. Each issue typically features five to twelve essays (ranging from three to fifteen pages in length), many of which were originally presented at Wordsworth-Coleridge Association and other academic association conferences. These conference collections have treated dialogue between male and female Romantic writers, natural knowledge in the Romantic age, and transatlantic Romanticism. In the fall, the journal provides reviews of the main books published during the previous year in British, American, and Continental Romanticism. The journal's website offers links to related Web resources, in addition to subscription and conference information, but no tables of contents. Contents can be accessed online, however, via the *Romantic Circles Bibliographies* page for the years 2000–2002.

Romanticism: The Journal of Romantic Culture and Criticism publishes both scholarly and critical work on Romantic literature and culture during the period 1750 to 1850. Each issue offers four to eight articles (twelve to twenty pages in length) on the major figures of the Romantic era, with Wordsworth and Coleridge perennial favorites. Recent articles have examined memory and irony in the literary annuals, the cosmic poetics of Wordsworth and Whitman, Clare's "sublime vision," and the idea of resistance in Barbauld and Milton. Occasional special issues have been devoted to the following: "Barbauld, Bloomfield, Clare"; "Coleridge, Wordsworth, Barbauld, Hamilton"; "S. T. Coleridge"; "William Hazlitt"; "Science and Second Sight"; "In 'Xanadu...': Coleridge, Wordsworth, and Other Matter"; and "Mary Shelly." The electronic journal *Romanticism on the Net* features *Romanticism*'s table of contents (1995–2003), although reviews are only listed from Volume 6 (2000).

Expanding beyond a British literary focus, the journal ***Prism(s): Essays in Romanticism*** emphasizes interdisciplinary studies of European Romanticism. *Prism(s)* is published annually for the International Conference on Romanticism, whose membership represents literature, history, philosophy, music, art history, and history of science disciplines. Each volume typically contains three or four essays (fifteen to thirty pages long) that treat canonical British, European, and occasionally American figures, as well as such topics as Weimar classicism, the persistence of Romanticism, Kant's ethics, representations of the Irish in Romantic drama, and Romantic women poets and the Bible. Recent issues have investigated the works of Shelley, Smith, Wordsworth, Coleridge, Austen, Baillie, Mary Shelley, Byron, Emerson, and Poe. Volumes 8–11 (2000–2003) also provide an assessment of the year's key and influential books in Romantic studies. Tables of contents (1993–current) can be read at the Society's website.

Also offering a broader investigation of Romantic-era literature, the ***European Romantic Review (ERR)*** is concerned with British, European, and American literatures and cultures during the years from 1760 to 1840. This journal features four to ten thematically focused essays each volume (ranging from ten to forty pages long) on such topics as Romantic drama, the sonnet, Byron and disability, Romanticism and the physical, and the picturesque. Recent issues have addressed works by Blake, Baillie, Brunton, Lee, Beddoes, Smith, Tighe, Coleridge, Wordsworth, Scott, Dacre, Austen, Lewis, Kant, Blake, Radcliffe, and Wollstonecraft. Each issue typically presents six book reviews; *ERR* is also used as a forum for selected papers from the North American Society for the Study of Romanticism (NASSR) annual conference. Tables of contents (2002–present) may be found at the publisher's website, in addition to subscription information to SARA, an e-mail contents alerting service provided by Taylor and Francis.

Described more fully in the Web Resources chapter, ***Romanticism on the Net: An Electronic Journal Devoted to Romantic Studies*** is an international peer-reviewed journal that publishes critical articles on all aspects of British Romantic studies. With contributors in the United States, Canada, Great Britain, Japan, Denmark, Ireland, and Australia, each issue presents four to seven essays as well as several reviews. Recent essays have investigated Wordsworth's "The Thorn" and the emergence of secular history, embedded narratives in *Frankenstein*, and the Romantic libido, as well as a special issue exploring the transatlantic poetess. The journal's website also features conference postings, in addition to links to Romantic studies journals and other related Web resources.

Several journals are devoted to individual canonical authors of the Romantic period, most of which are author association or society publications. The main purpose of these journals is to highlight articles about the author's life and work, serve as a forum for society members' scholarship, and to present information relevant to studies of the author. Although the contents vary for each title, many of these journals publish articles originally presented at society conferences, as well as book reviews, news, bibliographies, overviews of recent research, and notes of interest to scholars of that particular author.

Readers of *Blake* **"An Illustrated Quarterly"** will usually find a mix of scholarly essays, brief articles, book and exhibition reviews, reproductions, discussions, news, and notes of general interest. Recent articles have focused on Blake's engravings for Lavatar's *Physiognomy*, the lost Moravian history of Blake's family, and Blake, Bacon, and "The Devil's Arse." The Summer 2004 issue contains a checklist of publications and discoveries for 2003; typically the Spring issue features an overview of Blake's works sold during the preceding year, and also covers sales of works by artists considered to be part of his circle or followers. The website offers indexes to the journal's articles and reviews listed alphabetically (1977–present), a newsletter, Blakeana, and related Web resources.

The Byron Journal, an annual publication of the Byron Society, features articles and notes on Byron's work and life, in addition to conference reports, international Society news, "Byroniana" (a report from the sales rooms and booksellers), book reviews, a list of books received, obituaries, and letters to the editor. Each volume typically offers nine to eleven essays (five to fifteen pages in length) and seventeen to twenty-one reviews of critical studies, anthologies, and reference works about Byron, other Romantic authors, and Romanticism. Recent articles have examined Byron's influence on Berlioz, allusions to Shakespeare in *Don Juan*, and natural law and the state in *The Two*

Foscari. Shorter articles have provided transcriptions of recently discovered letters, a manuscript fragment, and documents found at Kingston Lacy House, Dorset. The journal's website includes a library of selected full-text articles from previous issues, tables of contents (1988–1989, 1991–1995, 1997–1999), conference announcements, and related news. *Romantic Circles* posts tables of contents for Volumes 27–30 (1999–2002).

The ***Charles Lamb Bulletin*** is a slim society publication that typically offers two to four essays each issue on aspects of Lamb's life and works, as well as on those of his contemporaries Wordsworth, Coleridge, and Hazlitt. The essays range from seven to twenty-five pages in length; recent studies have examined Lamb's representation of London, the suppression of Hazlitt and select British poets, and the religious opinions of Coleridge. Each issue also provides one or two book reviews, Society notes, and members' news. The former *Romanticism on the Net* server posts selected *Bulletin* contents (1995–1998, 2000) but they are not part of the new *RoN* site.

Focused on the life and works of Coleridge and his contemporaries, the ***Coleridge Bulletin*** publishes anywhere from two to sixteen articles each issue, three to twenty-five pages in length, as well as reviews. Recent articles have examined Coleridge and the Bible, mythology and polytheism in Coleridge's lectures, and Wordsworth's poetry and philosophy. The website features tables of contents (1992–present), and selected full-text articles (published in 1997–1999 issues), as well as links to Friends of Coleridge conference and membership information.

The ***John Clare Society Journal*** presents scholarly articles, notes, and reviews that treat the life and work of John Clare. Each volume usually offers five to nine articles (ten to twenty pages in length) on such recent topics as women's storytelling in Bloomfield and Clare, poetry and self-fashioning in 1790's Ulster, and peasant poets and the control of literary production. In addition, Volumes 18 and 19 (1999–2000) feature a checklist of critical publications about Clare published from 1993 to 2000. The online index lists articles, review essays, reviews, poems and settings, and illustrations alphabetically by author (1982–2003).

The only journal devoted to a female author of the period, ***Persuasions*** showcases articles about Jane Austen's works and their cultural context for both academic and "informed general readers." To reach these audiences, the journal publishes essays on themes like landscape views, articles about Jane Austen and other writers, conference papers concerned with specific novels (eight to twenty papers, four to twenty pages long), and a selection of miscellaneous articles on diverse topics (three to ten articles, four to twenty-five pages long). Each issue also includes the contents of the online journal and a bibliography of works and studies published during the previous year. *Persuasions: The Jane Austen Journal On-Line*, the society's electronic journal, features conference reports and papers, as well as additional articles about Austen's work and life. Recent essays have explored moral neutrality in *Mansfield Park*, salvation and society in the Georgian period, and the petticoat's significance in *Pride and Prejudice*. The latest issue posted (Winter 2002) includes a bibliography of Austen criticism for 2001. The journal is available for Volumes 20–23 (1999–2002). The website also offers a separately published "Occasional Papers" series.

Although not focused exclusively on one author, the *Keats-Shelley Journal* and the *Keats-Shelley Review* both publish articles primarily about Keats, Shelley, Byron, and their circles. The **Keats-Shelley Journal: Keats, Shelley, Byron, Hunt, and Their Circles** (*KSJ*) is devoted primarily to the later or second-generation Romantics. Indeed, most of the five to eight articles published in each volume (ranging from ten to forty pages in length) concern Keats, Percy Shelley, and Byron, although recent essays have also explored works by Mary Shelley, Tighe, Hays, Baillie, Hemans, Hogg, Leigh Hunt, and Peacock. The "News and Notes" section offers association meeting updates, Distinguished Scholar award introductions, grants, obituaries, and typically one to three shorter articles. Each volume also includes fifteen to twenty book reviews, as well as a list of books received. *KSJ* is known, of course, for its "Current Bibliography" which features articles, reviews, and book-length studies published during the preceding year about Keats, Mary and Percy Shelley, Byron, Hunt, Hazlitt, and their circles. The electronic version of the "Current Bibliography" (1994–1999) is posted at the *Romantic Circles* website <http://www.rc.umd.edu/reference/ksjbib/>; recent online *KSJ* bibliographies are now published as part of the *Romantic Circles Bibliographies* page. The "Current Bibliography" also continues to appear annually in print. The journal's website offers tables of contents (1952–forthcoming) as well as a link to the online bibliography.

The **Keats-Shelley Review** is published by the British-based Keats-Shelley Memorial Association, originally formed to preserve "la casa rossa" in Rome where Keats died. Each volume typically presents six to seven articles (ranging from one to thirty pages in length), with a particular emphasis on works by Keats and Shelley, as illustrated by recent essays on Keats's "Ode on a Grecian Urn" and Ovid's Pygmalion, natural and ethical necessity in Shelley's epistemology, comic possibilities in *The Cenci*, and the problem of Keatsian "Self." Other articles address the reception of Romanticism in Japan, Mary Shelley's

Frankenstein, and Byron's travels in Rome. Following association reports, the journal highlights that year's winning *Keats-Shelley* prize poems and essays, and offers a selection of seven to fifteen reviews. The *Romantic Circles Bibliographies* page posts contents for Volumes 13–15 (1999–2001) and the former *Romanticism on the Net* server has contents for Volumes 11–12 (1997–1998).

The Eighteenth Century

British Journal for Eighteenth-Century Studies (BJECS). British Society for Eighteenth-Century Studies, 1978–. 2/yr. ISSN: 0141-867X. Former title: Newsletter—British Society for Eighteenth-Century Studies (1972–1977). www.bsecs.org.uk/britjour.htm.

The Eighteenth Century: Theory and Interpretation (ECent). Texas Tech University Press, 1979–. 3/yr. ISSN: 0193-5380. Former titles: Studies in Burke and His Time (1967–1978); Burke Newsletter (1959–1967). www.sp.uconn.edu/~tec/ and www.ttup.ttu.edu/journals.html.

Eighteenth-Century Fiction (ECF). Published for McMaster University by University of Toronto Press, 1988–. Quarterly. ISSN: 0840-6286. www.humanities.mcmaster.ca/~ecf.

Eighteenth Century Life (ECLife). Duke University Press, 1974–. 3/yr. ISSN: 0098-2601. muse.jhu.edu/journals/eighteenth-century_life.

Eighteenth-Century Novel. AMS Press, 2001–. Annual. ISSN: 1528-3631. www.miscellanies.org/ams.

Eighteenth-Century Studies (ECS). Johns Hopkins University Press, 1967–. Quarterly. ISSN: 0013-2586. www.press.jhu.edu/press/journals/ecs/ecs.html.

Eighteenth-Century Women: Studies in their Lives, Work, and Culture. AMS Press, 2001–. Annual. ISSN: 1529-5966. www.miscellanies.org/ams.

Restoration and 18th Century Theatre Research (RECTR). Loyola University of Chicago, 1963–. 2/yr. ISSN: 0034-5822. Former title: 17th and 18th Century Theatre Research (1962). www.du.edu/english/rectr.htm.

Studies in Eighteenth-Century Culture (SECC). Johns Hopkins University Press, 1971–. Annual. ISSN: 0360-2370. asecs.press.jhu.edu/secc.html.

The eighteenth-century studies journals described here range from those that focus primarily on literature, to those that provide interdisciplinary explorations of eighteenth-century culture. Published by the

British Society for Eighteenth-Century Studies, the *British Journal for Eighteenth-Century Studies* is concerned mainly with British and, to a lesser extent, French literature, in addition to eighteenth-century cultural history. Each issue features three to ten essays, ranging in length from ten to thirty pages, and twenty to forty book reviews; many articles address canonical authors of the period. Sample articles relevant to the Romantic era include: "Allegory and April Foolery on the Eve of the French Revolution," "Shipwreck Narratives of the Eighteenth and Early Nineteenth Century: Indicators of Culture and Identity," and "Burke's Dagger: Theatricality, Politics, and Print Culture in the 1790s," in addition to articles on Wollstonecraft, Wordsworth, Blake, and Austen. The Society's website does not currently post the journal's contents and only issues published before 1999 are indexed in *MLAIB*.

Eighteenth-Century Fiction publishes critical and historical articles that examine "imaginative prose" from the period 1660 to 1832. British, French, and American literatures are the journal's primary focus, however other European literatures are examined occasionally as well. Each issue contains four to seven articles either in French or English, which usually range from twenty to thirty pages in length, and five to twenty reviews. In the past four years, issues have been combined to create special thematic issues, such as "The Edge of Fiction" (2004), "Fiction and Religion" (2003), and "Print Culture" (2002). Recent articles have addressed the sexual heroine in Eliza Fenwick's *Secresy* and Mary Robinson's *The Natural Daughter*, venereal disease in *Sense and Sensibility*, and Gothic fiction and the erotics of loss. The website currently features tables of contents for Volumes 1–17 (1988–2004).

Relatively new to the field, *Eighteenth-Century Novel* presents an annual book-length collection of critical essays regarding the prose fiction of the long eighteenth century, from 1688 to 1830. Most of the articles examine the work of British authors, although American authors also are covered. The journal encourages "research based on primary sources… [that] engage in significant critical dialogue with existing scholarly interpretations." To date, the volumes have offered twelve to sixteen essays, ranging from fifteen to forty-five pages in length, and three to six book reviews. Authors of the Romantic era treated include Radcliffe, Edgeworth, Walpole, Austen, Burney, Smith, Wollstonecraft, and Mary Shelley; other articles have investigated the oriental tale and popular politics in late eighteenth-century Britain, and botany and the novel of courtship. The AMS website features tables of contents for Volumes 1 and 2 (2001–2002).

Another new annual publication by AMS Press, *Eighteenth-Century Women: Studies in their Lives, Work, and Culture* features essays on all aspects of women's writings and lives in the long eighteenth century, with an emphasis on literary figures from, but not limited to Great Britain. The two volumes published so far offer thirteen and eleven articles (ranging from ten to forty-four pages in length); articles addressing Romantic-era figures cover the politics of sensibility in Helen Maria Williams's *Julia*, matrilineal descent in the Gothic novel, women writers and the literary marketplace, and Wollstonecraft's authorship of *The Emigrants*. Each issue also provides a selection of book reviews and an index. The publisher's website presents a description of the journal and tables of contents for both volumes.

Although concerned in general with the "literature, history, fine arts, science, history of ideas, and popular culture" of the long eighteenth-century from 1660 to 1800, *The Eighteenth Century: Theory and Interpretation* exhibits a preference for articles about British literature. In fact, recent essays have explored works by Lennox, Burney, Wollstonecraft, Blake, and Clare. Each issue typically presents three to five essays (ten to twenty-five pages in length), with occasional special issues that have focused on laboring-class poets, millennialism, and incest in Restoration and eighteenth-century England. One or two book review essays are also included per issue, as well as notes on the contributors. Volume 41:1 (Spring 2000) features author and subject indexes to Volumes 30–39. The website offers an index to contents for Volumes 31–39 (1990–1999). *The Eighteenth Century* is not indexed in *ABELL* as of November 2004.

In a category by itself, *Restoration and 18th Century Theatre Research* focuses specifically on British and European drama and staging of the late seventeenth and eighteenth centuries. *RECTR* presents three to seven essays each issue (ten to thirty-five pages in length), with occasional reviews and theatre notes. Although works by authors of the late eighteenth century are covered infrequently, the journal has published articles about the dramatic sameness of Sheridan and Coleridge, Baillie's *Basil* and its masquerade, the discourse of slavery in Colman's *Inkle and Yarico*, and Isaac Reed's diaries and the theatrical scene in eighteenth-century England. The website provides subscription and submission information only.

Eighteenth-century literature journals with an interdisciplinary focus include the wide ranging *Eighteenth Century Life* which publishes essays on all aspects of eighteenth-century culture, including the literature, art, history, and societies of Britain and Europe. Topics about North America were also addressed until 2002. Each issue typically contains four to six essays (ten to thirty pages in length), with one to two review essays, and a list of books received. Occasional special issues provide twelve to sixteen essays on themes such as "Exoticism and the Culture of Exploration," the "Cultural Topography of Food," and

"Ireland, 1798–1998: From Revolution to Revisionism and Beyond."
Romantic-era writers are profiled infrequently, but have appeared recently in essays concerning Godwin and contractarianism, Barbauld's
"The Mouse's Petition," the "evil father" trope in Gothic fiction, British travel accounts of America, and didacticism in the early Romantic
era. Many issues feature illustrations from print and art collections.
Although tables of contents (1996–present) may be viewed for free at
the *Project Muse* website, full-text is available for subscribers only.

Covering British, European, and North American cultures of the
long eighteenth century, *Eighteenth-Century Studies* (*ECS*) presents
articles with a range of critical approaches and disciplines. Each volume typically features three to five essays (ten to twenty-five pages in
length) grouped by such recent themes as "Hair," "Artistic Interac-
tions," "Critical Networks," "Spaces of Enlightenment," "Exploring
Sentiment," "Political Interventions," "Print Matters," "False Arca-
dias," "Aesthetics and the Disciplines," "Race and Slavery," and
"French Revolutionary Culture." A good portion of each issue is devoted to book reviews (nine to fourteen reviews), exhibition reviews,
occasional special forums, and a list of books received. Many essays
include illustrations. *ECS* is the official journal of the American Society
for Eighteenth-Century Studies. The website offers tables of contents of
forthcoming and special issues, as well as linked contents (1995/1996–
present) through *Project Muse.*

Published annually for the American Society for Eighteenth-
Century Studies, *Studies in Eighteenth-Century Culture* (*SECC*) highlights selected papers that were originally presented at the Society's
meetings. Each volume typically contains ten to fifteen essays (ten to
thirty pages in length) that examine topics in eighteenth-century culture
from a range of disciplines, including English, French, German, and
Italian literatures, history, art history, and women's studies. Grouped
thematically, recent essays have investigated women's credit, politics
and history, gambling and spending, national and international identi-
ties, the geography of the Enlightenment, and allegories of healing.
Since the journal addresses the long eighteenth century, many Romantic-era authors are featured; recent volumes have covered anti-slavery
poetry, the English Jacobin novel, as well as works by Wollstonecraft,
Baillie, Blake, and Burney. *SECC* also contains notes on the contributors and an index of persons, twentieth-century critics, and selected
concepts and keywords. The website posts tables of contents (1998–
forthcoming volume) and submission guidelines.

The Nineteenth Century

Nineteenth-Century Contexts (NCC). Interdisciplinary Nineteenth-Century Studies, with the assistance of the College of Arts and Sciences and the Dept. of English of Northeastern University, 1987–. Quarterly (1994–); formerly 2/yr (1987–1993). ISSN: 0890-5495. Former titles: Romanticism Past and Present (1981–1986); Milton and the Romantics (1975–1980). www.tandf.co.uk/journals/titles/08905495.html

Nineteenth-Century Feminisms (NCFe). Department of Modern Languages, King's College, 1999–. 2/yr. ISSN: 1481-840X. www.odyssey.on.ca/~ncf.

Nineteenth-Century Literature (NCF). University of California Press, 1986–. Quarterly. ISSN: 0891-9356; electronic ISSN: 1067-835. Former titles: Nineteenth-Century Fiction (1949–1986); Trollopian: A Journal of Victorian Fiction (1945–1949). Caliber .ucpress.net/loi/ncl and www.ucpress.edu/scan/ncl-e.

Nineteenth-Century Prose (NCP). Dept. of English, U.S. Naval Academy, 1989–. 2/yr. ISSN: 0160-4848. Former titles: Arnoldian (1975–1990); Arnold Newsletter (1973–1975).

Nineteenth-Century Studies (NCS). Southeastern Nineteenth-Century Studies Association, 1987–. Annual. ISSN: 0893-7931. www.selu.edu/Academics/Depts/English/NCS/frameset.html.

Nineteenth Century Theatre and Film (NCTR). Manchester University Press, 2002–. 2/yr. ISSN: 0893-3766. Former titles: Nineteenth Century Theatre (1987–2000); Nineteenth Century Theatre Research (1973–1986); NCTR Newsletter (1976–1979). www .manchesterunivesitypress.co.uk/information_areas/journals/19th%20century/nineteenth.htm.

The journals in this section offer broad investigations of nineteenth-century literature and culture. Since the Romantic era straddles both eighteenth and nineteenth centuries, it is worthwhile reviewing these titles even though Romantic authors are not the main focus. More literary than the others, the journal **Nineteenth-Century Literature** is concerned primarily with the major figures of nineteenth-century British and American literature. Following article abstracts, each issue presents three to four essays (fifteen to forty pages in length), five to seven reviews, a list of books received, and notes on the contributors. Authors of the Romantic period are addressed only occasionally due to the journal's broad coverage, but recent issues have explored "sublime translation" in Scott and Cooper, the poetics of giving in Landon's work, and the influence of exile on Byron's *Mazeppa*. The *UC Caliber* website

offers tables of contents (March 2001–current) and the former journal
site posts contents for Volumes 45–55 (1990–2000).

Nineteenth-Century Feminisms explores writing by and about
British and American women, as well as gender and cultural issues
from interdisciplinary perspectives. Covering the long nineteenth century from 1780 to 1918, each issue presents three to five essays, ranging from ten to thirty pages in length, in addition to a couple reviews.
Romantic-era authors have been discussed in articles that examine Barbauld and Wollstonecraft's contrary visions of women's rights, sover-
eignty and sexuality in Austen's *Emma*, and the pedagogical aims of
Hemans's *Records of Woman*. The journal's website offers article abstracts and tables of contents (1999–2001). *Nineteenth-Century Feminisms* is not indexed in *ABELL* as of November 2004.

Featuring explorations of British, American, and Continental non-
fiction prose, *Nineteenth-Century Prose* publishes seven to nine articles each issue which range from ten to thirty-five pages long, ten to
thirty book reviews, and occasional review essays. Many of the issues
are devoted to special topics, including Emerson, the picturesque, and
platform culture in nineteenth-century Britain. Recent issues have explored Hazlitt's "essayism," and the *Monthly Review* and Barbauld's
literary criticism. Volume 28:2 (Fall 2001) will be of particular interest
to Romantic scholars since it offers articles on reading Romantic autobiography, Romantic biography and reform, and articles on DeQuincey,
Keats, Lamb, and Hazlitt. Since the website is currently unavailable
(11/04), contents can be accessed through *MLA*. *ABELL* does not index
current issues.

Nineteenth Century Theatre and Film, formerly *Nineteenth Century Theatre*, provides essays, documents, bibliographies, and reviews
on the performing arts from the "'Age of Revolution' to the advent of
sound motion pictures." The journal adopts a broad view of performing
arts to include drama, dance, opera, music halls, the circus, and fair-
ground entertainment. Each issue offers two to five articles (ranging
from fifteen to thirty pages in length) and five to seven book reviews.
Romantic studies scholars will find a recent article on the English actor
Thomas Potter Cooke, reviews of dramas by Byron, Shelley, and Baillie, and the full text of the Gothic melodrama, *Camilla the Amazon* by
Jane Margaret Scott. The Manchester University Press website posts a
description of the journal and subscription information. As of November 2004, *MLA* only includes *Nineteenth Century Theatre* (1983–2000)
and *ABELL* continues to index the journal with its former title (2002).

Aiming to be both international and interdisciplinary in approach,
Nineteenth-Century Contexts strives to offer "innovative contextuali-
zations across a wide spectrum of nineteenth-century experience and

the critical disciplines that examine it," with an emphasis on works that investigate the nineteenth century in relation to "contemporary political flash points around the world." Even with this goal, most of the three to five articles presented each issue (ranging from fifteen to thirty-five pages in length) are written by English department faculty on works of British literature. To be fair, faculty from French, Russian, media, physics, history, and women's studies departments have also contributed. Recent Romantic-era articles have treated Southey's *Tale of Paraguay*, *Frankenstein* and polar exploration, Blake's environmental poetics, Romantic-period daily newspapers, the nation in Scott's *Guy Mannering*, and surveillance and space on the plantation in Lewis's *Journal of a West Indian Proprietor*. The June 2001 issue explored women's friendships and lesbian sexuality in the later eighteenth century. *NCC* also features five to six reviews, as well as black and white illustrations, including photographs, engravings, and text reproductions. The journal's website provides tables of contents (2002–present) and a full-text sample copy.

Also adopting a wide scope, **Nineteenth-Century Studies** features articles on the literature, art, history, music, and social sciences of nineteenth-century Britain, America, Europe, and the British Empire. Most of the four to seven articles published each issue (ranging from fourteen to thirty-six pages) focus on topics of the Victorian period, although two recent articles have investigated "breach of promise of marriage" court cases in the 1820s and Coleridge's "The Rime of the Ancyent Marinere." Volume 17 (2003) contains a special section on religion and culture. Each issue also typically contains review essays of pertinent books, exhibitions, and electronic resources, as well as a list of books received. The journal is currently published by the Nineteenth-Century Studies Association. The website offers tables of contents (1987–2004) and selected full-text articles.

Victorian

Victorian Literature and Culture (VLC). AMS Press, 1991–. 2/yr. ISSN: 1060-1503. Former title: Studies (Browning Institute) (1973–1990).   www.nyu.edu/gsas/dept/english/journal/victorian/ and journals.cambridge.org.

Victorian Periodicals Review (VPR). Research Society for Victorian Periodicals, 1979–. Quarterly. ISSN: 0709-4698. Former title: Victorian Periodicals Newsletter (1968–1978). www.utpjournals.com/ jour.ihtml?lp=vpr/vpr.html.

Victorian Poetry (VP). West Virginia University, 1963–. Quarterly. ISSN: 0042-5206. Poetry 1830-1914. vp.engl.wvu.edu/ and muse.jhu.edu/ journals/victorian_poetry.

Victorian Studies: An Interdisciplinary Journal of Social, Political, and Cultural Studies (VS). Indiana University, 1957–. Quarterly. ISSN: 0042-5222. iupjournals.org/victorian/ and muse.jhu.edu/journals/ victorian_studies.

Although the few journals described in this section are concerned primarily with the authors and culture of Victorian Britain, scholars working with figures whose careers continued on through the nineteenth century may want to consult these journals for relevant articles. *Victorian Literature and Culture* (*VLC*) publishes six to twelve articles each issue on the literature and culture of post-1830 Britain, one to four review essays, and selections from critical works in progress. Many of the issues focus on a specific theme, including Victorian taxonomies, boundaries, religion, fashions, construction of Victorian classes, and Victorian aesthetics and aestheticians. *VLC* also published the annual "Robert and Elizabeth Barrett Browning Annotated Bibliography" until 1998; Volume 31:2 contains the cumulative index to the bibliographies (1972–1998). Since the journal's primary emphasis is on the Victorian period, only scholars working with issues and authors from 1830 on will find the articles of potential use. Both the NYU and Cambridge University Press websites present tables of contents (1991–present) and (1999–present) respectively.

Stressing the importance of periodicals in understanding the "history and culture of Victorian Britain, Ireland, and the Empire," *Victorian Periodicals Review* provides scholarly articles on the editorial and publishing history of Victorian periodicals. Offering two to six articles each issue (fifteen to thirty pages in length), recent issues have covered the personification of Father Thames in the campaign for public health reform, political comments in the *Quarterly Review* after Croker, and the educative reading pursuits of the ladies of Edinburgh from 1865 to 1885. Volume 37:2 (2004) is devoted to the nineteenth-century press in India. In addition to book reviews, the journal also publishes the "Research Society for Victorian Periodicals Bibliography" (Volume 35:4, 1999–2001), and corrections to the *Wellesley Index*. Tables of contents (1994–present, excluding issues 34:1–2) are available at the University of Toronto website.

Victorian Poetry covers British and colonial poetry of the Victorian period from 1830 to 1914. Each issue contains four to eight articles (ranging from six to thirty-five pages long), with occasional issues devoted to special topics, including: the "Future Direction of Victorian

Poetry Scholarship"; "Science and Victorian Poetry"; "Australian poetry"; "William Morris"; and "Coventry Patmore." As to be expected,
most articles treat Victorian poets but some are relevant to Romantic
studies. One recent article explores post-Romantic ideologies and Victorian poetic practice, another presents a newly discovered poem by
Thomas Lovell Beddoes, and others examine Shelley's reputation in
the 1880s and 1890s, as well as the friendship between Hemans and
Wordsworth. Each fall the journal publishes an overview of the previous year's work in Victorian poetry. The website presents the full text
of Volumes 35 and 36 (1997, 1998) and the Morris and Patmore issues
of Volume 34 (1996). Tables of contents are available for free at *Project Muse* (2000–present) but full-text access is by subscription only.

True to its title, ***Victorian Studies: An Interdisciplinary Journal
of Social, Political, and Cultural Studies*** publishes articles (ranging
from fifteen to thirty-six pages in length) on all aspects of Victorian
British culture, with an emphasis on literary figures. The two to five
essays in each issue range from studies of Brontë, Trollope, and Eliot to
examinations of Victorian sensation theater, charity, and honeymoons.
The journal features an extensive selection of twenty-five to forty book
reviews per issue, as well as occasional longer review essays and book
forums. *Victorian Studies* is known for the summer issue's annual
"Victorian Bibliography," a list of "noteworthy" editions, critical studies, and journal articles published during a particular year (with a two
year time lag). Since 1998, the "Victorian Bibliography" is now published only electronically and can be searched for the years 1999 to
2002 at *Victorian Bibliography Online* <http://iupjournals.org/vicbib/
index.html>. The Indiana University Press journal site offers tables of
contents (Autumn 1996–present) and selected full-text articles. *Project
Muse* presents contents (1999–present), with full-text articles available
for subscribers only.

General

ELH (ELH). Johns Hopkins University Press, 1934–. Quarterly. ISSN:
     0013-8304. Former title: ELH: A Journal of English Literary His-
     tory (1934–1955). Volumes 4–16 (1937–1949) contain "The Ro-
     mantic Movement: A Selective and Critical Bibliography for
     [1936–1948]." muse.jhu.edu/journals/elh.
English Language Notes (ELN). University of Colorado, 1963–. Quar-
     terly. ISSN: 0013-8282. Supplement to Volumes 3–17 (1965–
     1979) "The Romantic Movement: A Selective and Critical Bibliog-
     raphy for [1964–1978]." www.colorado.edu/journals/eln.

Essays in Criticism: A Quarterly Journal of Literary Criticism (EIC). Oxford University Press, 1951–. Quarterly. ISSN: 0014-0856. www3.oup.co.uk/escrit.

Gothic Studies. Manchester University Press, 1999–. 2 or 3/yr. ISSN: 1362-7937. www.manchesteruniversitypress.co.uk/information_areas/journals/gothic/Gothic.htm.

MLQ: Modern Language Quarterly: A Journal of Literary History (MLQ). University of Washington, 1940–. Quarterly. ISSN: 0026-7929. Former title: *Modern Language Quarterly* (1940–1992). depts.washington.edu/mlq.

Modern Language Review (MLR). Modern Humanities Research Association, 1905–. Quarterly. ISSN: 0026-7937. Former titles: Modern Language Quarterly (1900–1904); Modern Quarterly of Language and Literature (1898–1899); Modern Language Quarterly (1897). www.mhra.org.uk/Publications/Journals/mlr.html.

New Literary History (NLH). Johns Hopkins University Press, 1969–. Quarterly. ISSN: 0028-6087; E-ISSN: 1080-661X. muse.jhu.edu/journals/nlh.

Philological Quarterly (PQ). University of Iowa, 1922–. Quarterly. ISSN: 0031-7977. Published "The Romantic Movement: A Selective and Critical Bibliography for [1949–1963]" in Volumes 29–43 (1950–1964).

PMLA: Publications of the Modern Language Association of America (PMLA). Modern Language Association of America, 1888–. 6/yr. ISSN: 0030-8129. Former titles: Transactions of the Modern Language Association of America (1884/1885); Transactions and proceedings of the Modern Language Association of America (1886–1887). www.mla.org.

Review of English Studies: A Quarterly Journal of English Literature and the English Language (RES). Oxford University Press, 1925–. Quarterly; 5/yr in 2003. ISSN: 0034-6551. www3.oup.co.uk/revesj.

Scottish Studies Review (ScSR). Association for Scottish Literary Studies, 2000–. 2/yr. ISSN: 1475-7737. Former titles: merged Scottish Literary Journal (1974–2000) and Scotlands (1994–1998). www.arts.gla.ac.uk/ScotLit/ASLS/FrameSet.html.

SEL: Studies in English Literature, 1500–1900 (SEL). Rice University, 1961–. Quarterly. ISSN: 0039-3657. www.sel.rice.edu/ and muse.jhu.edu/journals/studies_in_english_literature.

Studies in Scottish Literature (SSL). University of South Carolina Press, 1963–. Annual (1978–); Quarterly (1963–1975). ISSN: 0039-3770. www.sc.edu/library/scotlit/ssl.html.

Women's Writing (WoWr). Triangle Journals Ltd., 1994–. 3/yr. ISSN: 0969-9082. www.triangle.co.uk/wow.

This general section highlights journals that cover more than one literary period; several journals also address American and European literatures in addition to British literature. The journals have been selected for the frequency with which articles on Romantic- and Regency-era figures and topics appear, as well as for their standing as important journals in the field. Of course numerous journals occasionally publish articles relevant to Romantic studies, many more than just the few journals recognized here, so it is important to search a comprehensive database like *MLAIB* to be sure of conducting a thorough literature review.

The highly respected journal *ELH* features essays primarily on the major figures of British literature from Chaucer to authors of the early twentieth century, with some inclusion of American and later figures as well. Each issue contains nine to eleven articles, typically twenty to forty pages in length, and no book reviews. Authors of the Romantic era are covered frequently; the latest issues have explored works by Hogg, Hemens, Blake, More, Baillie, Mary and Percy Shelley, Godwin, Edgeworth, Coleridge, Wordsworth, and Scott, in addition to an investigation of allegory in recent critical accounts of Romanticism. Volumes 4–16 (1937–1949) contain "The Romantic Movement: A Selective and Critical Bibliography" for the years 1936 to 1948. *Project Muse* offers tables of contents (1993–present), and full-text access for subscribers. The subscription database *JSTOR* makes full-text issues available from 1934–1994.

Philological Quarterly publishes critical articles on classical and modern languages and literatures, with most articles devoted to pre-twentieth-century English canonical figures and works. Each issue typically provides five or six articles, ten to forty pages in length, and a list of books received. Authors of the Romantic era are treated on a regular basis and recent articles have addressed theatrical spectatorship in *Mansfield Park*, an unrecorded letter by Wordsworth, and medieval sources for Keats's *La Belle Dame sans Merci*. *PQ* acquired responsibility for "The Romantic Movement: A Selective and Critical Bibliography for the Year" from *ELH*, and published it for the years 1949–1963 in Volumes 29–43 (1950–1964). Although the journal does not have its own website, contents can be accessed through *MLAIB*.

Covering English and American literature from all literary periods but with an emphasis on canonical works, *English Language Notes* offers seven to ten articles each issue, usually five to fifteen pages in length, that treat textual interpretation "supported by biographical, historical, and bibliographical documentation." Recent articles on Romantic-era figures include "The Bee-Politics in Wordsworth's 'Vernal Ode,'" "Body as Epitaph: Byron's Reclamation of England through Allegra," and "Charlotte Smith and the American Agrarian Ideal," in addition to articles on Mary Shelley, Wordsworth, Austen, and Keats. Each issue also features several book reviews and occasional lists of books received. "The Romantic Movement: A Selective and Critical Bibliography" was published by *ELN* as a supplement to Volumes 3–17 (1965–1979) and covers the years 1964 to 1978. Contents for the current issue only are posted at the journal's website.

Although the following journals offer a broad coverage of British literature, they are noted here for their tendency to feature articles relevant to Romantic studies. The journal *Gothic Studies* examines literary and cultural aspects of the Gothic from the eighteenth century through the present. Many issues are thematic in focus and have explored female Gothic, modern and postmodern Gothic, Gothic drama, and monstrosity and anthropology. Each issue provides four to twelve articles (ten to thirty pages in length), and several brief book reviews. Readers will find Romantic-era authors covered frequently, including Fenwick, Wollstonecraft, Lewis, Walpole, Mary and Percy Shelley, Baillie, Hogg, Maturin, Dibdin, and Planché. The website features abstracts (1999–present) with full-text article access for institutional subscribers. *Gothic Studies* is not indexed in *MLAIB* or *ABELL* as of November 2004.

Modern Language Quarterly publishes articles on the "relationship of literary change or historicism to feminism, ethnic studies, cultural materialism, discourse analysis, and all other forms of representation and cultural critique." The three to six articles each issue, fifteen to forty pages in length, treat works in British, American, and European literatures from the medieval period to contemporary texts. Occasional special issues have been devoted to national literary histories, periodization, and reading for form. Although the coverage is broad, Romantic-era authors are discussed with regularity. Issues published in 2004 explored works by Hays, Wollstonecraft, Barbauld, and Wordsworth. Tables of contents are posted at the website (1990–forthcoming), with abstracts available for most articles from 2000 forward. The tables of contents may also be searched by keyword.

With an emphasis on "literary criticism rooted in historical scholarship," *Review of English Studies* features articles on English literature and language, including American and post-colonial literatures in English. Each issue contains four to six articles (five to thirty pages long), most of which concern figures and works from the English literary canon, and twenty to twenty-five reviews with an occasional review essay. Articles relevant to Romantic studies are published frequently; recent examples include "'Meditative Morality': Wordsworth and Samuel Daniel" and "*Madoc*, 1795: Robert Southey's Misdated Manuscript." Formerly each May, June, and now September issue presents the winning *RES* prize essay. Tables of contents (1996–present) and abstracts (1998–present) are available at the website, however, full-text access from 2001 on is limited to subscribers only.

SEL: Studies in English Literature offers essays on English literature presented quarterly by literary period: the winter issue covers the English Renaissance, spring is Tudor and Stuart drama, summer addresses the Restoration and eighteenth century, and autumn is devoted to the nineteenth century. Each issue contains eight to ten articles (fifteen to thirty-five pages long), a useful discussion of recent studies in that particular literary period, and a list of books received. Romantic studies scholars will find relevant articles in both the summer and autumn issues. A recent article in the 2003 eighteenth century issue compared Baillie's and Burke's aesthetics, with a discussion of the play *De Monfort*. Articles in recent nineteenth century issues have treated the works of Percy and Mary Shelley, Austen, Coleridge, Lamb, and Scott. The website features tables of contents (1995–present); full-text access from 1999 to the current issue is available to subscribers of *Project Muse*.

Focusing on the works of primarily British women authors who wrote before 1900, **Women's Writing** features articles from "theoretical and historical perspectives, and contributions that are concerned with gender, culture, race and class." Each issue contains usually seven to nine articles (ranging in length from ten to twenty pages) and several book reviews. Many of the issues are devoted to special topics, including "Popular Fiction," "Sex, Gender, and the Female Body," "Scottish Women's Writing," and "Dissenting Women, 1350–1800." Romantic studies scholars will find individual issues that treat the authors Robinson, Shelley, Austen, and Wollstonecraft, as well as issues on female Gothic writing and the Romantic period. The website offers tables of contents and abstracts (1994–2002) and full-text articles (1997–2002).

Scholars interested in Walter Scott or Robert Burns will want to review two journals, *Scottish Studies Review* and *Studies in Scottish Literature,* which concentrate on Scottish authors and works from all literary periods. Published annually, **Studies in Scottish Literature** offers a collection of fifteen to thirty articles each issue that range from five to twenty pages long, as well as book reviews, notes and documents, and an index. Articles on Scott and Burns are featured regularly, such as "Roseneath: Scotland or 'Scott-land'? A Reappraisal of *The Heart of Midlothian*," "Freedom and Responsibility in *The Bride of*

Lammermoor," and "Robert Burns and William Wordsworth: Positioning of a Romantic Artist in the Literary Marketplace." Journal contents for the years 1991 to 1993, 1996, and 1998 are available at the University of South Carolina website. More recent contents can be accessed through *MLAIB* or *ABELL.*

More interdisciplinary in emphasis, *Scottish Studies Review* features articles on Scottish literature and culture, including art, architecture, history, music, and philosophy. Most of the six to eight articles published each issue are on literary topics; the journal also presents book reviews, author interviews, and an overview of the year's publications. Romantic-era authors are represented in such recent articles as, "Scott's Critique of the English Treason Law in *Waverley,*" "From Caledonia to Albania: Byron, Galt, and the Progress of the Eastern Savage," and "Competing Idylls: Fergusson and Burns." *Scottish Studies Review* is the successor to the *Scottish Literary Journal* and *Scotlands* and is published by the Association for Scottish Literary Studies. The website presents an index to articles (2000–present).

This final group represents important literary studies journals that should not be overlooked when investigating Romantic authors and topics. Confessing itself an "English journal with an Oxford bias," *Essays in Criticism: A Quarterly Journal of Literary Criticism*, which was founded by the eminent scholar F. W. Bateson, offers critical articles on works of English literature from all literary periods. Each issue typically presents one to three articles (fifteen to twenty-five pages in length), several book review essays, and "Critical Opinion" discussions of such topics as Browning and translationese, and the biographical imperative. The April issue usually features the F. W. Bateson Memorial Lecture, given in 2003 and 2002 by Linda Colley and Stefan Collini. Issues in 2004 examined fatal women of Romanticism, Clare's awkwardness, and editing Wordsworth's fragments. The cumulative index to Volumes 1–50 lists many articles and reviews for Romantic canonical figures, as well as for the subject Romanticism. The journal's website makes available tables of contents (1996–present) and full-text PDF articles from 2000 to the present for Oxford University Press subscribers.

Modern Language Review, the flagship journal of the Modern Humanities Research Association, publishes articles on medieval and modern English, French, Germanic, Hispanic, Italian, and Slavonic literatures, as well as linguistics, comparative literature, and critical theory. Each issue contains nine to thirteen articles (ranging in length from eight to twenty-five pages), in addition to more than one hundred book reviews. Since the scope ranges so widely, articles about Romantic-era figures are limited. However, the July 2004 issue contained an article about Fanny's gaze and the construction of feminine space in *Mansfield Park*, the July 2003 issue featured unpublished letters from Joseph Cottle to Robert Southey, and the July 2002 issue presented articles about German women writers in the 1820s and about the republication of Wordsworth's Napoleonic sonnets in 1840. Each issue also concludes with article abstracts. The MHRA website offers a sample article and links to the current issue's table of contents and article abstracts through *IngentaConnect* (www.ingentaconnect.com). Full-text availability is limited to subscribers only.

With an emphasis on theoretical investigations, *New Literary History* features thematically focused issues on such topics as theorizing genres, ethics and narratives, anonymity, and reconsiderations of literary theory, literary history, and cultural authority. Each issue presents eight to twelve articles (ranging from ten to thirty pages in length) and a list of books received. Recent articles related to Romantic-era figures include "Romantic Satanism and the Rise of Nineteenth-Century Women's Poetry," "The Paradox of the Anthology: Collecting and Différence in Eighteenth-Century Britain," and "'Unboastful Bard': Originally Anonymous English Romantic Poetry Book Publication, 1770–1835." As part of *Project Muse*, the journal's website features free tables of contents (1995–present) and full-text articles for subscribers.

PMLA, the Modern Language Association of America's journal, presents a broad range of articles concerned with language and literature from "all scholarly methods and theoretical perspectives." Each issue contains usually three to eight articles (twelve to twenty pages in length), Society news, and shorter articles in such sections as "theories and methodologies," "talks from the convention," and "the changing profession." The May issue also features the Nobel lecture. Recent articles relevant to Romantic studies include, "Relocating Inwardness: Historical Distance and the Transition from Enlightenment to Romantic Historiography," "'Children of Liberty': Idealist Historiography in Stael, Shelley, and Sand," and "'Islanded in the World': Cultural Memory and Human Mobility in *The Last Man*." Information about the journal can be retrieved from the society's website; full-text issues are available by library subscription only (2002–present).

Conclusion

This overview of pertinent British Romantic and literature journals will help you to become familiar with the principal journals in the field and obtain a sense of each journal's scope and theoretical stance. Again, it is not a comprehensive list. Although you can consult selected journal websites for recent contents, you should also search both *MLAIB* and *ABELL* in order to identify a greater range of relevant articles for your topic or figure. Since journals are often the first venue for new scholarship, they play an important role in most literary research. Consequently, you will need to be knowledgeable about the trends, authors, and theoretical approaches currently being explored in Romantic studies journals. Journal literature can also be used to assess how Romantic scholarship has changed and developed over time. Journals are a key component to this type of understanding and can be a forum for your own contribution to the field.

In the following chapters, the emphasis will shift from modern reference works and resources that can be used for studying literature of the British Romantic period to resources specifically concerned with primary materials of the eighteenth and nineteenth centuries and the secondary tools to help you investigate these materials. The chapters on contemporary reviews, eighteenth- and nineteenth-century journals, microform and digital collections, and manuscripts and archives will describe the historical context of the Romantic period. Moreover, these chapters will recommend specific sources and the best practices to be applied when conducting research with primary materials.

Note

1. Erdman, David V. "Foreword." *The Romantic Movement Bibliography, 1936–1970: A Master Cumulation from ELH, Philological Quarterly and English Language Notes.* Edited by A. C. Elkins, Jr. and L. J. Forstner. 7 vols. (Ann Arbor, MI: Pierian Press in association with R. R. Bowker, 1973), vii.

Chapter 6
Contemporary Reviews

We think so favorably of this performance that it is with some reluctance we decline inserting it among our principal articles, but the productions of the press so continually multiplied, that it requires all our exertions to keep tolerable pace with them.

"Notice of *Sense and Sensibility*,"
The British Critic, 39 May 1812, p. 527

In committing this Work to the judgement of the Public, the Editors have but little to observe.
    It will be easily perceived, that it forms no part of their object, to take notice of every production that issues from the press: and that they wish their Journal to be distinguished, rather for the selection, than for the number of its articles.

"Advertisement,"
The Edinburgh Review, 1 October 1802, no page number

Although both the above statements were published in the nineteenth century, the two publications represent the differences between eighteenth-century (*The British Critic*) and nineteenth-century (*The Edinburgh Review*) reviewing philosophies. In the eighteenth century, editors of review journals believed comprehensive coverage was crucial while in the nineteenth century selectivity was more desirable. The two most important book review publications in the eighteenth century, *The Monthly Review* and *The Critical Review*, set the standard for review journals by attempting to identify and review all books published. The editors of these journals felt it was part of their mission to be inclusive. Publishing burgeoned and the task became overwhelming, as illustrated by the quote from *The British Critic*.
    At the beginning of the nineteenth century, *The Edinburgh Review* was born and with it a new philosophy towards reviewing: selectivity rather than comprehensiveness. This goal enabled reviewers to examine

a few chosen books and to write longer, more in-depth analysis. Over the course of the first half of the nineteenth century selective review journals became the standard, replacing the inclusive old guard. But with selectivity came exclusion. Because of the new philosophy, anonymous, unknown, or non-mainstream authors were overlooked: "the important new writers who appeared between 1802 and 1820— Jane Austen, Byron, Hazlitt, Hunt, Keats, Scott, Shelley—none were first recognized in the *Edinburgh* or the *Quarterly*."[1]

Each of the reviewing policies had strengths and weaknesses. Although eighteenth-century review methods meant books of dubious quality were evaluated, as a result new and as yet undiscovered authors were brought to the attention of the public. Quarterlies such as *The Edinburgh Review* did evaluate later works by the authors mentioned above, but the survival of the eighteenth-century review journals well into the nineteenth century allowed many authors of the Romantic era to be noticed from the beginnings of their literary careers. However, Frank Donoghue points out the struggle comprehensive reviewing caused eighteenth-century editors: although the publishers of *The Monthly Review* and *The Critical Review* hoped the critical assessments they printed would sway the public to improve its taste in literature by selecting the books receiving the highest praise, the public responded by buying the books it found most interesting and not necessarily those deemed worthwhile by the monthlies.[2] Selective reviewing allowed the editors of the *Edinburgh Review* to focus only on those writings determined to be most important at the expense of alternative voices. Thus, the struggle between comprehensiveness and quality began to be resolved, and slowly over the next few decades the old style eighteenth-century reviews died out. However, as a result of these philosophies coexisting during the Romantic era, a rich and broad range of published reviews, from brief comments to extensive analysis, were published and illustrate the contemporary response to a large number of literary works from the time period.

Short but helpful information about review practices and profiles of review journals can be found in some of the reference tools we cover in this volume. In *Index to Book Reviews in England*, Foster provides a valuable overview about review publishing. As mentioned in Chapter 2, volume 110 from the series *Dictionary of Literary Biography* titled *British Romantic Prose Writers, 1789–1832*, has an appendix on literary reviewing during this era, with chapters on individual review journals. *British Literary Magazines: The Romantic Age, 1789–1836*, discussed in Chapter 7, provides profiles on eighty-four of the literary journals from this time.

Although no single source exists which exhaustively covers contemporary critical reception to literary works of the Romantic era, there are several excellent reference tools to begin the process. Various scholarly projects have produced indexes and bibliographies to provide access to the periodical literature from that time. Rather than leaf through decades of periodicals every time one needs to identify contemporary reviews, invaluable reference books such as Forster's *Index to Book Reviews in England, 1775–1800*, Ward's series of volumes titled *Literary Reviews in British Periodicals: A Bibliography*, covering the years from 1789 to 1826, and *Romantics Reviewed* have been compiled to allow scholars to find references to periodical and newspaper commentaries. The specialized series *Critical Heritage* and *Critical Assessments* cite contemporary reviews and responses for authors with established critical histories such as Byron, Austen, and Wordsworth. Ultimately, the thorough scholar or the scholar in search of more obscure authors may need to browse through periodicals and newspapers, but by starting with the following, much time and effort will be saved.

Contemporary Reviews in British Periodicals

Forster, Antonia. *Index to Book Reviews in England, 1775–1800*. London: The British Library, 1997.

Garside, Peter, James Raven, and Rainer Schowerling, eds. *The English Novel 1770–1829: A Bibliographical Survey of Prose Fiction Published in the British Isles*. 2 vols. New York: Oxford University Press, 2000.

Reiman, Donald H., ed. *The Romantics Reviewed: Contemporary Reviews of British Romantic Writers*. 9 vols. New York: Garland, 1972.

Ward, William S., comp. *Literary Reviews in British Periodicals, 1789–1797: A Bibliography with a Supplementary List of General (Non-Review) Articles on Literary Subjects*. New York: Garland, 1979.

―――. *Literary Reviews in British Periodicals, 1798–1820: A Bibliography with a Supplementary List of General (Non-Review) Articles on Literary Subjects*. 2 vols. New York: Garland, 1972.

―――. *Literary Reviews in British Periodicals, 1821–1826: A Bibliography with a Supplementary List of General (Non-Review) Articles on Literary Subjects*. New York: Garland, 1977.

Antonia Forster and William S. Ward have completed two separate
projects to identify and index book reviews published in British periodicals between 1775 and 1826. Forster's volume, *Index to Book Reviews in England, 1775–1800*, indexes reviews for nearly five thousand works of poetry, fiction, and drama reviewed during the years
covered. An excellent introduction provides the background, politics,
and practices of eighteenth-century journals publishing book reviews.
Forster selected a core of twenty-seven primarily English journals: a
mix of standard periodicals devoted to reviewing contemporary publications (such as *The Monthly Review* and *The Critical Review*), the
important periodicals carrying substantive reviews (*Gentleman's
Magazine* and *London Magazine*), and thirteen periodicals with reviews
of secondary importance (*Annual Register* and *New Annual Register*).
The volume is arranged alphabetically by author or, if unknown, by
title. Entries include publication information for each title followed by
reviews listed in order of importance. Using *A Dictionary of British
and American Women Writers 1660–1800*, Forster identified authors
for works by women previously listed as anonymous.

In *Literary Reviews in British Periodicals, 1789–1797: A Bibliography*, *Literary Reviews in British Periodicals, 1798–1820: A Bibliography*, and *Literary Reviews in British Periodicals, 1821–1826: A
Bibliography*, Ward indexes reviews of literary works and critical essays about authors and genres. Coverage is almost exclusively British
for fiction, poetry, drama, and non-fiction prose published in the years
from 1789 to 1826. These volumes provide indexing to literary reviews
in over ninety periodicals and in two newspapers, *The Champion* and
The Examiner. Ward does not provide a list of periodicals in his indexes, which would have been helpful as a source for periodical title
verification. However, the breadth of journal coverage in the first two
decades facilitates access to a wide variety of contemporary responses
and makes the lack of a periodical list more inconvenient than detri-
mental.

The overlap between Ward's first volume and Forster's for the
years 1789–1797 is extensive, but it is worth checking both if the opportunity arises. Each is of very high quality and accuracy with detailed
information providing unexpected avenues for research exploration.
For example, one key difference between these sources is the way
anonymous writers are identified. Forster integrates anonymous works
by title into the alphabetic list while Ward lists all under the heading
Anonymous. Ward uses a variety of sources in an attempt to identify
authors of some anonymous works, including *Dictionary of Anonymous
and Pseudonymous English Literature*, *New Cambridge Bibliography
of English Literature*, and the *National Union Catalog pre-1956 Im-*

prints, while Forster uses Janet Todd's *A Dictionary of British and American Women Writers, 1660–1800* (Rowman and Allanheld 1985). Consequently a work may be attributed to different authors by the two compilers: the reviews for *Selima* are listed under Margaret Holdford's name in Forster and in Ward under Harriet Ventum. As a result of such preliminary detective work by Forster and Ward, the researcher has names connected with specific works and titles of bibliographic and biographical sources to use for additional information. On the surface, these two sets of reference works appear to be straightforward guides to Romantic-era review literature, but close attention to details by each compiler make these works rich sources of information.

Romantics Reviewed provides reproductions of reviews for the works of the major Romantic poets and selected literary figures, including Wordsworth, Coleridge, Byron, Keats, Shelley, Hunt, Godwin, Hazlitt, and Mary Shelley, published in the important review periodicals and journals of the late eighteenth and early nineteenth century. The set consists of nine volumes divided into three parts: A (Lake District Poets), B (Byron and Regency Society Poets), and C (Shelley, Keats, and London Radical Writers). Each section is arranged by periodical and then by reviews in chronological order. Reiman adds headnotes identifying the item reviewed and at times includes a description of the quality *(perceptive* or *obtuse, well* or *badly written)* of review the book received. He also includes concise background history about each journal and its biases.

The arrangement of the volumes, by magazine and then chronologically by author and work reviewed, makes the work cumbersome for those researching by author. However, the table of contents does list titles of single works reviewed while the index offers more access points to authors and titles covered both singly and as a group, so access to author and title are still possible. Scholars, especially those without easy access to journals themselves, will appreciate the convenience of reproductions of the original reviews as well as the groupings of reviews by publication: both allow the researcher to read the contemporary response to a work and to compare that with the reception of other canonical Romantic works within the same publication. This type of comparison can reveal biases inherent in the journal not clearly seen from a single review and help place a single work within the larger picture.

The English Novel 1770–1829: A Bibliographical Survey of Prose Fiction Published in the British Isles is not an index to reviews but does provide useful information in this area of research. While the two volumes list chronologically the novels published between 1770 and 1829, each entry also includes any references, either publication announcements or full reviews, to *The Monthly Review* and *The Critical Review* in the eighteenth century and to *The Edinburgh Review* and *The Quarterly Review* in the nineteenth. If the novel is indexed by Ward, that information is included as well.

Author-Specific Sources

Bentley, G. E, Jr. and Martin K. Nurmi. *A Blake Bibliography: Annotated Lists of Works, Studies, and Blakeana*. Minneapolis: University of Minnesota Press, 1964.

Bentley, G. E., ed. *William Blake: The Critical Heritage*. Boston: Routledge & K. Paul, 1975.

Littlewood, Ian, ed. *Jane Austen: Critical Assessments*. 4 vols. Mountfield, East Sussex: Helm Information, 1998.

Bibliographies and critical guides to specific authors will often provide bibliographic information for contemporary reviews and responses. These types of works exist mainly for canonical figures and not for lesser-known authors or for authors who do not have a continuous record of reviews and criticism up through the present. Because these works are focused upon the author and not the periodical, reviews and responses other than those found in serial publications may be covered, including letters and references in books. The following are examples of types of literary bibliographies.

A Blake Bibliography: Annotated Lists of Works, Studies, and Blakeana, a standard resource, states that every attempt was made to list everything published by and about William Blake prior to 1863, when modern interest in his life and works began. Blake's works, biographies about him, books he owned, and critiques are included. After 1863, the bibliography is more selective. Although larger in scope than just reviews and criticism, this invaluable source identifies late eighteenth- and early nineteenth-century discussions of Blake. Unfortunately for the scholar searching for the early reviews, the bibliography is arranged by author rather than by date. The volume, *William Blake: The Critical Heritage*, part of a Routledge series including literary figures from various countries and eras, is another type of bibliography. It is arranged by topic, then in chronological order, and provides bibliographic essays describing public and private responses to Blake's writings, art, and life and includes text from the original sources. These types of bibliographies push beyond the standard periodical responses to literary works and provide access to alternative contemporary perspectives on literary figures.

Of potential value are the *Helm Information Critical Assessments of Writers in English* series, published by Helm, which reproduce the text of criticism from contemporary views up to recent analysis. Each set in the series comprises four volumes of selected essays to provide students with a historic overview of criticism. These expensive, labor intensive sets focus on canonical authors. Thus far Jane Austen is the only figure represented from the Romantic era.

There are several strategies for finding bibliographies dedicated to specific authors.

- Search the library catalog. Examples of keywords searches to execute in an online library catalog include:

    > *william blake and critical heritage*
    > *william blake and bibliograph**
    > *jane austen and critical assessments*

- *The Dictionary of Literary Biography* series, published by Gale, often includes standard bibliographies
- Marcuse's *A Reference Guide for English Studies* lists standard bibliographies published prior to 1990 for selected British authors

Identifying and Locating Eighteenth- and Nineteenth-Century Periodicals

Crane, Ronald S. and Frederick B. Kaye. *A Census of British Newspapers and Periodicals 1620–1800.* Chapel Hill, NC: University of North Carolina Press, 1927.

Ward, William S. *Index and Finding List of Serials Published in the British Isles, 1789–1832.* Lexington: University of Kentucky Press, 1953.

Because many of the periodicals have common, generic titles, it is best to verify the publication needed. Two excellent resources for bibliographic identification are Crane's *A Census of British Newspapers and Periodicals 1620–1800* and Ward's *Index and Finding List of British Serials, 1789–1832.* These provide basic publishing information, including editor, to help identify the correct title, and symbols for libraries owning some volumes of the journal. To locate the journals publishing the reviews, verify the title of the journal using such resources and note unique details about the publication. For example, a title-phrase search on *monthly review*, limited to English language, in *WorldCat* yields 169 records. Ward's volume provides the journal's full title when it was published between 1790 and 1825: *Monthly Review: or, Literary Journal*, information that allows the researcher to search on the title and reduce the number of results in *WorldCat* to two records. Both of these records are for microfilm of the journal. To find print copies of the journal, the search strategy can be expanded. For example, although Crane's volume is not as detailed as Ward's in terms of title changes, it does list editors; in this case the editor is Griffiths. Combining the previous search with the keyword *griffiths* yields seven records for both print and microfilm versions of the *Monthly Review.*

Once you are confident about the source needed, search local libraries for the periodical title and, if not found, request via Interlibrary Loan. Because journals from the late eighteenth and early nineteenth centuries may not have unique titles or may have slight title changes, they may be difficult for ILL to identify. To expedite ILL requests, provide the staff of that department with the OCLC number found using *WorldCat*. As illustrated by the *Monthly Review* results above, supplying the OCLC number may be complicated because there are at least seven records to choose from, and you may not know which would be the best one to select. Ask a reference librarian for assistance determining the best OCLC or other standard number to use.

If these methods do not provide you with the materials needed, Chapter 7, "Eighteenth- and Nineteenth-Century Journals and Newspapers," will provide additional reference tools to help identify and locate periodicals. Because libraries do not always catalog individual parts of major microfilm collections, also consult Chapter 8, "Microforms and Digital Collections," for titles of eighteenth- and nineteenth-century literary periodical microfilm collections which may include the periodicals sought.

Conclusion

Forster and Ward have done an invaluable service to research in the Romantic era by indexing the contemporary reviews of all literary figures they could identify, and even those they couldn't. Other scholars have also contributed to our knowledge about the reputations of literary figures during their own time by identifying and reprinting reviews and other types of contemporary responses. It isn't as easy to research non-review articles in periodicals from this age, because the basic resource we take for granted—the article index—does not exist for the majority of journals and newspapers published between 1775 and 1830. The indexes which do exist are difficult to use. Romantic researchers, therefore, owe a great deal of gratitude to the scholars who created the resources examined in this chapter, for these essential works make further inquiry into the Romantic-era literature much easier and more rewarding. In the next chapter we will tackle the much tougher challenges of identifying journals and newspapers published during the Romantic period, and explain techniques for finding articles in those publications.

Notes

1. Roper, Derek. *Reviewing Before the Edinburgh, 1788–1802* (Newark, NJ: University of Delaware Press, 1978), 41.

2. Donoghue, Frank. "Colonizing Readers: Review Criticism and the Formation of a Reading Public" in *The Consumption of Culture 1600–1800: Image, Object, Text,* ed. by Ann Bermingham and John Brewer (New York: Routledge, 1995), 66–67.

Chapter 7
Eighteenth- and Nineteenth-Century Journals and Newspapers

Serial publishing in England grew steadily during the Romantic era and introduced a variety of publications reflecting the diverse philosophies and even partisan politics of the editors and publishers, as well as the wide-ranging tastes of the public. As the medium had not yet been defined, there were no standards established to govern how a serial publication would look or what it would contain. National, regional, and audience-specific publications were published in the form of dailies, weeklies, monthlies, quarterlies, and annuals, some lasting only for a few issues while others became British institutions. Because of these variable characteristics, the periodical literature from this era can prove challenging for the Romantic researcher to manage and to access.

A combination of factors allowed the serial publishing industry to grow steadily during the Romantic era, including an established literate society which consumed the publications and technological advances in printing presses and papermaking which made bulk publishing easier and cheaper. Scholars may argue about the true availability of these publications to the population as a whole, but enough consumer demand existed across the nation to support regional as well as metropolitan publications. To illustrate the growth of newspapers alone, London had four dailies and about six tri-weeklies in 1760 and by 1811 had a total of fifty-two papers, including morning, evening, tri-weekly, bi-weekly, and Sunday newspapers.[1] These figures do not include the London newspapers which came into being and disappeared during the intervening years. These short-lived publications should not be overlooked or dismissed as longevity may not determine the usefulness of a serial to a project; an ephemeral publication from a specific geographic area or one intended for a particular audience could prove more relevant than a long-lived London daily. Therefore, depending upon the project, the researcher may need to consult as many directories as possible to identify necessary publications.

Serial publications were an important means of communication in British society during the Romantic period, but they do not represent a coherent voice nor indicate the existence of a harmonious national atmosphere for the era as a whole. The various publications provided news about politics, commerce, and crime as well as reviews and announcements about leisurely activities such as literature, theatre, and sports. People who could not afford subscriptions or were not literate had access to serial publications at coffeehouses, which had served as public arenas for discussion and information since late in the seventeenth century. However, the public was not homogenous; a wide range of publications were produced for particular readers as well as general publications intended for several segments of society. There were serials for sportsmen, for the aristocracy, for the working classes, and for specific political parties. For example, the *Lady's Monthly Museum*, *Lady's Magazine*, and *La Belle Assemblée* were produced for aristocratic women, defining and addressing issues of femininity and duty in terms of class, while *British Lady's Magazine* was originally established for instruction, including news and issues concerning politics, science, and literature, and intended specifically for women. The content of the magazines was designed to appeal to the class or the interests of the women targeted. Shaping these journals' philosophical stance through editorial policies and selection of contributors was a means of establishing a particular image for the publication and for its readers. The connection between publication and audience was sometimes made ambiguous as some of the readers wrote pieces for the magazines, and by becoming involved in the production of the publication, blurred the line between reader and writer.[2]

As discussed in Chapter 6, early nineteenth-century review journals, such as *The Edinburgh Review*, were intentionally different in character and scope from the eighteenth-century publications, such as *The Monthly Review*, but they were also deliberately distinctive from each other as well. Among the nineteenth-century literary periodicals, the competition and philosophical rivalries could be intense: the Whig *Edinburgh Review* was countered by the Tory *Quarterly Review* and later another Tory publication, *Blackwood's Edinburgh Magazine*; the Evangelical *British Review* set itself up to fill the gap neglected by *The Edinburgh Review* and *The Quarterly Review*. In an extreme example of the fierce disagreements between editors, John Scott, editor of the *London Magazine*, died in a duel over his severe criticism of *Blackwood's Edinburgh Magazine*. Although Scott's demise was atypical, arguments between publishers, writers, and reviewers could be very heated and personal.

In the midst of these issues about audience and image, other outside forces provided challenges for editors and publishers to keep in business. Newspapers especially struggled to exist in an era of heavy taxation, government censorship, and fierce competition for audience and advertising dollars. Understanding the climate in which a publication existed, its audience, including rival audiences, and economic and political challenges, will shed light upon the contents of particular publications and trends of the industry as a whole. The above overview illustrates the broad issues facing and influencing serial publications and publishing, which in turn will have an impact upon the research strategies for using this type of material.

Today, it is often difficult to differentiate between Romantic-period magazines and newspapers because the rules for calling a publication one or the other were very fluid. No single directory exists which comprehensively lists the titles of all serial publications. Researchers will find that indexes and finding aids to the contents of periodicals are limited; moreover these sources provide access to articles mainly in the most well-known monthly and quarterly periodicals, while the only newspaper currently indexed is *The Times*. Although plans to digitize the serial publications of this era are in development, at present a mixture of traditional print resources, electronic subscriptions, and Web-based sources are necessary to identify and access this type of material. To ease the Romantic scholar into accessing the serial literature, this chapter begins with the most basic research strategies—finding articles by subject—and then proceeds to describe resources for identifying a broad range of periodicals within a geographic area or those intended for a specific audience and outlines strategies for finding articles within these publications.

Finding Articles

Balay, Robert. *Early Periodical Indexes: Bibliographies and Indexes of Literature Published in Periodicals before 1900*. Lanham, MD: Scarecrow Press, 2000.

Houghton, Walter E., ed. *The Wellesley Index to Victorian Periodicals, 1824–1900*. Toronto: University of Toronto Press, 1966–1989.

Palmer's Index to the Times Newspaper. 1790–June 1941. 100 vols. Vadux: Kraus Reprint, 1965–1966.

Poole, William Frederick. *Poole's Index to Periodical Literature*. 6 vols. 1802–1906. Boston: Houghton, 1888–1908. Rev. ed. Boston: Houghton, 1891. Reprint, New York: Peter Smith, 1938. Available online via www.paratext.com/.

Shattock, Joanne, ed. *The Cambridge Bibliography of English Literature*. 3rd ed. Vol. 4: 1800–1900. New York: Cambridge University Press, 1999.

The Times Digital Archive, 1785–1985. Farmington Hills, MI: Thomson-Gale. www.gale.com

Watson, George, ed. *The New Cambridge Bibliography of English Literature*. 2nd ed. Vol. 2: 1660–1800. Cambridge: Cambridge University Press, 1971.

A limited number of general indexes have been published which provide subject access to the periodical and newspaper literature of the Romantic era. In the last chapter we described how to find review articles, and in this chapter we will concentrate on how to find other types of articles. At present, the core early nineteenth-century magazine article indexes are *Poole's Index to Periodical Literature* and *The Wellesley Index to Victorian Periodicals, 1824–1900*, which both provide limited but important access to the contents of major journals of the time. The *(New) Cambridge Bibliography of English Literature* and topical bibliographies are another means of accessing the periodical literature, although coverage is not as complete as in a standard index. In *Early Periodical Indexes: Bibliographies and Indexes of Literature Published in Periodicals before 1900*, Balay has compiled an annotated bibliography to the bibliographies and indexes which index periodical articles prior to 1900. The use of any of these research tools, even the electronic versions of *Poole's* or *Wellesley*, requires patience because none are not easy to use and do require diligence on your part.

William Frederick Poole was a nineteenth-century librarian with a vision about bibliographic control over the materials housed in the library. Periodicals posed a particular problem. Libraries across the United States stored the serials but no subject access existed. Early in his career, Poole created a list of articles by subject for the students at Yale. In 1848 a limited run of this resource was published as *An Alphabetical Index to Subjects, Treated in the Reviews, and Other Periodicals to Which No Indexes have been Published* (Society of Brothers in Unity, Yale College, New Haven) and in 1853, made more widely available as *An Index to Periodical Literature* (Boston: Norton, 1853). In 1876, a project to update the list and expand it was born. Poole organized a group of librarians to divide up a core list of periodicals, including some British titles, and, based upon the title of the article, assign subjects to the articles. In 1877, an article reveals the importance of this endeavor, which still holds true today:

> We may sometimes desire to find a certain given article or, perchance, one by a well-known author; but so many contributions are anonymous, and so little are the contents of our periodicals known, that this will seldom happen. Further, the titles of these essays are very misleading, more so even than those of books, and it will be very seldom that we search for a particular title. What we most desire is to obtain all the matter on a given *subject*, regardless of the *title* of the piece, but with the author's name attached, if known, as a guarantee of its worth, or at least as an index to its reliability. [3]

What had been lacking, and what Poole provided, was subject access to the periodical literature of the nineteenth century, including a portion of the Romantic era.

Available both in print and online by subscription, ***Poole's Index to Periodical Literature*** provides subject access to 479 nineteenth-century periodicals published from 1802 to 1906. The index can be difficult to use but realizing its foibles will help make searching more rewarding:

- The index is arranged by subject, but the headings are not standardized. Therefore researchers need to search under a variety of possible terms.
- The entries are abbreviated and do not include the full title for the article but rather include a few words at most to indicate the content of the article. When the indexer felt the article title was inadequate, a better title was assigned.
- When originally published, the index had no author index. Authors, not always accurately identified, were listed in parenthesis following the entry. A separate author volume was published in 1971, but no attempt was made to verify or regularize spelling.
- Poole did not approve of the sporadic numbering system used by journals, or of the variant titles which cropped up during the century. Instead of including the publication year or in some cases the actual volume number for the magazine, Poole decided to create a numbering scheme for the volumes and directed librarians to put labels on the journals which reflected his renumbering scheme. In addition he would use only the most well-known title for the journal. These decisions may have simplified the compilation of the index, but today complicates the process for the researcher because, by changing such basic details as the journal title and volume, the scholar is

required to verify this information before going forth to locate the article. As a means of alleviating these problems, the *Poole's Index Date and Volume Key* and the *Transfer Vectors for Poole's Index to Periodical Literature* were created to provide researchers with the correct titles, volumes, and years for the journals.

- Only the first page of the article was referenced, with no indication of the article's length.

- Stories, poems, and plays were indexed by title, reviews of fictional works were indexed by authors, and reviews of nonfiction works were indexed by subject. Most of these problems were corrected when the Web version of the index was created: the author index was integrated, volume numbers corrected, and years added, but it still lacks pagination.

Poole mainly indexed American periodicals, but twenty of the forty-five periodicals in *Poole's* index, published between 1802–1830, were from England and Scotland, including *The Edinburgh Review* (beginning in 1802), *Methodist Magazine* (1802), *Christian Observer* (1802), *Eclectic Review* (1805), *Quarterly Review* (1809), *Monthly Review* (1817), *London Magazine* (1820), *Westminster Review* (1824), *Foreign Quarterly* Review (1827), and *Fraser's Magazine* (1830).

Poole's is available both in print and via the World Wide Web by subscription. If available through your library, we recommend the electronic version: the author index has been integrated with the subject index, dates have been added to the citations, and known inaccuracies corrected. For example, a reference to "Northanger Abbey and Persuasion" by R. Whatley was cited in the print version of *Poole's* as published in "*Quar.* 24:352," which would have been about 1820 and during the Romantic era. In the electronic version, this citation was corrected to "*Old and New*, 7 (1873): 352."

However, both the electronic and print versions of *Poole's* can be awkward to use. In the electronic version, the default result display is by relevancy. This can be overridden by limiting searches to a specific year and sorting by year, author, or title. In both versions, author as subjects are listed with their full forenames (Austen, Jane; Scott, Sir Walter) while authors of the articles are listed by initials. Therefore researchers who wish to find articles about Scott search by keyword using his whole name while those wanting articles by him search *scott, sir w.*—an author search on *scott, walter* yields no results because the correct entry for him is "Scott, Sir W." In both print and electronic versions, only the initial page number is provided, a flaw which should have been corrected in the electronic version, but was probably an expensive endeavor to undertake. And, as innovative as *Poole's* reference tool was at the time, and as valuable as it continues to be when re-searching the periodical literature of the time, subject headings are not standardized. Even in the electronic version, which is searchable by keywords, the Romantic scholar may need to use a variety of terms to locate relevant citations. For example, when investigating religious topics, you would need to search the words *religion, spirituality, baptism, bible, christian, methodist,* and *catholicism.*

Literary scholars do benefit from the fact that *Poole's* was compiled later in the nineteenth century, since by then some anonymous authors had been identified, such as Jane Austen, and the author as subject therefore searchable. In an index such as *Periodicals Contents Index (PCI),* a database which at present provides access to a few eighteenth- and early nineteenth-century periodicals, compilers indexed what was on the page of the publication and did no verification work to identify authors. Therefore, if using *PCI,* the researcher will need to know which year a novel such as *Emma* was published to try to find references to the work, for Austen's name is not associated with the articles written. Whereas with *Poole's* the possibility exists that the anonymous person was identified. (At the time this volume is being written, *PCI* doesn't cover enough unique titles to warrant inclusion in our research guide as a primary research tool, but as it grows it may prove more valuable. It will be worth your time to consult the resource if available, for new citations are continually being added.)

The online version of *Poole's* is unquestionably superior to the print in terms of combining keywords to find relevant citations, searching by year, and searching by author. The online version includes the year an article was published, as well as volume and page number, and the author index is integrated into the whole; in the print version, only the volume and page number are included and the author index is in a separate volume and cumbersome to use. To locate the year an article was published using the print copy of Poole's: 1) use the *Chronological Conspectus of the Serials Indexed* (which may not be accurate) located at the front of each volume; 2) consult the separate *Transfer Vectors* which lists titles of journals indexed and years and volumes covered; and 3) consult the *Date and Volume Key,* a master list of journals, dates, and volumes which attempts to correct the errors found in the *Chronological Conspectus.* The print *Cumulative Author Index* is an alphabetic list of the authors identified within the subject volumes, but an author with variant spellings may have more than one entry, and the entries include only the volume and page number for the location of a citation in the main volumes, with no indication about the title or subject of the author. The print version of this invaluable resource requires patience and diligence to use, but it is well worth the effort if not available online.

The Wellesley Index to Victorian Periodicals, 1824–1900 lists the tables of contents of forty-three British periodicals. Seven of the journals included are indexed before 1830: *Blackwood's Edinburgh Magazine* (from 1824), *Eclectic Review* (1824), *Edinburgh Review* (1802), *Quarterly Review* (1824), *Foreign Quarterly Review* (1827), *Fraser's Magazine for Town and Country* (1830), *London Review* (1829), *The New Monthly Magazine* (1821), and *The Westminster Review* (1824).

Wellesley lists tables of contents for major quarterly and monthly Victorian British periodicals. Using publisher records, archives, and a variety of other resources, the compilers of the index researched each article included thoroughly to provide the most accurate information possible about the identity of the author. Poetry published in the journals is excluded from the project, but book reviews are included. When the title of the article is imprecise, a subject is provided in brackets. Notes providing evidence to support authorship are listed after the author's name in the entry.

Wellesley is available in both print and on CD-ROM. The five-volume print version of the reference tool includes the table of contents and authors, but no keyword access. Each subsequent volume includes corrections for the previous volumes. The CD-ROM incorporates both the author index and the corrections into the database, and provides keyword searching to the tables of contents. Articles are not classified by subject in either version. Valuable introductory essays to each journal title describe the history, editorial practices, and political biases of that publication. We hope the database will one day be Web-based to provide remote access and to take advantage of more sophisticated search software. The CD-ROM software is very clunky to search; rather than pulling all the records together to be displayed and printed as a block, the software displays abbreviated bibliographic information in a pop-up "Search Results" box with no total number of hits. Instead of allowing each citation to be displayed in full from this list, you must highlight the desired item and then the software finds the citation within the table of contents. To know which volume and year the article is in, you scroll up to the heading for the table of contents. When using this database, read the help screens carefully to understand how to search, retrieve, and display results.

Together *Poole's* and *Wellesley* provide preliminary, and perhaps satisfactory, broad access to a few of the major journals of the era. *Poole's* indexes more journals than *Wellesley*, while the author identification, article titles, dates, and page numbers in *Wellesley* are more accurate. Searching the table of contents of articles by keyword can always be challenging, and, as neither use controlled vocabulary, both must be searched using a variety of keywords. The brainstorming exercise described in Chapter 1 is very important under these circumstances. And even these two resources, which attempt to use the titles of the articles as much as possible, give different results even when indexing the same article. For example, a search on the keyword *marriage*, limited to the years 1802–1830, will retrieve the same citations, but there are discrepancies in titles and dates. When such discrepancies occur, use the information from *Wellesley* because that is more likely to be accurate, but keep the *Poole's* information available in case this proves not to be the case. And, however frustrating this may sound, although neither the print nor the electronic version of either resource is easy to use, they do provide the best access to the more general periodicals published during the time.

Indexes published in the annual volumes of periodicals can provide in-depth access to contents. If working on a particular journal, take the time to browse through the tables of contents and indexes, if present, to find relevant articles. Some of these entries are quite descriptive and may help in the process of identifying pertinent sources. Also, check bibliographies of current scholarly works you discover for references to articles from the era.

Unfortunately, however, for the majority of publications, including newspapers, the only way to find articles may be to scan the publication page by page. At present, *The Times* of London has the only index available for a newspaper. **Palmer's Index to the Times**, available in print, microform, CD-ROM, and through Chadwyck-Healey as an online subscription, is the only index to a newspaper from the Romantic era currently in existence. When complete, *Palmer's Full Text Online, 1785–1870* will allow researchers to search for relevant articles using the online index and then link to digitized images of the full articles. At present the project provides access to articles from 1800–1870. Thomson Gale offers a digital version of the newspaper through *The Times Digital Archive, 1785–1985* which allows the full-text of over 7,682,300 records to be keyword searched and the articles displayed digitally. In addition, *The Times Digital Archive* allows articles to be limited by a wide variety of criteria, including advertising, by topic such as business or entertainment, editorials and commentary, news, and people (including birth, marriage, and death announcements). Both *Palmer's* and *The Times Digital Archive* can be used to establish when certain events were reported, and thus can serve as a rough index to other newspapers of the time that may have reported on the same events. You can also use chronologies (see Chapter 2 and the Appendix) of British history or culture to determine dates or relevant events and then, in turn search newspapers for reports. As digitizing projects continue to be developed, more newspapers could become available via the Web, either by subscription or through cooperative initiatives by cultural institutions such as libraries and universities, and access to articles by topic made easier. For the latest information about digitization projects, monitor the websites discussed in Chapter 10 and consult with your reference librarian.

The Cambridge Bibliography of English Literature, revised as *The New Cambridge Bibliography of English Literature* and currently being revised once again as *The Cambridge Bibliography of English Literature*, is a standard print bibliography for literary researchers (see Chapter 4). The chronological arrangement allows the scholar to browse through the bibliographic history of an author or a topic. Although not comprehensive, this resource could prove valuable for locating early writing about an author or topic.

Balay, in *Early Periodical Indexes: Bibliographies and Indexes of Literature Published in Periodicals before 1900*, categorizes and annotates a wide variety of indexes, from the standard to the obscure, which provide some access to periodical articles from around the world published prior to 1900. This volume is the result of Balay's long interest in identifying articles within publications from earlier eras and the frustration of trying to do so successfully. Because indexes, even today, do not adequately address this gap in research, *Early Periodical Indexes* includes a large number of bibliographies which cover articles, books, and other publications. The volume is arranged in six broad categories: General; Humanities; History and Area Studies; Social and Behavioral Sciences; Science and Technology; and Library and Information Science. *Poole's* is listed in the general index section under *General*, which is further subdivided by country where general indexes are available. *Wellesley* is listed under General–>Indexes–>Britain. The subject divisions are subdivided by discipline ("Literature" under "Humanities," for example), by specialization within the discipline (e.g., Jewish Literature, Rhetoric, Science Fiction) or geographic location (United States–>Native Americans; Europe–>Britain). You can find possible reference sources to help in researching languages, philosophy, religion, art, music, history, education, sociology, law, chemistry, biology, medicine, and many other fields of study. Works are not limited to English language but include resources from other countries. The work is much broader in scope than the Romantic era, but a valuable "Dates of Coverage" section at the end arranges most of the indexes and bibliographies in broad chronological order of the periodicals indexed. As expected, the majority of the resources are from the Victorian era and later; however, there are gems in this volume which can aid the researcher willing to seek out alternative resources. The annotations are very thoughtful and helpful with descriptions of the content, analysis of strengths and weaknesses, and when the resource is difficult to use, suggestions for using the resource effectively. Balay's *Early Periodical Indexes* is invaluable.

Identifying Newspapers and Periodicals

British Library Newspaper Archive, at www.bl.uk/collections/news papers.html (accessed 7 December 2004).

Crane, Ronald S. and Frederick B. Kaye. *A Census of British Newspapers and Periodicals, 1620–1800*. Chapel Hill, NC: University of North Carolina Press, 1927.

English Short Title Catalogue (ESTC). Mountain View, CA: RLG. www.rlg.org.

Gibson, Jeremy, compiler. *Local Newspapers, 1750–1920, England and Wales, Channel Islands, Isle of Man: A Select Location List*. Birmingham, England: Federation of Family History Societies, 1987.

Harrison, Royden. *Warwick Guide to British Labour Periodicals, 1790–1970: A Check List*. Atlantic Highlands, NJ: Humanities Press, 1977.

North, John S., ed. *The Waterloo Directory of English Newspapers and Periodicals, 1800–1900*. 10 vols. Waterloo, Ont.: North Waterloo Academic Press, 1997.

———. *The Waterloo Directory of Scottish Newspapers and Periodicals, 1800–1900*. 2 vols. Waterloo, Ont.: North Waterloo Academic Press, 1989.

———. *The Waterloo Directory of Irish Newspapers and Periodicals, 1800–1900*. Waterloo, Ont.: North Waterloo Academic Press, 1986.

RLG Union Catalog. Mountain View, CA: RLG. www.rlg.org.

Shattock, Joanne, ed. *The Cambridge Bibliography of English Literature*. 3rd ed. Vol. 4: 1800–1900. New York: Cambridge University Press, 1999.

Stewart, James D., Muriel E. Hammond, and Erwin Saenger. *British Union Catalogue of Periodicals*. 4 vols. Hamden, CT: Archon Books, 1968.

Sullivan, Alvin, ed. *British Literary Magazines: The Romantic Age, 1789–1836*. Westport, CT: Greenwood Press, 1983.

Titus, Edna Brown, ed. *Union List of Serials in Libraries of the United States and Canada*. 3rd ed. 5 vols. New York: H. W. Wilson, 1965.

Ward, William S. *British Periodicals & Newspapers, 1789–1832: A Bibliography of Secondary Sources*. Lexington, KY: University of Kentucky Press, 1972.

Ward, William S., comp. *Index and Finding List of Serials Published in the British Isles, 1789–1832*. Lexington, KY: University of Kentucky Press, 1953.

Watson, George, ed. *The New Cambridge Bibliography of English Literature*. 2nd ed. Vol. 2: 1660–1800. Cambridge: Cambridge University Press, 1971.

WorldCat. Dublin, OH: OCLC. www.oclc.org/firstsearch/.

Using a combination of bibliographies and checklists, researchers can effectively identify titles of periodicals and newspapers available during the Romantic era. No single source exists which will provide the information, but it is possible to make an effective start with the tools available. Broadly, most directories in this section define a serial as anything which was intended to be published over time, with an indefinite ending point. Therefore books, which were often published in parts over a prescribed period of time, would not be included but annuals, published without a known ending date, would. None of the directories claim to be all inclusive and error free. Therefore the scholar needs to be diligent when focusing on this era and attempting to identify and locate relevant serials. In addition, since only the selected titles were indexed by *Poole's* and *Wellesley*, it is important to remember that titles were included for indexing based upon later ideas about the historical importance of the serials.

As a point of entry into this arena, William S. Ward created two selective volumes which allow the scholar to begin identifying both newspapers and periodicals published during the relevant time period. The ***Index and Finding List of Serials Published in the British Isles, 1789–1832*** is a list of periodical and newspaper titles culled from the *Union Catalog of Serials* (*UCS*), the *British Union Catalogue of Periodicals* (*UCP*), and Ward's own personal research. Brief bibliographic entries include dates of publication and volume numbers, when available, as well as references back to holdings listed in the *UCS* and *UCP* or libraries Ward has identified as holding the titles. Although entries are very brief, it remains a standard source for this time period. The strictly alphabetic list does not allow publications by location or type to be easily identified, but this volume, used in conjunction with others in this section, will allow the researcher to compile an initial list. Because microfilm and digitizing projects make such rare materials more widely available, libraries other than those listed may hold the title desired in alternate formats, so do not rely upon the locations as the only libraries which own the title.

In addition to the *Index*, Ward also compiled a bibliography of secondary sources about the periodicals and newspapers, the people who published them, and the role of such publications in society during the Romantic era. *British Periodicals and Newspapers, 1789–1832: A Bibliography of Secondary Sources* is divided into six sections: general bibliographies, general studies, periodicals (including newspapers), people, places, and special subjects (printing, production, advertising, stamp tax, and literary forms). Of particular value is the list of general bibliographies, which include lists of finding aids compiled and published from early in the nineteenth century forward. Much of the scholarship may be dated, but again this volume provides an entry into the era and serves as a good starting point for identifying the publications and people involved.

When completed, *The Waterloo Directory of English Newspapers and Periodicals, 1800–1900*, *The Waterloo Directory of Irish Newspapers and Periodicals, 1800–1900*, and *The Waterloo Directory of Scottish Newspapers and Periodicals, 1800–1900* will comprise the most comprehensive directories of newspapers and periodicals covering all subjects published in the nineteenth century. As these will be the definitive resources for identifying publications for the early part of the nineteenth century, the directories reveal how incomplete all other resources are for identifying serial titles. Five series of *The Waterloo Directory of English Newspapers and Periodicals, 1800–1900* are planned. The first series, a ten-volume set, lists over twenty-seven thousand entries; the fifth series is projected by the authors to include over 125,000 serial titles published during the century. The ongoing project will attempt to identify and locate all these titles.

Entries for the directory sets list: title; alternate titles; title changes; volumes; dates; place of publication; editor; proprietor; publisher; printer; contributors; size; price; circulation; frequency; description and comments; and selected locations for holdings. Both the Scottish and English directories include some facsimiles of title pages. Indexes cover subject, place, and people. The Web-based version of the English set allows a more flexible means of searching: not only can it be searched by title, but the advanced search allows you to compile a list of titles by date and location. For example, a list of serial publications from Bath published between 1790 and 1830 can be pulled together using the software. To be included in this directory, publications must either have ended or started (or both) in the nineteenth century, which means some eighteenth-century titles, such as *The Monthly Review* and *The Critical Review*, are listed. These sets are the most thorough directories available for the nineteenth century. At present, no eighteenth-century equivalent exists, so you must use other available resources, such as Ward, Crane, *NCBEL*, *WorldCat*, *RLG Union Catalog*, and *ESTC* to identify and locate those publications from 1775 to 1799.

Crane's *A Census of British Newspapers and Periodicals 1620–1800*, published in 1927, overlaps with Ward's *British Periodicals and Newspapers, 1789–1832* at the end of the eighteenth century but does have some unique titles listed. Both Crane and Ward list titles alphabetically and include very brief bibliographic and holdings information. Crane's contains two features which add value to his volume: a chronological list of entries by year so that scholars can identify by date which titles were available each year from 1620 through 1800, and a brief list of publications by location, including titles published outside London. As with Ward's directory, the holdings information is no longer entirely valid, and therefore this volume serves as a place to gather preliminary information which can then be supplemented by other directories and online databases.

No comprehensive collection of Romantic-era newspapers exists in one library, but the *British Library Newspapers* contains a rich collection of titles. Newspapers are housed in both the main library in St. Pancras, London, and at the **British Library Newspaper Archive** at the Colindale Avenue location in North London. Newspaper holdings in both locations are searchable online via the newspaper catalog, available through the British Library website. The collections include all national daily and Sunday newspapers from 1801 forward and some provincial newspapers. For titles prior to 1801, the British Library purchased the Burney Collection in 1818 which included seven hundred volumes of newspapers published between 1603 and 1817 (for more information about this collection, see Chapter 8). To identify potentially relevant titles, scholars need to use the Web-based newspaper catalog. At present, searching is limited to words in the place name or title. Results may be sorted by title, place, or year. Although search results will not be flawless, searching by place name can be valuable. A keyword search on *london*, and date search limited to the start year *1770*, the end year *1830*, sorted by date, yields over three hundred records in chronological order for newspapers published in London between 1770 and 1830. The records include brief information about the publication: start and end dates, holdings for the British Library listed, and some title changes. For more complete information, the title should be cross checked with other resources listed in this section, such as one of the online catalogs or, if published after 1800, in North's *The Water-loo Directory of English Newspapers and Periodicals.*

The New Cambridge Bibliography of English Literature *(NCBEL)* is currently being revised to become the third edition of the reference tool and renamed *The Cambridge Bibliography of English Literature (CBEL).* This standard resource (see Chapter 4) provides selective lists of newspapers and periodicals from 1660 to 1800 (Volume 2 of the *NCBEL*) and 1800–1900 (Volume 4 of the *CBEL*, 3rd edition). However, because no additional titles were added to the third edition, if you have access only to the earlier edition you can rely on that source. It's unknown at this point if additional titles will be added to Volume 2 once the new edition is published. In Volume 2, sections are arranged in chronological order from the earliest through the end of the eighteenth century and include periodicals and newspapers published in London and outside London by geographic area. The list can be used in conjunction with Ward's *British Periodicals and Newspapers, 1789–1832* and Crane's *A Census of British Newspapers and Periodicals, 1620–1800* to identify potential titles.

In *NCBEL*, an attempt has been made to categorize the periodical publications by type: "Periodical Essays Published in London by Themselves, in Newspapers, or in Magazines and Miscellanies," "Magazines, Miscellanies, Learned Journals and Reviews Published in London 1660–1800," "Annuals," "London Newspapers," "Manuscript Letters," "Miscellaneous London Serials," and separate sections, divided by the English provinces, Scotland, and Ireland, for "Periodical Essays," "Magazines and Miscellanies," and "Newspapers." Outside London areas are further divided geographically. Every attempt has been made to include dates of publication. For the volume covering the nineteenth century, the contents of the newspaper and magazine section include: daily papers; London morning and evening papers; provincial papers; Scottish and Irish dailies; weekly papers; Sunday papers; unstamped and radical journals; weekly literary reviews; religious, agricultural, financial, sporting, humorous, and juvenile newspapers; monthly magazines; quarterly magazines; and annuals and yearbooks. The lists in *NCBEL*, although selective, are valuable for identifying newspapers and periodicals by geographic location and type, not just by title. The lists are arranged in chronological order from when the periodical first started, so that the scholar can scan the list to see which titles might fall within the Romantic time period. However, because there are no solid definitions differentiating the types of publications, it is strongly recommended that you examine all the different sections of this resource in case something of interest is categorized in an unexpected section.

Online union catalogs, such as OCLC's *WorldCat*, the Research Library Group's *RLG Union Catalog*, and *Copac*, and printed union lists of serials, such as *Union List of Serials* and *British Union Catalogue of Periodicals* are valuable as secondary resources for verifying titles, dates, and possible locations of materials. *WorldCat* can be searched by place of publication, range of dates from 1775 to 1830, and limited by type of publication (serial). This search will retrieve records for materials in print or on microform. If a library has cataloged the individual titles of a microfilm collection and uploaded their records into *WorldCat*, then a title such as *The Patriot, or, Political, Moral, and Philosophical Repository*, which is reproduced on microfilm as part of the collection *Rare Radical and Labour Periodicals of Great Britain*, can be located. The *English Short Title Catalog*, available on CD-ROM and via the Research Library Group's *RLG Library Resources*, is a bibliography of publications from 1475–1800 and includes records for nearly four thousand newspapers and other serials. The CD-ROM can be searched to limit results by date and keyword (using *j journal* to focus on periodicals). In addition, this resource will list the locations of the publication, and, if included as part of a microform set, the title of the collection. Read Chapter 8 for more information about locating microform collections.

British Literary Magazines: The Romantic Age, 1789–1836 lists annotated entries for relevant publications from the Romantic period and describes the audience and scope. Periodical entries include *Edinburgh Review*, *Eclectic Review*, *Quarterly Review*, *London Magazine*, *Westminster Review*, *Foreign Quarterly Review*, and *Fraser's Magazine*. The editor attempted to include titles which are representative of, or which began and ceased publication during, the Romantic era. Each of the eighty-four titles covered provides a two- to three-page profile, indexes and location sources when available, bibliographies, and publication history. Such a source is invaluable for condensing the history of a broad range of literary magazines for easy referral about the history of the publication itself, as well as the complex relationship between journals. "Appendix A" lists periodical titles from the previous volume, *British Literary Magazines: The Augustan Age, 1698–1788*, which were still relevant in the Romantic age and therefore of interest to the Romantic scholar, including journals such as the *The Monthly Review* and *The Critical Review*.

In addition to the above, researchers should seek out specialized directories and bibliographies to newspapers or periodicals by subject. Historical society publications such as Jeremy Gibson's *Local Newspapers, 1750–1920, England and Wales, Channel Islands, Isle of Man: A Select Location List* or specialized lists such *Warwick Guide to British Labour Periodicals, 1790–1970: A Check List* are examples of resources which focus on niche publications. To find specialized publications such as these, use the techniques covered in Chapter 3 and search union catalogs by keyword, combined with such terms as *bibliography, check list, union lists* or *history* to find potentially useful records. Follow promising Library of Congress subject headings to see if more resources of a similar nature exist. For example, to find lists of newspapers in Durham, searching the keywords *durham and newspapers and bibliography* in *WorldCat* will lead to records with relevant titles, as well as subject headings assigned within the records.

Conclusion

Although a great deal of research has been done on some aspects of the Romantic era, there are still enormous gaps in our knowledge of primary source materials such as periodicals. Lack of standard indexes to this literature provides research challenges for scholars. No directory accurately or comprehensively lists the publications from the time. The scholar of this era needs to approach such research with patience and creativity, and to be willing to figure out how to effectively use as many resources as possible to discover relevant materials. A combination of Web-based and traditional print indexes, bibliographies, directories, checklists, online catalogues, and even chronologies are required to research the serial literature of the day.

Notes

1. Black, Jeremy. *The English Press, 1621–1861* (Thrupp, Stroud, Gloucestershire: Sutton, 2001), 74.

2. Beetham, Margaret. *A Magazine of Her Own? Domesticity and Desire in the Woman's Magazine 1800–1914* (New York: Routledge, 1996), 19.

3. Biscoe, Walter S. "The Improvement of Poole's Index" in *American Library Journal*, 1, no. 8 (April 30, 1877), 280.

Chapter 8
Microform and Digital Collections

Access to primary source materials, including books, journals, manuscripts, and documents, can be challenging because these types of materials may be rare or even unique and available only in special collections or archives. However, these same primary sources could also be available in a microform collection or through a digitization project.

Microforms were used during the twentieth century as a means of providing wider access to rare materials and preserving the originals from excessive use. At the beginning of the twenty-first century, digitization began to replace microforms as the technology of choice because, in addition to preservation, this technology made access to documents easier, with distribution over the Internet, and it made full-text searching of older texts possible. Large scale projects to convert major microform collections into electronic format were undertaken by commercial publishers. Digitization also allowed cultural institutions such as universities, libraries, archives, and museums to scan and disseminate works from their collections. Scholars, working with microform collections which had not yet been converted, were able to capture the images electronically using digitization technology.

Here at the beginning of the twenty-first century, we are in a transition period in which the Romantic scholar will need to be comfortable using both microforms and digital images. In the foreseeable future, both formats will continue to co-exist as conversion of all microforms to digital form will take time and will be expensive. Despite the advantages of digitization, microforms are still being created because the format is easier to manage and sell. Both formats allow librarians to purchase access to and researchers to view and consult rare primary source material. For the Romantic researcher, both technologies will provide valuable access to the publications of that era.

Microforms have various formats, including fiche, film, microopaque, and ultra-microfiche. At present microfiche and microfilm appear to be the most stable format for a couple of reasons: because the technology is simple, requiring a lens, a light, and a screen onto which an image can be projected, and because librarians continue to invest in this technology. Micro-opaque proved to be the least dependable format, for the technology to use this format fell out of favor and the equipment to view the cards ceased to be manufactured. The images were printed on white cards and the image reflected onto a screen. Ultra-microfiche allowed publishers to put a lot of pages on a single fiche, which saved some space, but the format required a very powerful lens which still did not always magnify the image to an acceptable degree.

Neither micro-opaque nor ultra-microfiche formats are being used for new microform projects. However, with the twenty-first century, the digital age has revived even the unusable micro-opaque. The technology being used to create digital collections on a large scale is also available to the individual scholar. Digitizing microform readers allow researchers to scan and save images as PDF, GIF, JPEG, and TIF files from the microform. The files can then be enhanced using optical character recognition (OCR) software, a computerized process which, without retyping the text, transforms a digitized image of text into ASCII characters that can be imported into a word processing program and made searchable. For the fonts of the eighteenth and nineteenth centuries, the use of OCR can be problematic because they are not as easily recognizable or standardized as today's fonts, but the option is available for the individual and is being used in large digitization projects. Because of the high quality of the images which result even from projects done by individuals for their own use, scans are very detailed. For example, in the past, researchers using newspapers on microfilm would have to print out the page in parts and then tape the results together. With a digital scanner, the entire page of a newspaper can be captured and then, using appropriate software, the image can be magnified to allow the researcher to zoom in on the relevant article on the page. Digitization allows scholars much more flexibility in using the microform collections at their disposal and to manage such images using electronic means of storing, scanning, and keyword searching the materials.

Cataloging of microform and digital collections varies according to the policies of the library who owns the materials. One common practice is to catalog the collection as a whole and provide one record in the library catalog; this is called a "collection-level record." If only one record represents the entire collection, the individual parts of the collection cannot be searched online and you need to find another means for accessing the content, such as a print or electronic finding aid. Another common practice is to buy the cataloging records for the individual parts of the collection and load these into the library catalog. In this case each record will have the specific microform number within the collection or, if in digitized form, a link to the electronic version of the resource. Microforms are usually kept together physically in one location within a library, and are often arranged by access numbers (a numbering system based upon the order in which the materials were acquired) rather than call numbers.

The library may have purchased parts of a collection rather than the entire set. Also, many newspapers and periodicals can be purchased individually in microform. In these cases, the parts or the individual titles will be cataloged and records made available in the library catalog. Because of cataloging rules, these records will contain the title of the complete microform collection, but this does not mean the library owns the whole collection. If you want to use the whole collection for your research project, and if you cannot determine whether the library owns the entire collection, consult with the reference librarian.

In the case of microform reproductions of newspapers and periodicals, if the finding aids to the collection don't provide article-level access, consult Chapters 6 and 7 for recommendations for indexes and bibliographies which do allow you to search for articles by keyword or subject. Digitization projects are much more likely to allow keyword searching on the article title at a minimum, and may even allow full-text searching. Whether the serial is in microform or in digitized form, you may still be required to use the core indexes, such as *Poole's* or *Wellesley*, to find articles. Remember, whether *The Edinburgh Review* is available in print or on microfilm, it is the same serial, and you will need to use the techniques discussed in Chapters 6 and 7 to do article-level searching

If your library doesn't own the collection you wish to use, you can request the microforms through interlibrary loan. If you need to consult the finding aid to determine which microfilm reels or microfiche cards you need, you can try to borrow the finding aid via interlibrary loan first.

Finding Microform and Digitized Collections

"Bibliographies and Guides." *Library of Congress Microform Reading Room* at www.loc.gov/rr/microform/bibguide.html (accessed 7 December 2004).

Dodson, Suzanne Cates, ed. *Microform Research Collections: A Guide.* 2nd ed. Westport, CT: Meckler Pub., 1984.

Frazier, Patrick, ed. *A Guide to the Microform Collections in the Humanities and Social Sciences Division of the Library of Congress.* Washington, DC: Library of Congress Humanities and Social Sci-

ences Division, 1996. Online at www.loc.gov/rr/microform/guide/
intro.html (accessed 7 December 2004).
Guide to Microforms in Print, updated annually. Munich: Saur.
*Internet Library of Early Journals: A Digital Library of 18th and 19th
Century Journals*, 1990s, at http://www.bodley.ox.ac.uk/ilej/ (ac-
cessed 7 December 2004).
RLG Union Catalog. Mountain View, CA: RLG. www.rlg.org.
WorldCat. Dublin, OH: OCLC. www.oclc.org/firstsearch/.

Microform and digitized collections can be made up of periodicals,
newspapers, books, pamphlets, papers, manuscripts, letters, archival
materials, images—in other words, anything which can be published in
paper form can be captured to film or scanned into a file. Twentieth-
and twenty-first-century technologies do bring a wealth of resources to
the researchers, but many digitization and microform projects are based
upon the meticulous bibliographic research and collecting habits of
previous generations. For the researcher this means the idiosyncrasies
or the extensiveness of a collection may depend on the individuals be-
hind the original collecting or bibliography. To discover which microform collections your library holds, consult with the reference librarians. The library's website may have a list of microform collections
available. If you know the title of the collection you want, search your
library catalog by the title to see if it is owned. To discover the scope of
the microform collection itself, read any accompanying materials, such
as the finding aid or a reference book describing major microform collections.

Finding relevant microfilm collections requires consultation with
librarians and requires a variety of reference resources. Because the
individual contents of microform collections are not always cataloged,
conventional library catalog searches may not be successful. For example, a search in the online library catalog may not reveal that the first
edition of Mary Shelley's novel *Frankenstein* is available in the ultra-
microfiche collection titled, *The Microbook Library of English Literature*. You will have to know how to find this out. Therefore, you must
use a combination of print and online databases to find possibly relevant collections.

Working with a reference librarian knowledgeable about microforms is the most effective way to start researching for relevant resources available in these types of special collections. By consulting
with the librarian, you can describe your project to discover if any collections exist which fit your requirements. In addition, check standard
microform reference books such as **Microform Research Collections:
A Guide** or **Guide to Microforms in Print**. Large research libraries

often have Web pages which describe the holdings of special collections and finding aids available, including microforms. For example, the Library of Congress Microform Reading Room *Bibliographies and Guides* Web page provides links to finding aids and descriptions of special microform collections owned by the library. One finding aid, *A Guide to the Microform Collections in the Humanities and Social Sciences Division of the Library of Congress*, was published in paper in 1996 and is also available and updated electronically via the Library of Congress website. Although this finding aid describes a wide variety of collections beyond those which cover the Romantic era, such a publication does include and can help identify potentially useful sources. In this guide, the subject index (on the Web page, use the link *Index A–J* and *Index K–Z*) includes the headings "English Literature, Great Britain—History," "Great Britain—Imprints," and "Great Britain—Politics and Government." Under these headings are listed titles of collections. Descriptions are brief, but provide enough information to allow a researcher to pursue finding out more about the contents. For example, the *Home Office Papers and Records...(George III, correspondence, 1782–1820)* documents "various levels of British social and political life, covering a long period of war with revolutionary France, and various domestic eruptions, including Luddite actions, food riots, labor disturbances, and the assassination of Prime Minister Spencer Perceval (in 1812)."[1] The arrangement on the 172 microfilm reels is chronological with a reel guide on each film, but no print finding aid exists. In a case such as this, it will be necessary to examine the film for the years of interest. To find the collection, search your library catalog first, then, if not available, local library catalogs and finally union catalogs such as *WorldCat* and *RLG Union Catalog* to order the desired microfilm via interlibrary loan. Although not an efficient means of searching, you can consult the websites of standard microform and digital publishers, such as Thomson Gale, Adam Matthews, or ProQuest (which includes UMI and Chadwyck-Healey), to see which collections they have available.

No directories to digitization collections have been compiled as yet. Most of the commercial or major cultural projects can be discovered by talking with reference librarians, searching union catalogs, or exploring Romantic-era scholarly websites. Many projects are still under development or in the process of being completed. The *Internet Library of Early Journals* is an example of an early cooperative endeavor. Through the collaboration of several British universities—Oxford University, Birmingham, Leeds and Manchester—20-year runs of three eighteenth-century and three nineteenth-century periodicals were scanned and the text enhanced by the use of OCR software to make the journals full-text searchable. The project was intended to explore the feasibility of creating a digitized database of early journals. No new material was added after 1999 and, of the six titles, only two very briefly touch on the beginning of the Romantic era: *Annual Register* (1758–1778) and *Philosophical Transactions of the Royal Society* (1757–1777). The project is interesting, however, for the reports explain the different approaches to digitizing journals and what, in the early stages of such projects, must be considered. The problems of OCR technology and older fonts are addressed by the use of fuzzy matching software, a technology which will find an approximate word match rather than an exact match in the text. Such a project, although small in scope, may prove useful to the Romantic scholar for both the content and for the descriptions of technologies required to digitize texts from this era of publishing.

Often you don't need to know how to find entire microform collections. Generally, if a book or serial is needed, a search for the title within the library catalog or a union catalog is sufficient to identify the resources for retrieval purposes, including requests through the interlibrary loan department. However, special collections of materials available in microform or digitized collections may not be cataloged separately within a library or union catalog, and the contents only listed in a finding aid. For example, the *English Literary Periodicals* microfilm collection has a printed guide to the titles included in the collection titled *Accessing English Literary Periodicals*, and a CD-ROM to search the article titles. Or, as we explained earlier in this chapter, an individual library may own the title in a microform, but only have a "collection level record"—a record which describes the whole collection, not the individual parts—in the catalog. Because cataloging policies for microform and digital collections differ from library to library, the individual parts of a collection may be available elsewhere; union catalog such as *WorldCat* or *RLG Union Catalog* are the best place to look for individual parts of a collection. Therefore it is important to learn how to search for and to read collections records within library catalogs.

Figure 8.1 is a record in *WorldCat* for *The British Critic* published between 1793–1826 and available on microfilm.

Figure 8.1. Modified *WorldCat* record for *The British Critic*.

The British critic
1793–1826
English Serial Publication : Periodical : Quarterly (every 3 months):
Microform 88 v. : ill. ; 22 cm.
London : Printed for F. and C. Rivington,
      Title: The British critic

Publication: London : Printed for F. and C. Rivington,

Year: 1793-1826

Frequency: Quarterly, Oct. 1825-Oct. 1826; Former: Monthly, May 1793-June 1825

Description: Began with vol. 1 (May 1793); ceased with [3rd ser.] v. 3, no. 5 (Oct. 1826).; 88 v. :; ill. ;; 22 cm.

Language: English

Series: Variation: *Early English newspapers ;; 283-297, 1358-1362.*

Main Series: Early English newspapers

SUBJECT(S)

Descriptor: Theology—Periodicals.

Geographic: Great Britain—Religion—Periodicals.

Note(s): Imprint varies./ Description based on: Vol. 7 (1796)./ Reproduction: Microfilm./ Woodbridge, Conn. :/ Research Publications./ microfilm reels ; 35 mm./ (Early English newspapers ; 283-297, 1358-1362).

Accession No: OCLC: 8630262

Source: *WorldCat*, via *FirstSearch.*

This record is for the title which is part of the microfilm collection *Early English Newspapers* (see bold, italics text in Figure 8.1). To find this periodical, first search by the title of the periodical in your library catalog, then, if that fails, search by the title of the collection to see if it is owned. As always, consult with a reference librarian if you need further assistance. If your library does not own the collection, search a union catalog such as *WorldCat* or *RLG Union Catalog* on the title of the journal. Once you find the appropriate record, note the numbers of the reels you will need to request, in this case reels 283–297 and 1358–1362 (see bold, italics text in Figure 8.1).

If the individual parts of the collection are not cataloged, you will need to work with a reference librarian to discover if a finding aid exists and if it can be borrowed. For example, *The British Critic* is also available in the microfilm collection *English Literary Periodicals*. The following record is a collection level record, which tells us the collection exists.

Figure 8.2. Modified *WorldCat* **record for** *English Literary Periodicals.*

English literary periodicals
1951-1977
English Book : Microform **969 microfilm reels** ; 35 mm.
Ann Arbor, Mich. : University Microfilms,

Availability:	Check the catalogs in your library. Libraries worldwide that own item: 52
Title:	**English literary periodicals**
Corp Author(s):	University Microfilms International. ; Accessing English literary periodicals.
Publication:	Ann Arbor, Mich. : University Microfilms,
Year:	1951-1977
Description:	**969 microfilm reels ; 35 mm.**
Language:	English
SUBJECT(S)	
Descriptor:	English literature—Periodicals. English periodicals. Periodicals on microfilm.
Note(s):	**Accompanied by printed guide with title: Accessing English literary periodicals.**
Material Type:	Microfilm (mfl)
Accession No:	OCLC: 22860959

Source: *WorldCat*, via *FirstSearch*.

We've highlighted, using bold, the microform collection title, description, and notes. The record indicates there are 969 microfilm reels, but there is no list of titles included within this record. Therefore, if you do not find a record for the individual item, try searching for and, if necessary, requesting through interlibrary loan the printed guide listed in the "Note(s)" field, *Accessing English Literary Periodicals.*

Microform and Digitized Collections

Cox, Susan M. and Janice L. Budeit. *Early English Newspapers: Bibliography and Guide to the Microfilm Collection.* Woodbridge, CT: Research Publications, 1983.

Early British Periodicals. 902 microfilm reels. Ann Arbor, MI: University Microfilms International, 1970–1979.

The Early English Newspapers, Burney Collection. 1,207 microfilm reels. New Haven, CT: Research Publications, 1978.

Eighteenth Century Collections Online (ECCO). Detroit, MI: Gale Group. www.gale.com.

The Eighteenth Century: Guide to the Microfilm Collection. Woodbridge, CT: Research Publications, 1984.

Eighteenth-Century English Provincial Newspapers. 125 microfilm reels. Brighton, Sussex, England: Harvester Press Microform Publications, 1985–1991.

English Literary Periodicals. 969 microfilm reels. Ann Arbor, MI: University Microfilms, 1951–1977.

English Short Title Catalog (ESTC): 1473–1800. CD-ROM. 3rd ed. Farmington Hills, MI: Gale, 2003.

Hoornstra, Jean and Grace Puravs, eds. *A Guide to the Early British Periodicals Collection on Microfilm with Title, Subject, Editor, and Reel Number Indexes.* Ann Arbor, MI: University Microfilms International, 1980.

The Microbook Library of English Literature. 7,000 ultra–microfiche. Chicago: Library Resources Inc., 1979.

The Nineteenth Century. Cambridge: Chadwyck-Healey. c19.chadwyck .co.uk (accessed 7 December 2004).

Palmer's Full Text Online, 1785–1870. Cambridge: Chadwyck-Healey. historyonline.chadwyck.co.uk.

Project Gutenberg, 1971, at promo.net/pg/ (accessed 30 November 2004).

Puravs, Grace, Kathy L. Kavanagh, and Vicki Smith, eds. *Accessing English Literary Periodicals: A Guide to the Microfilm Collection with Title Subject, Editor, and Reel Number Indexes.* Ann Arbor: MI: University Microfilms International, 1981.

Three Centuries of English and American Plays, 1500–1830. 5500 micro-opaque cards. New Canaan, CT: Readex, 1953–1962. Later republished on 6890 microfiche.

Three Centuries of English and American Plays: Microfiche Collection Checklist. New Canaan, CT: Readex, 1991.

Three Centuries of English and American Plays, A Checklist. England 1500–1800, United States 1714–1830. New York: Hafner Pub. Co., 1963.

The Times Digital Archive, 1785–1985. Farmington Hills, MI: Thomson-Gale. www.gale.com.

None of the microform or digitization projects produced to date have focused exclusively upon the Romantic era, but the years 1775–1830 are included in larger projects. Below are descriptions of a selective list of microform and electronic resources valuable to the Romantic scholar. We have listed both collections and finding aids in the bibliography at the head of this section.

The *Eighteenth Century Collections Online (ECCO)* is a major project in which 150,000 titles published in Great Britain and its colonies between 1701 and 1800 have been digitized and the text of each made searchable. To allow for the vagaries of eighteenth-century fonts and variant spellings, fuzzy searching is available. The *Eighteenth Century Short Title Catalog* compiled by the British Library was the basis for identifying materials to be included in the project. The documents were microfilmed from the original, and then the digitized images were created from the microfilm. Both the microfilm and the digitized collection are packaged and sold in the following subject modules: History and Geography, Social Science and Fine Arts, Medicine/Science/Technology, Literature and Language, Religion and Philosophy, Law, and General Reference. Finding aids include the *English Short Title Catalog (ESTC)*, available on CD-ROM and online, and *The Eighteenth Century: Guide to the Microfilm Collection* available in print form. Because libraries may not have purchased the entire collection, do use any finding aids available to conduct a comprehensive search and identify which items, not available in your library, may be borrowed via interlibrary loan on microfilm. This resource offers the richest access to monographic publications from the end of the eighteenth century, including the major and minor writers with works published 1800 and earlier: works by Coleridge, Wordsworth (with four editions of the *Lyrical Ballads*, two from 1798 and two from 1800), Wollstonecraft, Radcliffe, Scott, Godwin, Paine, Blake, Burns, Hannah Cowley, and Burney.

The Nineteenth Century is a microfiche collection of over 28,000 titles. Published by Chadwyck-Healey, in cooperation with The British Library, the collection aims to reproduce the English-language works published between 1801 and 1900 using the collections at The British Library as the basis. The program is designed to reproduce the nineteenth-century texts not easily available to scholars and to preserve the materials published after 1845 which are deteriorating due to the use of wood-pulp paper. Because of the large volume of works published during the century, the collection is being overseen by Robin Alston who has developed a plan to focus on reproducing resources necessary to current teaching and research. Thus far Alston's program has produced sub-collections within *The Nineteenth Century* which include: *The General Collection* (described as works about human life and ideas); *Women Writers*; *Art and Architecture*; and collections of books on economics, children's literature, Ireland, British colonization, China, linguistics, publishing, and evolution and creation. Chadwyck-Healey provides a free online catalog to the collection via their website. Restricting the search in the catalog to the years 1795–1830 yields 3570 records sorted by the sub-collections listed above. You can search for individual titles of the collection, which may have been cataloged separately and which may be available in your library. If not available in your library, search by title or author in a union catalog such as *World-Cat*, or, to find the whole collection, search the title field for *nineteenth century*, by publisher *chadwyck healey*, and limit the search to *microform*.

Started by Michael Hart in 1971, **Project Gutenberg** currently provides free access to over ten thousand electronic texts of literary works. The e-books are not digitized versions of the print editions, but are text versions of books which are in the public domain. The project's stated goal is to provide wide access to books electronically, but does not desire to create standard editions of electronic texts. Because the texts must be free of copyright, more obscure editions may be used, which can be problematic for scholars. Therefore, if the information is provided, you need to pay attention to which edition of the text is used. Volunteers enter the text in a format which is low-tech enough to allow broad access to the database. This site may prove valuable for scholars who don't have access to some of the texts available, but the texts on this site are not authoritative and therefore must be approached with caution.

Three Centuries of English and American Plays 1500–1830 and **Library of English Literature** are examples of literary microfilm collections which include some relevant materials for the Romantic scholar. *Three Centuries of English and American Plays* contains two subsets which may be useful: *Three Centuries of Drama 1751–1800*, with approximately 1,312 plays from the Romantic era and *Three Centuries of Drama 1737–1800 Larpent Collection* with roughly 400 plays. Published originally in micro-opaque, and then reprinted on microfiche, the collections provide access to late eighteenth-century plays. Each microform version has it's own print finding aid: **Three Centuries of**

English and American Plays, A Checklist. England 1500–1800, United States 1714–1830, the guide to micro-opaque collection, and *Three Centuries of English and American Plays: Microfiche Collection Checklist*. Many of these texts are not readily available in print, so the microforms may be the only means of reading the texts if access to the *ECCO* database, or the microfilm of *The Eighteenth Century*, are not available.

The *Library of English Literature* is an ultra-microfiche collection with approximately eight hundred works published during the Romantic era. Unlike *ECCO*, this collection is highly selective. It includes first editions of literature, collected works, such as Andrew Marvell and John Milton, Sir Walter Scott's edition of *The Works of Jonathan Swift* from 1814, history, biography, and letters. Based upon the recommendations of a panel of academics, listed in the front matter, the stated purpose of the collection is to meet the needs of both undergraduate and graduate students by including major texts on a broad range of subjects from the Anglo-Saxon through Edwardian periods. There are no explanations for inclusion of one edition over another—for example, why film the second edition of "The Lady and the Lake" and the first edition of Scott's "Lay of the Last Minstrel"? The value of this collection will depend upon what resources are necessary. It is worth consulting but is not a primary tool for research.

At present, microfilm access to periodicals and newspapers is more prevalent than online access, but this will change as digitization initiatives get underway. Currently, the microform collections titled *Early British Periodicals*, *Eighteenth-Century English Provincial Newspapers* (including Bath, Derby, and Ipswich), *English Literary Periodicals*, *British Periodicals in the Creative Arts*, and *Early English Newspapers* each contain titles from a wide variety of magazines and newspapers published in Great Britain, including publications from the Romantic era.

The *English Literary Periodicals* (*ELP*) microfilm collection covers 341 titles from 1681 to 1914, roughly eighty-seven titles from the Romantic era between 1770 and 1830. This collection is based upon a bibliography compiled by Professor Richmond Bond of the University of North Carolina. In the late 1940s, Professor Bond coordinated a project between scholars and UMI to identify titles for inclusion in this microfilm collection.[2] The bibliography and, as a result, the microfilm collection, include periodicals from various geographic locations within Britain, different frequencies of publication (from daily to semi-annual to irregular), various lengths of publication life (a few issues to decades), and from a broad range of subjects, including theater, literature, history, social sciences, politics, and economics. Titles which were deemed to be more easily available in American libraries, such as *Blackwood's Edinburgh Magazine* and *Edinburgh Review*, were excluded. Periodicals range from the standards of the time, including *Monthly Review, Critical Review, Scots Magazine* and the title it merged with later, *Edinburgh Magazine and Literary Miscellany, London Magazine*, to periodicals which existed for just a short run but which are representative of the era. The print finding aid to this collection, by Puravs, Kavanagh, and Smith, is titled ***Accessing English Literary Periodicals: A Guide to the Microfilm Collection with Title Subject, Editor, and Reel Number Indexes***.

Early British Periodicals (*EBP*) is a supplement to *ELP*, consisting of 168 additional serial titles published between 1681 and 1921, about fifty published between 1775 and 1830. This collection was selected by Dr. Daniel Fader, Professor of English Literature, University of Michigan. The scope of periodicals covered includes literature, slavery, religion, history, philosophy, politics, and art, and two major literary publications, the *Quarterly Review* and *Edinburgh Review*, excluded from the *English Literary Periodicals* collection, are present. Others included are *The Gentleman's Magazine*, Leigh Hunt's periodicals, *The Reflector* (1810–1811) and *The Liberal Verse* (1822–1823), regional publications (*Irish Magazine*), anti-slavery publications (*Anti-Slavery Monthly Reporter*), nationalistic (*The Anti-Gallican*), business (*The Bee*), women (*La Belle Assemblée*), political (*Anti-Jacobin*), and religion (*The Arminian Magazine* or *Methodist Magazine*). This collection provides a broader perspective on the issues of the day and, together with *English Literary Periodicals* provides access to a representative number of titles for researchers to peruse. The print finding aid for this collection, compiled by Hoornstra and Puravs, is titled ***A Guide to the Early British Periodicals Collection on Microfilm, with Title, Subject, Editor, and Reel Number Indexes***.

Newspapers may be available in microfilm, either as individual titles or as part of a newspaper microfilm collection. As discussed in Chapter 7, *The Times* of London is available on both microfilm and through two digital collections, *Palmer's* and *The Times Digital Archive*. ***The Times Digital Archive*** allows you to view the image of an article either as an individual image or as part of the entire page. Therefore, you can see the article in isolation or choose to see where on the page it was published by displaying the full image. For other newspapers, searching by title in a union catalog is the easiest method to discover if a microfilm for an individual newspaper title is available. Because some academic libraries may not catalog the individual titles of a newspaper microfilm collection, searching in a large union catalog such as *WorldCat* or *RLG Union Catalog* allows you to increase your chances of finding a record for the specific newspaper you want, and will provide you with the name of the microfilm collection should a microfilm version be available. For the Romantic era, one microfilm collection, *The Early English Newspapers*, includes two newspaper collections, with additional newspapers supplementing these two core collections to total about 1,300 titles. In 1818, the British Library purchased the library of Dr. Charles Burney, which comprised about seven hundred volumes of newspapers published between 1603 and 1817, the year of Burney's death. About eighty-five titles from the late eighteenth century are filmed, including *Bath Chronicle* (1784, 1787–1789), *Morning Chronicle* (1791–1800), and *True Briton* (1793, 1794–1800). Because of the murky definition of what constitutes a newspaper as opposed to a journal, some titles we may today consider journals are included, and these titles are the few which reach into the nineteenth century: *British Critic, Gentleman's Magazine,* and the *Annual Register.* In 1865 the Bodleian Library at Oxford University purchased what later became the second core collection for this microform set: the London newspaper collection of John Nichols, which included publications from 1672–1737. The microfilm collection has a finding aid, *Early English Newspapers: Bibliography and Guide to the Microfilm Collection*, and the individual titles are searchable in *WorldCat*. Another microfilm collection of newspapers is the *Eighteenth Century English Provincial Newspapers* from the British Library, which includes titles from Bath, Derby, Ipswich, and Newcastle. Yet another collection, *Eighteenth Century Journals* from the Hope Collection at the Bodleian Library, Oxford, provides images of newspapers and journals throughout the century.

In addition, the eighteenth-century newspaper portion of the Burney Collection is in the process of being digitized and OCR processed from the microfilm copy held by the British Library. The project, titled *Digitizing the Burney Collection of Early English Newspapers* <www.cbsr.ucr.edu/> is being done in partnership with the British Library by the Center for Bibliographic Studies at the University of California, Riverside, which is funded by a grant awarded by the National Science Foundation. The British Library is also currently planning a project, *Newspaper Digitisation Project: British Newspapers 1800–1900*, which will provide free access to a variety of important national, regional, and local British newspapers <www.bl.uk/collections/british newspapers1800to1900.html>.

Conclusion

Microfilm and digitization projects are not limited to books and serial publications. Other types of materials which can be found in microfilm collections include Parliamentary papers, *London Directories from the Guildhall Library, Playbills and Programs from London Theatres 1801–1900 in the Theatre Museum, London,* and *English Cartoons and Satirical Prints.* But, as digitization projects continue to be implemented, the possibility that the documents required are available online increase. You will need to be creative about discovering what riches are available by consulting with a reference librarian, searching union catalogs, asking scholars in the field, and browsing appropriate websites. Technology is changing access to historic documents, books, journals, and manuscripts so rapidly it is impossible to determine what will be available in just a couple of years, so the best practice of all is to keep asking for help.

Notes

1. Frazier, Patrick, ed. *A Guide to the Microform Collections in the Humanities and Social Sciences Division of the Library of Congress* (Washington, DC: Library of Congress, 1996), 108.

2. Bond, Richmond. "English Literary Periodicals to Form New Microfilm Series," *Library Journal,* 76, no. 2 (January 15, 1951), 125–128.

Chapter 9
Manuscripts and Archives

Manuscript and archival research are very different from and more complex than traditional library research. Since the materials are usually unique and irreplaceable, they require careful handling, are kept in secured areas, and are organized according to different cataloging rules. Consequently, researchers may need to consult published or unpublished guides, called "finding aids," instead of a traditional library catalog to identify records. Because the documents may have been sold or distributed by other means, even documents originating from a single source could be geographically scattered and located in libraries, archives, or private collections around the world. In the case of some of Keats's poems, a single manuscript could be in several libraries. In this instance it is known that a couple of his friends cut the manuscripts they owned into strips and gave these away as souvenirs.

> Several of the ten leaves of the original draft of "I stood tip-toe upon a little hill" were cut into fragments by [Charles] Clarke when he owned the manuscript. All but three fragments and one entire leaf have been located.... Most of the surviving bits are widely scattered, in six different libraries in three different countries. Two of the bits have been published as facsimiles but remain unlocated and a third is in private hands.[1]

In the archive itself, scholars may be limited to the number of items used at one time, and retrieval of the materials from secured areas often can be time consuming. For preservation purposes and security reasons, pens, notebooks, and even coats may not be allowed in the room where the materials are consulted. Laptops may be allowed, but handheld scanners will most likely be prohibited. Scholars must do a great deal of preliminary research to identify and locate the desired materials, and once the archive is located, learn the rules for using the archive. Because of the unique challenges archival research offers scholars, we will cover the basic best practices and tools; however, it takes practice, good planning, and patience to be an efficient and effective archival researcher. In this chapter, we will discuss the process of using archives first, and follow that with an overview of resources and techniques for discovering where archival materials may be housed.

General Information about Archives

There are no clear-cut definitions for identifying various types of archives. An archive is a generic term referring to a collection of records, created in any format, of enduring historical value. In the world of archives, a "record" is a document which can include: a film of a live stage production, a typewritten letter, a sound recording of an oral history, a photograph, a handwritten speech, a poem created on a word processor, or a contract between a publisher and an author. An archive can comprise everything from public records (e.g., governmental correspondence or corporate ledgers) to personal papers (e.g., author's manuscripts, letters, diaries, or notebooks) to sound and film materials. The commonalities among these seemingly disparate materials are that they are unique or rare, primary sources, housed in secured areas, and that access is mediated by professionals and limited to scholars with legitimate research projects.

   Public record collections can be very inclusive, including every piece of paper generated by or submitted to an organization: company shipping records, military records, letters written to the government by citizens, or minutes of an association or non-profit organization. Vital records are a form of public record: births, deaths, marriages, and divorces. Manuscript collections are a subset of archives and typically include personal papers of an individual or family. Traditionally these documents were handwritten, but today they can be in any format, including audio or electronic. However, archival materials don't fall into neat categories. Documents such as the *Magna Carta* or Lincoln's *Gettysburg Address* are each considered a manuscript and a public record. Making fine distinctions between what is considered a public record or a manuscript isn't necessary because, even with the differences, personal papers and public records have more in common with each other than they do with other types of library resources. Any archival record requires similar techniques for discovery and use.

Best Practices for Archival Research

The more you know about your topic prior to visiting an archive, the more effective use you can make of the collection. Don't start your research at an archive or manuscript collection because it is best first to have a firm grasp of the secondary literature available on your topic and a well-defined focused research plan. The former will provide you with a strong foundation for your archival research. If someone else has already done an analysis on an aspect of your topic, you can build upon that research.

The more you know about the context within which an archival collection would have existed, the more efficient you will be about using the archive, recognizing important threads of information, and staying focused. Also, through careful research using secondary sources you will begin to discover which archives may prove to be most useful in your research because authors of scholarly secondary resources generally specify which institutions they used and which individuals within those institutions proved most knowledgeable. A solid background and clues about valuable archives will assist in creating a focused plan. By defining your project carefully, you can rule out certain parts of the collections you visit and sift through the materials which would be most fruitful for you, thus efficiently spending your time and energy. As an added benefit, it is easier to apply for funding with a well-defined project.

Archival research can be challenging for a variety of reasons. Once at the site, retrieval of the documents may take several hours, depending upon the institution. As mentioned above, the collection has been gathered and organized in a manner different from book collections. The resources are not arranged for your research project, so you may have to patiently sift through a great deal of irrelevant materials to find the pieces you need. For example, if you are working on marriage laws in the early part of the nineteenth century and public responses to those laws, you may have to sift through all letters written by concerned citizens to the government during a year to ferret out those addressing the impact of the law.

Beyond working with the raw data which has not been interpreted, the documents themselves may offer challenges which slow the process: the ink used to write the letter may be faded and the early nineteenth-century penmanship may be difficult to decipher; or perhaps data has been preserved on negative microfilm and can only be viewed via an old microform reader with no printing facilities available. In addition, it is easy to get distracted by tangential finds or, unfortunately, you may find nothing at all because there may be no records, since not all papers of every person or organization have been preserved. Such time-consuming challenges need to be considered during the planning stages of the project because they will have an impact upon how much time will be necessary to use a collection. If you are traveling abroad and have limited time, the more prepared you are the more you will accomplish.

The best practices for archival research include patience, flexibility, and preparedness. This type of research generally requires traveling to another location for the materials, so plan ahead. Archives have shorter hours than traditional libraries and may be closed at specific times of the year. Archives may require special permission to use the materials and all have rules to preserve the materials from damage and to prevent theft. It is best to correspond with the archivist or librarian prior to your visit to see if the materials you wish to consult are available for use. A good first step is to see if the archive has a website with information about access, hours, regulations, and contact names. If an e-mail address is listed for inquiries, ask about the specific types of records or manuscripts you need. If no website exists, consult the directories listed below for an address or ask a librarian for assistance.

Whether the archive you wish to use is internationally renowned or a small special collection in a library, the same rules of etiquette may apply and are worth observing whenever possible. In a smaller special collection, you could get personal attention from the archivist knowledgeable about the contents of the collection, but in a larger institution, you may be on your own. To illustrate the process for accessing a manuscript archive, let's review the procedures for using the British Library, which is one of the most restrictive.

The British Library

The British Library is a library of last resort, meaning that you have exhausted other library collections. If you gain admittance to the British Library, you cannot borrow the materials but must use the collections on site. To discover the procedures for access, check for an institutional website. There is a section in the British Library website <www.bl.uk> under the heading *Manuscripts Reading Room* titled "Preparing for your visit," which explains the steps necessary to access their collections in general, and then specifically addresses use of manuscripts. First you need to apply for a "reader pass" to allow you to use the collections. Acquiring a reader pass requires proof that you have exhausted other library collections, that you need to use the collections on site, and that your research need is legitimate. You can apply for the reader pass either in person or submit an application for advance approval by mail. In either case, you will need to present proof of identity such as a driver's license or a passport once you arrive at the library and proof of your status as a researcher. For the latter, bring a letter of support, written on institutional letterhead, from your department chair, dean, or academic advisor. The letter must explain your project and the desired outcome (e.g., book, article, dissertation), state your connection to and/or status at the institution with which you are affiliated, and confirm that you are a scholar or student in good standing at your institution.

Once your application has been accepted and you have a reader's pass which allows you to access the Manuscripts division, you may use the Manuscripts Reading Room and the collection, but with some potential exceptions. If you wish to use specific manuscripts, send a request in advance of your visit to verify that the materials you wish to use are available. Include a signed recommendation letter from your advisor, chair, or dean which states his or her status and affiliation, explains your project, and specifies the manuscripts and related materials you will need to consult. In the case of fragile or important manuscripts, be prepared to be told you may only be allowed to use a microfilm or facsimile of the manuscript. Take a copy of your letters with you when you visit the library so that, if by chance you discover a manuscript you didn't know existed, your letters will help the curator determine if your research warrants access to any restricted documents.

In addition to the procedures for access and use of the collections, the British Library website has contact information for the various departments within the library, including e-mail addresses, rules for using the collections, and issues concerning copyright. Scanner pens, ink wells, food, drink, scissors, knives, highlighters, tape, matches, bags over a certain size, and umbrellas are prohibited. There is a cloak room where such items can be checked. Clear plastic bags are provided for carrying those items allowed into the Reading Rooms. Laptops, with some restrictions about the use of electronic library resources, are permitted. The Manuscript Collection regulations state that pencils are the only writing implements allowed, that manuscripts may be used only by the person to whom the items have been issued, how the materials are to be handled, and the procedures and copyright governing the reproduction of manuscripts.

These rules of use illustrate some of the types of issues you may need to face in your research. The best advice is to check for a website for rules of access and contact information. The Web has definitely made communication with archives and special libraries much easier than in the past.

Locating Relevant Archives and Manuscripts

Ash, Lee and William G. Miller, comps. *Subject Collections: A Guide to Special Book Collections and Subject Emphases as Reported by University, College, Public, and Special Libraries and Museums in the United States and Canada.* 2 vols. 7th ed., rev. and enl. New Providence, NJ: R. R. Bowker, 1993.

Cameron, Kenneth Neill, ed. *Shelley and His Circle.* Cambridge: Harvard University Press, 10 vols. 1961– .

Croft, Peter J., Theodore Hofmann, and John Horden, ed. *Index of English Literary Manuscripts.* 4 vols. New York: Bowker, 1980–1999.

Dictionary of Literary Biography. Detroit: Gale Research Co.

Foster, Janet and Julia Sheppard, eds. *British Archives: A Guide to Archive Resources in the United Kingdom*, 4th ed. New York: Palgrave, 2002.

Matthew, Henry C. G. and Brian Harrison, eds. *Oxford Dictionary of National Biography: From Earliest Times to the year 2000.* 61 vols. Rev. ed. New York: Oxford University Press, 2004.

Sutton, David C., ed. *Location Register of English Literary Manuscripts and Letters: Eighteenth and Nineteenth Centuries.* 2 vols. London: British Library, 1995.

WorldCat. Dublin, OH: OCLC. www.oclc.org/firstsearch/.

A great deal can be discovered about an archive or manuscript collection from its website, including descriptions of the collections, finding aids, digitized images of parts of the collections, and even, as is the case with the British Library, an online catalog for the manuscript collection. The online environment is proving to be a valuable means for archivists to communicate with potential visitors and for scholars to conduct research remotely. But what are the best techniques for discovering who holds the manuscripts or archives you wish to use? For the Romantic-era scholar, we recommend the following resources and search strategies.

For locations of personal papers and manuscripts by an author, the **Oxford Dictionary of National Biography** (Chapter 2) is an excellent place to start, for this reference tool attempts comprehensive coverage of biographical information on major and minor British figures of note, and includes, when possible, locations of papers and manuscripts. However, this information may not be comprehensive enough in the case of some authors and therefore further research is required. The introductions to or the acknowledgment sections of the standard editions or standard biographies for the author are another important place to look because generally the author or editor of these editions will state which collections were consulted and who helped with the research. Search for facsimile editions of the authors' works in your library collections and in *WorldCat*: a keyword search on your author's name and the keyword *facsimile** or *manuscript** will allow you to find monographs or microforms of manuscripts. For example, Garland has published a series of facsimiles titled *Manuscripts of the Younger Romantics* and the National Library of Scotland in Edinburgh has published *The Sir Walter Scott Manuscripts* on microfilm. Look for a website devoted to your author, or, if all else fails, ask on an electronic listserv. General information about collections of manuscripts and papers can be found by author in the **Dictionary of Literary Biography**, also described in Chapter 2.

There are few directories to manuscripts and letters for British authors, but those which exist are invaluable resources. The **Index of English Literary Manuscripts** lists manuscript locations for about thirty authors active in the Romantic era, and includes locations for the manuscripts wherever they are found. The relevant volumes are Volume 3 (1700–1800) in four parts, and Volume 4 (1800–1900) in three parts up through the author Patmore. The highly selective list of authors, derived from *The Concise Cambridge Bibliography of English Literature, 600–1950* (Cambridge, 1965), includes Burney, Blake, Burns, Radcliffe, Walpole, Wollstonecraft, Austen, Byron, Carlyle, Clare, Coleridge, De Quincy, Edgeworth, Hazlitt, Keats, and Lamb. The project was suspended after Volume 4, Part 3, so the last entry is for Coventry Patmore, which means the remaining authors in *The Concise Cambridge Bibliography of English Literature, 600–1950*— Wordsworth, Shelley, Scott, Mary Shelley, and Robert Southey—are not present. The volumes are arranged in alphabetical order by author with an introductory overview of the manuscripts available, some provenance, followed by a listing of the individual manuscripts, description, and location with manuscript number. A typical overview describes the history of the manuscripts and discusses facsimiles, standard editions, lost manuscripts, forgeries, substantive collections, provenance of collections, autographs, and transcripts.[2]

In the chapter devoted to Fanny Burney we discover that most of her literary manuscripts are in the Berg Collection at the New York Public Library. She bequeathed her papers, which are at Yale, to Charles Parr Burney and the rest to Charlotte Francis Barrett which are located in both NYPL and the British Library. Subsequent sections of the introduction provide short histories of the manuscripts by type (e.g., verse, novels, dramatic works, diaries, and notebooks) and conclude with a bibliography listing the printed versions of the letters and diaries, a catalog of the family correspondence, biographies, and a summary of the Burney manuscripts. In the Burns entry we find a review of forgeries. As quoted above, the Keats chapter describes how and why some of his manuscripts are in fragments. Because of the fate of his manuscripts, the introduction to the chapter discusses the facsimile edition of Keats's manuscripts, edited by Jack Stillinger, which includes both handwritten manuscripts, or autographs, by Keats and authoritative transcripts of the poems by Richard Woodhouse; both the autographs and the transcripts are included in the location list. Jane Austen's novels were probably destroyed after being used as the printers' copies. The British Library and the Pierpont Morgan Library hold most of Austen's remaining manuscripts. The largest Byron collection, including manuscripts, proofs, notes, and letters he sent to the publisher, is with the London publisher John Murray, which began publishing the poet's works in 1812. The largest Keats collection is at Harvard. The largest collection of Coleridge manuscripts is in the British library, including books from his library, many containing his marginalia. The entries in *Index of English Literary Manuscripts* can be rich in detail about the fates of authors' personal papers.

The *Index of English Literary Manuscripts* is invaluable for those seeking the manuscripts of any of the authors covered, but, because each entry is a microcosm of what can happen to an author's papers and what issues need to be considered when using a manuscript collection, the volumes are very helpful even if the author isn't included. The provenance of the collection can help you realize why some materials may be present and not others. What is missing from the collections and why? Papers may not have been preserved and could have been burned or destroyed by family, friends, or publishers for a variety of reasons. Where can manuscripts be found besides libraries and archives? Perhaps, if the publisher still exists, they have an archive containing correspondence with the author or even the manuscripts themselves. Did the author leave a will? Was there an executor for the estate who may have disposed of the papers or had some other effect on the collection? By browsing through the entries, you can start to realize quickly the variety of challenges faced when conducting manuscript research and can formulate questions to help understand the historical context and origins of the documents.

Location Register of English Literary Manuscripts and Letters: Eighteenth and Nineteenth Centuries is a two-volume, computer-generated directory of manuscript locations, arranged by author and listing the literary manuscripts and letters found in about four hundred libraries and archival repositories in England, Scotland, Ireland, and Wales. The directory is much more comprehensive in terms of the number of authors included in the *Index of English Literary Manuscripts*, but it is limited to the selected repositories surveyed and visited by the team of compilers and, therefore, the holdings for institutions outside Britain and Ireland or in private collections are not listed separately. Each entry includes the title or descriptive title of the piece, location, manuscript number, date, and, if known, physical description (e.g., autograph, photocopy, microfilm). Some entries are more complete than others because the compilers sometimes had to rely on finding aids to the collections for details, so information such as physical description may be missing. The date the manuscript was added to the database is included up through July 1994 when the content of this resource was completed. If notable collections for the author exist elsewhere, this is placed in a headnote to the author's entry. For example, the headnote for Byron describes the major collections and papers in the private archive at John Murray, and the North American library holdings at the University of Texas, Pierpont Morgan Library, Pforzheimer Library, New York Public Library, Yale University, Princeton University, the Huntington Library, and University of Pennsylvania. This is followed by an entry with 260 items listed under his name, and an additional ten entries in which he was the recipient of letters. Literary manuscripts, speeches, notebooks, and even a draft of his will are listed first, followed by a chronological list of individual letters or collections of letters, including those in microform and photocopies.

Neither of the Shelleys were included in the *Index of English Literary Manuscripts* because the last volume wasn't published. The *Location Register* lists the manuscripts, other documents, and letters. The items held in the Bodleian Library at Oxford University, one of the largest Shelley collections, are listed separately in this resource, including the Abinger papers held on deposit, such as the autograph draft manuscript of *Frankenstein*. Outside the British libraries, the important collection of Mary Wollstonecraft Shelley papers are in the Pforzheimer Library, the Huntington, Washington University, Duke University, University of Iowa, Harvard University, and the Berg Collection of the New York Public Library. Percy Shelley's papers are in the same collections, and also at the University of California, Berkeley, University of Texas, and the Pierpont Morgan Library.

It is worth identifying institutions which have systematically built Romantic collections: British Library, Bodleian, Yale, and the Berg Collection at New York Public Library. The Pforzheimer Collection has the Shelley and His Circle collection. Harvard has the Keat's Room. The Huntington Library has the Larpent Collection of plays produced between 1737 and 1824 (see Chapter 8 to find the microform collection). The Pierpont Morgan has a broad collection of British literary and historical manuscripts. Princeton University has the Robert Taylor collection of American and British nineteenth- and twentieth-century authors.

For example, according to the *Location Register*, the Pforzheimer Collection at New York Public Library has holdings, and in some cases significant collections, for Percy Shelley, Mary Shelley, Byron, Wollstonecraft, Godwin and others from the Romantic era. According to the website for the collection, Carl H. Pforzheimer, Sr. (1879–1957) was interested in the Romantic era and collected manuscripts and papers of Shelley and his circle, including contemporary writers, and Mary Shelley's parents. In addition to the manuscripts and papers, the collection includes related documents and publications from the era in the sciences, biography, politics, dictionaries, grammars, almanacs, and directories. Materials about women are another important feature of this collection, which are being collected to enhance the extensive holdings of documents of both Mary Shelley and her mother Mary Wollstonecraft. The major manuscripts of the collection are treated in a multivolume scholarly catalog, **Shelley and His Circle**, with extensive notes and facsimile images of the manuscripts included. The books in this collection are located by searching CATNYP, the online library catalog for Research Libraries of the New York Public Library system, with notes in the records telling patrons that special permission is required for admission to the collection.

Subject Collections: A Guide to Special Book Collections and Subject Emphases as Reported by University, College, Public, and Special Libraries and Museums in the United States and Canada, by Lee Ash and William G. Miller, is a two-volume directory of special collections in libraries in the United States and Canada. The most current edition is from 1993, so there may be newer collections developed which are not included, but these volumes are good for discovering established collections. The information compiled is derived from questionnaires distributed to libraries and supplemented by additional research done on the part of the authors. Depending upon the information provided by the institution, the contents of the entries may be sketchy or they may be more descriptive.

The resource lists all types of special collections in libraries in the United States and Canada, from computers to history to science to the environment, and does include authors and literary movements such as Romanticism. Entries are arranged by subject heading or name. Each entry is subdivided geographically by United States states followed by Canadian provinces and, within the geographic area, subdivided by the library. Typical entries contain contact information, holdings, a general description of the relevant collection, including whether the collection is cataloged, if manuscripts and/or pictures are present, number of volumes, number of linear feet, and notes to further clarify the contents of the collection. For example, under "Byron" we find that Duke University owns various editions, under "Crabbe, George" that Ohio University holds a representative collection of first and other early editions, and under "Cowper, William" that Princeton University has 500 books and pamphlets in the General Rare Book Collection and nine cubic feet of material by and about Cowper in the Manuscripts division. There are no listings for Anna Letitia Barbauld, John Thelwall, or Amelia Opie, but all three are included in the *Location Register.*

Subject Collections is good as a supplementary tool to the *Index of English Literary Manuscripts* and the *Location Register,* but because it has a much broader scope, the set is not focused on British authors and their manuscripts and the entries are more general. It can be helpful for discovering pockets of Romantic collections around the United States and Canada, whereupon the institutional websites may be used to obtain more detailed information about relevant collections.

The fourth edition of **British Archives: A Guide to Archive Resources in the United Kingdom** is a directory to archives. The volume includes repositories which hold an accumulation of records emanating from a single source, thus providing a historical record of an institution or individual. In addition, *British Archives* also lists *artificial collections* which have consciously been put together, usually around a subject area or a type of material, but which have not accumulated naturally over the course of time (ix).

The information in more than twelve hundred entries was gathered from questionnaires and supplemented by direct contact with the institutions, or by consulting their website. There are archives listed for literature, national and local government agencies, business organizations, schools, religious groups, associations, botanic gardens, museums, science expeditions, military campaigns, anti-slavery groups, and more. Because of the large number of privately held collections, small local archives, and museums in Britain, no attempt has been made for comprehensive coverage. Instead, this resource aims to identify collections from as many places as possible which are relatively accessible to the public. The volume is arranged by city and, within each city, in alphabetical order by institution, and includes an alphabetical index to institutions and a general subject index.

A typical entry lists the name of the repository, address, telephone number, fax, e-mail, website, contact name, hours of operation, access restriction, historical background for the institution and/or collection, major collections, non-manuscript materials (e.g., plans, drawings, photographs, maps, sound archives, films), finding aids, reproduction facilities (e.g., photocopying, photography, microform reader/printers), and published guides. The information gathered is very practical and concisely presented, and the content is directed at and organized for archival researchers who wish to get a basic understanding of a collection. The authors of *British Archives* caution that the information was as accurate as possible at the time of publication, but that there may have been changes, so details should be verified with the institution itself.

The entry for the Wordsworth Library in Grasmere provides a brief paragraph giving the background of the collection. The major and non-manuscript collections held include: verse, prose, and correspondence of Wordsworth, his family, and circle; papers associated with the poet and the Lake District; paintings, drawings, and prints; and various editions, biographical, and critical works about Wordsworth and his contemporaries. The types of finding aids available at the library are listed. Permission to use the collections may take three to four weeks, and photocopying must be arranged. At the time this edition was compiled, either the library had no website or that information wasn't provided in the questionnaire, but using Google we found the site by searching *"Wordsworth Library"* (in quotations to search the phrase). Titled *Wordsworth Trust*, the website provides descriptions of the Wordsworth library collections, an online searchable catalog to the collections, and the most current contact information.

For additional sources, consult Marcuse's chapter, "Archives and Manuscripts," in *A Reference Guide for English Studies* (see Chapter 2). Although the volume covers directories and guides published before 1990, the lists of printed catalogs and the guides to collections in individual manuscript repositories remain valuable because the resources have evaluative annotations and the collections for individual repositories are succinctly described. Some entries include information about several printed sources for a single repository which may be consulted, providing the scholar with a variety of avenues to explore. Sections of the chapter which may be especially helpful for the Romantic scholar are: "General Guides to the Location, Study, and Use of Archives and Manuscripts," "British Repositories," "American Repositories," "English Studies–Manuscripts," and "British Archives."

Websites for Locating Archives and Manuscript Collections

Abraham, Terry, comp. *Repositories of Primary Sources*, 1995, at www.uidaho.edu/special-collections/Other.Repositories.html (accessed 6 December 2004).

ArchivesUSA. Ann Arbor, MI: Proquest Information and Learning Co. archives.chadwyck.com/.

The ARCHON Directory, at www.archon.nationalarchives.gov.uk/ archon/ (accessed 6 December 2004).

British Library Manuscripts Catalogues, at www.bl.uk/catalogues/ manuscripts.html (accessed 6 December 2004).

DocumentsOnline, at www.documentsonline.pro.gov.uk/ (accessed 6 December 2004).

Guide to the Contents of the Public Record Office. London: H. M. Stationery Office, 1963–1968.

Index of Manuscripts in the British Library. 10 vols. Teaneck, NJ: Chadwyck-Healey, 1984–1986.

Index to Personal Names in the National Union Catalog of Manuscript Collections, 1959–1984. Alexandria, VA: Chadwyck-Healey, 1988.

Index to Subjects and Corporate Names in the National Union Catalog of Manuscript Collections, 1959–1984. Alexandria, VA: Chadwyck-Healey, 1994.

The National Archives, at www.nationalarchives.gov.uk/ (accessed 6 December 2004).

The National Archives Catalogue, at www.catalogue.nationalarchives .gov.uk/search.asp (accessed 6 December 2004).

National Register of Archives. London: The National Archives. www .nra.nationalarchives.gov.uk/nra/ (accessed 6 December 2004).

National Union Catalog of Manuscript Collections (NUCMC), 1997, at www.loc.gov/coll/nucmc/nucmc.html (accessed 11 December 2004).

Nickson, Margaret A. E. *The British Library: Guide to the Catalogues and Indexes of the Department of Manuscripts*. 3rd rev. ed. London: British Library, 1998.

Once the archive or collection desired has been identified, use the website to discover how to search the archive. As we just learned, the Wordsworth Trust has a small database to search the library contents. However, collections within libraries may not have records included in traditional library catalogs because the standards for cataloging unique materials are very different. Many websites for special collections will indicate which parts, if any, of a special collection will be found in the online catalog, and may provide finding aids rather than searchable databases to browse the contents. Searching either the print or online databases will prove to be very different from conventional library catalogs.

The **British Library** has both printed catalogs as well as a separate catalog for the Western manuscripts accessions from 1753 to the present. The online catalog records are being created from scanned images of the printed catalogs, which are based upon the traditional cataloging of the department. The traditional cataloging includes two parts, *indexes* (personal names, place names, subject terms) and *descriptions* (a narrative description including content, date, physical details, bibliography, and provenance); the two parts are searchable by two different engines, allowing the indexes to be searched by name or selected subject and the descriptions to be searched by keyword or manuscript reference. The descriptions can provide keyword access to the manuscripts collections because this field is often used to describe the author's occupation, rank, or even relationship with another individual. If looking for references to the Elgin marbles, for example, the descriptive cataloging may reveal the contents of a letter on the topic while the indexing will not. An extensive "Search Tips" Web page and an online "User Guide" provide advice how to search each effectively, including why certain searches fail. It is worth consulting both for more successful searching. Because the project to provide online access to all the print catalogs is underway, it is advisable to consult the website for the most recent information. A ten-volume set, *Index of Manuscripts in the British Library*, is a name and title index to the collections up through 1950, and M. A. E. Nickson's *The British Library: Guide to the Catalogues and Indexes of the Department of Manuscripts* describes the various catalogs for parts of the manuscript collections. Online searching may be done from remote locations, but identifying the manuscripts does not mean they can be requested online, nor that access will be provided. Once you know what you need to use, follow the requirements for access as spelled out on the website to find out if you may use the collections and the documents.

The largest governmental archive in the United Kingdom is *The National Archives*, formerly the Public Records office, in Kew outside London. This institution houses and cares for the state and central court documents of Britain, from the eleventh century to the present. The website contains a "Planning Your Visit: Useful Information for Visitors" page, with the following recommendations: verify that The National Archives has the materials desired; check the opening hours; plan your day carefully because only three items may be requested at a time and the last orders must be placed by 4 pm; register online to save time; and order up to three documents in advance. Visitors must bring proof of identity to obtain a "Reader's Ticket," the pass into the archives, which is good for three years and must be presented at every visit. Bringing background information on the topic being researched is vital so that staff can be more helpful. Only pencils and ten pieces of loose paper may be brought in, including documents, so it is highly recommended that notebooks, ring binders, or laptop computers be used for writing purposes. Other advice concerns securing valuables, paying for copies of documents, the availability of food and drink, and which clothing would be appropriate because of climate control.

The online *Catalogue*, formally called *PROCAT*, contains over 9.5 million records which are arranged by the department creating the documents. It is worth reading the help and search tips screens to understand the structure of the catalog and how to search it effectively, but in an archive such as this, the foundation of knowledge about the project will prove invaluable. For example, if searching for documents about Luddites, a search on *luddit**, limited to the dates *1800–1820*, finds four items. Since it seems there should be more, it might be that the term *luddite* was not widely used at the time to describe this group of people. The riots started in 1812, but a keyword search in the *Times Digital Archives* does not show the use of the word Luddites until 1813, even though there were several stories published in 1812 about the riots. Therefore, try to use terms to describe the actions of the Luddites, the geographic locations they inhabited, and the type of work they did. Now try reconstructing the keyword search as follows, limiting to the years 1800–1820: *riot OR riots OR wool OR machin* OR mill OR mills* (note Boolean operators must be in capital letters). This search is too broad and retrieves too many false drops, so refine the keyword search, again limiting to the years 1800–1820*: riot OR riots.* This retrieves sixty-three hits, which are more relevant. Finally, refine the keyword search by specifying a geographic location, limited by the same years as above: *riot* AND york** finds nine records.

The three-volume set titled ***Guide to the Contents of the Public Record Office*** describes the records in The National Archives up to the mid-1960s which provides a breakdown of the numbering system that may prove valuable for understanding the records retrieved. The Luddite records fall under the documents number TS and are part of the Treasury Solicitor and King's (Queen's) Proctor papers which dealt with the various legal proceedings by that department. "They relate to state trials, the preservation of public peace, escheats and administration cases, and a great variety of other business."[3]

In addition to the online catalog, prepared search strategies have been created to find the more popular topics researched at The National Archives, including specific searches to retrieve records for the battles of Trafalgar and Waterloo, and leaflets which describe the collections for popular topics such as lunatic asylums from the eighteenth through the twentieth centuries, the domestic state papers of George III (which, as was discussed in the Chapter 8, "Microform and Digital Collections," are also available on microfilm), and the Royal Navy operational records from 1660 to 1914.

The documents at The National Archives can be consulted onsite. Depending upon the restrictions for use, the documents may be in paper or in microform. However, if you are able to identify the desired records remotely, the documents may be ordered and purchased as photocopies or digital images from *DocumentsOnline*, which allows researchers from abroad to use the collections without traveling there. Beyond these individual requests, The National Archives is working on a variety of digitizing projects to allow broader access to important and popular parts of their collections. One such project is the online digital images of wills for famous people, including Lord Byron, Percy Shelley, and Jane Austen, which can be purchased for a fee. This is a subset of a much larger project which provides digital images to all Prerogative Court of Canterbury wills in The National Archives, covering the period from 1384 to 1858, and which can be purchased from *DocumentsOnline*.

The *Historical Manuscripts Commission* (HMC) is the advisory body on archives and manuscripts relating to British history. In April 2003 the HMC and the Public Records Office were merged to form The National Archives. While The National Archives is the caretaker for the governmental archives, the HMC maintains the *National Register of Archives* (*NRA*), which is the central resource for researchers who need to identify and locate relevant records. The HMC does not hold any manuscripts itself. Instead, the NRA houses 43,000 unpublished catalogs and descriptions of collections on British history. An online database can be searched by personal, family, corporate, or geographic name. A personal name search on *austen, jane* yields one entry with eight records attached: a reference to the chapter in *Index of Literary Manuscripts, Volume 4*, and the letters, manuscripts or papers held in the Pierpont Morgan, British Library, and Bodleian Library. Entries are very brief, but this may be an important source for finding papers on minor literary figures.

The *HMC* is also responsible for the two parts of *ARCHON*, the electronic directory of repositories in the United Kingdom and abroad and the portal to archival initiatives and projects, including digitization projects, online finding aids, and archival descriptive and conservation standards. In the *ARCHON* directory, repositories are listed by institutional name or by region. A search on *wordsworth* finds the "Wordsworth Trust," with address, e-mail, and URL. Items found in the NRA database link out to ARCHON for directory information, such as contact information, e-mail addresses, and Web links to websites for collections. For example, in the NRA list for Jane Austen, the brief entry lists about sixty letters and papers that can be found in the Pierpont Morgan Library, with location, contact information, and a link out to the institution via the ARCHON directory. Therefore, the NRA can be used to identify collections of interest, and ARCHON provides directory information about the institutions and links out to their websites.

The ARCHON Portal provides links out to digital initiatives, projects, and resources and is searchable by title, keyword, or region. For example, in the ARCHON Portal, under the keyword digitization, links can be found to such intriguing projects as "From History to Herstory: Yorkshire Women's Lives Online, from 1100 to the Present," "Spinning the Web: The Story of the Cotton Industry," and "The Voice of Radicalism" in northeast Scotland from 1800 to 1930.

Developed by Terry Abraham at the University of Idaho, ***Repository of Primary Sources*** is a large directory of Web links to archives, manuscripts, rare books, photographs, and other primary sources from around the world. The links are arranged geographically by continent and then by country. Under the country are links to websites alphabetically by institution. Under "Additional Lists" are links to other directory websites by country, such as *ARCHON*, *Archives Hub: Gateway to Archive Collections Held in UK Universities and Colleges*, and *Largo: Libraries and Archives Research Guide Online–London*. Each of these websites has a unique focus within the larger world of archives and, although the links found may be duplicated in other directories of websites, they may also lead to new sites of interest. It is worth exploring this site for some potentially useful links.

Manuscripts from the Romantic era can also be found in a wide variety of United States libraries and collections, so the ***National Union Catalog of Manuscript Collections*** (*NUCMC*) may prove a valuable resource to collections cataloged within this program, as well as those cataloged via RLG and OCLC. *NUCMC* is a free-of-charge cooperative program for cataloging archival collections in repositories within the United States and its territories, coordinated by the Library of Congress and intended to assist archives unable to deposit their own records into RLG or OCLC. Once cataloged, the records are then deposited in and searchable using RLG. In addition, the Library of Congress provides free access to the primary source materials files, called *Archival and*

Mixed Collections (*AMC*) within the RLG database and *Mixed Materials* within OCLC, because institutions that are not part of the free-of-charge cooperative cataloging program use either one or the other to catalog their collections and therefore both must be searched. RLG and OCLC cannot be searched together, so you must use both. The *NUCMC* program began in 1959 and started depositing records into RLG in 1986. Records created prior to 1986 are not available online via this free interface, although the records can be search from 1959 to the present in the commercial database *ArchivesUSA*. A two-volume set, ***Index to Personal Names in the National Union Catalog of Manuscript Collections, 1959–1984*** and the three-volume set ***Index to Subjects and Corporate Names in the National Union Catalog of Manuscript Collections, 1959–1984***, provide access to the printed volumes of *NUCMC* not covered by the online database. The volumes for 1985 and 1986 have to be searched separately.

Conclusion

The world of archival research is in a dynamic transition period. The advent of the Web has had a tremendous impact upon the scholar's ability to locate relevant archival materials and to contact the archives for assistance. In the past, much of the work was done by regular mail, but websites and e-mail have made communication much faster and information about collections easier to locate. In addition, as illustrated by the *DocumentsOnline* resource at The National Archives, digitization projects and document delivery are changing how archival materials themselves may be accessed and distributed. At present, printed directories, standard editions, and bibliographies continue to play an important role because, in these sources, the information about authors' papers are centralized in just a few places. But as these sources become dated, the Web will become even more pivotal. In the end, whether the finding aids or documents are available in print, in microform, or in digital format, you need to have the patience and skills to create and execute a thoughtful, knowledgeable plan to navigate through the primary source materials. The nature of the materials themselves will not change despite advances in technology, and therefore the best practices recommended in this chapter will continue to be valuable.

Notes

1. Rosenbaum, Barbara, comp., *Index of English Literary Manuscripts*, vol. 4, pt. 2, *1800–1900 Hardy-Lamb* (London: Mansell Publishing, 1990), 330.

2. Bellardo, Lewis J. and Lynn Lady Bellardo, comps., *A Glossary for Archivist, Manuscript Curators, and Records Managers* (Chicago: Society of American Archivists, 1992), 4 and 35. In this context, the term "autograph" is defined as "a manuscript, signed or unsigned, in the hand of the author, or a typescript signed by the author." A transcript is "a copy or reproduction, in so far as the resources of Script and/or typography allow, of an original document, with the exception that abbreviations, if their interpretation is clear, may be extended."

3. *Guide to the Contents of the Public Record Office*, vol. 2, *State Papers and Departmental Records* (London: Her Majesty's Stationery Office, 1963), 302.

Chapter 10
Web Resources

Resources for studying Romantic-era literature comprise a lively presence on the Web. The student new to Romantic literature studies will find numerous sites that provide introductory materials to the period, including: biographical information about canonical and non-canonical authors; full-text editions of Romantic poetry, fiction, drama, and prose; and historical and cultural contextual sources. Graduate students may be particularly interested in using electronic scholarly journals, online bibliographies of recent Romantic literature publications, and discussion lists to stay abreast of current scholarly debate and trends in the field. The Web is becoming an excellent resource for accessing texts previously only available on microfilm or in special collections, as more libraries make digital copies of published and unpublished texts available online. Some of these online editions also have the distinct advantage of being searchable by keyword. In addition, students may want to take advantage of online reference tools, such as union library catalogs in the United Kingdom and the United States, and both general Romantic studies and author-specific chronologies and bibliographies. Although Web resources will not meet all of your research needs, they can serve as excellent complementary tools to traditional reference materials. This chapter will describe the current core websites for Romantic-era studies, and will present a selection of additional sites to illustrate the range of available Romantic resources.

The Web presents a distinctive search environment from an online database such as *MLA International Bibliography*, or even your library catalog. Unlike these resources, websites are not governed overall by controlled vocabulary or an authoritative entity. In contrast to literature databases that strictly index scholarly materials, the Web is home to a wide variety of resources, only some of which will be relevant to academic research. Given these factors, a search for resources on the Web will have a very different outcome than if you search in a controlled database environment. Although you may not always retrieve relevant materials in a database, the number of irrelevant hits from a general Web search will likely be significantly greater. However, if you decide to use a general search engine to identify resources for your research project, evaluate the source according to the following criteria to ensure that it is appropriate:

1. Authority. Is the site based at an academic or government institution? Is it authored or edited by someone with expertise in the field?
2. Currency. When was the site last updated and how frequently is it maintained? Is the information time sensitive?
3. Scope. What is the subject matter and range of coverage? Who is the intended audience for the website (undergraduates, scholars, high school students)?
4. Objectivity. What, if any, particular bias does the author possess? How does that affect the website's content?
5. Accuracy. How accurate is the material presented? Can it be verified in other sources?

You can use these same criteria to evaluate any potential resource, print or electronic, that you are considering for your research.

Scholarly Gateways

Fraistat, Neil, and Steven E. Jones, general eds. *Romantic Circles*, at www.rc.umd.edu (accessed 20 November 2004).

Gamer, Michael. *Romantic Links, Electronic Texts, and Home Pages*, at www.english.upenn.edu/~mgamer/Romantic (accessed 20 November 2004).

Liu, Alan. *Voice of the Shuttle: Romantics*, at vos.ucsb.edu/browse.asp?id=2750 (accessed 20 November 2004).

Lynch, Jack. *Literary Resources–Romantic*, at andromeda.rutgers.edu/~jlynch/Lit/romantic.html (accessed 20 November 2004).

Although at some point you may want to search the entire World Wide Web, the best place to begin your exploration of Romantic websites is to consult a scholarly gateway in which a subject specialist has compiled links to a selection of recommended resources.

Alan Liu's highly regarded site, **Voice of the Shuttle: Romantics** *(VoS)*, offers the researcher a very good introduction to the range of scholarly sources available for the study of Romantic-era literature on the Web. *VoS* is organized in nine sections: general Romanticism; authors, works, and projects; selected topics; post-Romanticism; course syllabi; criticism; Romantic literature journals; listservs and newsgroups; and conferences. Most, but not all, of the resources listed are briefly described and some of the major sites include links to their individual components. Although the majority of author resources presented are for canonical figures, you will find textual, biographical, and critical resources for nearly one hundred authors from the Romantic period. The topical section offers websites on the French revolution, the Gothic, the sublime, slavery, women, and Romanticism and information technology. You can rely on *VoS* to guide you to interesting sites with relevant scholarly value.

Two other notable Romantic literature gateways, Lynch's *Literary Resources* and Gamer's *Romantic Links, Electronic Texts, and Home Pages*, provide thematically arranged selections of similar literary and cultural background sites. Although there is a lot of site overlap, in particular between *VoS* and *Literary Resources*, it is worth checking more than one gateway on the chance of coming across a unique source. In distinction from the others, Gamer's site posts his own editions of selected Romantic-era electronic texts and a directory of Romantic scholars' personal home pages in the United States, Canada, and Europe. All three of the gateways discussed in this section are edited by university English professors. Use a Romantic literature gateway to become acquainted with the types of websites available and to identify specific resources that pertain directly to your research.

More than a gateway and considered one of the premier sites for Romantic literature studies, **Romantic Circles** serves as a microcosm of the various scholarly resources available on the Web. This one site offers the following valuable research materials: electronic editions of works by selected Romantic-era authors; a bibliography of current and forthcoming publications in Romantic studies; tables of contents for important journals in the field; full-text chapters from selected Romantic studies Cambridge University Press publications; full-text book reviews of current scholarship; an online journal, *Romantic Circles Praxis Series*; bibliographies, indexes, and chronologies; recommended websites; an online MOO (Multi-User Domain Object Oriented) entitled Villa Diodati for live-time professional and casual discussion; and special online features and conference announcements. You will find here searchable, peer-reviewed editions of Anna Laetitia Aikin's *Poems (1773)*, Mary Shelley's *The Last Man*, and Percy Shelley's *The Devil's Walk*, in addition to full-text critical articles from the *Praxis Series* that investigate such pairings as Romanticism and neo-classicism, poetics, ecology, contemporary culture, law, and conspiracy. Be sure to check the "Bibliographies" section to stay abreast of recent books and journal articles in the field, and the "Reviews" section for critical assessments of new works. Designed specifically to assist students and scholars,

Romantic Circles likely will be an integral component to your research online.

Electronic Text Archives

Bartleby.com, at www.bartleby.com (accessed 20 November 2004).

British Poetry 1780–1910: An Archive of Scholarly Electronic Editions, at etext.lib.virginia.edu/britpo.html (accessed 20 November 2004).

British Women Romantic Poets, 1789–1832, 29 October 2004, at www.lib.ucdavis.edu/English/BWRP (accessed 20 November 2004).

Chawton House Library and Study Centre, at www.chawton.org (accessed 20 November 2004).

Crochunis, Thomas C. and Michael Eberle-Sinatra, general eds. *British Women Playwrights Around 1800*, 15 June 2004, at www.etang.umontreal.ca/bwp1800 (accessed 20 November 2004).

Fay, Elizabeth. *The Bluestocking Archive*, at www.faculty.umb.edu/ elizabeth_fay/toc.html (accessed 20 November 2004).

Lancashire, Ian, general ed. *Representative Poetry Online,* at eir.library.utoronto.ca/rpo/display/index.cfm (accessed 20 November 2004).

Modern English Collection, at etext.lib.virginia.edu/modeng/modeng0 .browse.html (accessed 20 November 2004).

Oxford Text Archive, 25 June 2004, at ota.ahds.ac.uk (accessed 20 November 2004).

Voller, Jack G. *The Literary Gothic*, 20 November 2004, at www.litgothic.com/index_fl.html (accessed 20 November 2004).

Electronic editions of canonical poetry and prose are the most prevalent type of Romantic literary studies Web resources. Numerous online archives provide full-text editions by the principal authors of the period, and individual author sites also feature full-text Romantic-era novels, poems, and prose. When using an online edition, be sure to note the following: source, publication date, and publisher of the edition being used; the authority of the editors (who is hosting the site—a university, an academic library, or a commercial organization); and if the text is subject to editorial review (are there notes, an introduction, links to a glossary or related materials). Freely available electronic texts on the Web are frequently works whose copyrights have expired. Online works range from plain ASCII text presentations to HTML and SGML versions to digitally scanned reproductions of works like Blake's illustrated manuscripts. Take care to choose an online edition to match your needs. Reading for pleasure, close textual analysis, and critical assessment will require texts with different levels of scholarly reliability.

The University of Virginia's *Electronic Text Center* possesses two online collections available to the public that are relevant for studying Romantic literature. The ***Modern English Collection*** features works by Austen, Barbauld, Blake, Coleridge, Godwin, Lewis, Peacock, Scott, Mary and Percy Shelley, Wollstonecraft, and Wordsworth as part of its broader collection of titles ranging from 1500 A.D. to the present. ***British Poetry 1780–1910: An Archive of Scholarly Electronic Editions*** offers selected poems by Cristall, Polwhele, Robinson, and Coleridge. A few of the texts in these collections include book cover and page images, as well as illustrations, and Cristall's *Poetical Sketches* is enhanced with a critical introduction. The *Electronic Text Center* also maintains the *Samuel Taylor Coleridge Archive* <http://etext.lib .virginia.edu/stc/Coleridge/stc.html>.

Aiming to collect "high-quality electronic texts for research and teaching," the ***Oxford Text Archive*** offers more than 2,500 texts in twenty-five different languages. Students will find here freely available public domain works by Austen, Blake, Byron, Coleridge, Mary Shelley, Wollstonecraft, and Wordsworth; however, Thomas Paine's *Rights of Man* and Percy Shelley's *Prometheus Unbound* require permission from the depositor in order to be accessed. The collection can be browsed by author, title, or language, or searched by various fields. Although most of the archive's collection is in SGML, the texts can also be downloaded in ASCII, DOS ASCII, and occasionally HTML and XML formats. Diskettes, data cartridges, and CD-ROM versions of the texts are also provided for a fee. If you are interested in requesting a text that requires permission, you will need to allow enough time for a hard copy of the order form to be submitted by regular mail to Oxford, United Kingdom. Also note that the *OTA* recommends viewing its texts with Microsoft's Internet Explorer.

Representative Poetry Online*,* based at the University of Toronto Libraries, provides approximately 2,900 full-text English language poems by poets from the Old English period to the present. Based on several editions of Alexander's *Representative Poetry*, an anthology designed for students at the University of Toronto, this online version highlights works by Barbauld, Beddoes, Blake, Bowles, Burns, Byron, Carlyle, Clare, Crabbe, Coleridge, Cowper, Hemans, Hunt, Keats, Lamb, Landon, Opie, Peacock, Percy, Robinson, Scott, Shelley, Smith, Southey, and Wordsworth. The poems may be accessed by the following means: alphabetical or chronological poet indexes; title, first line, or last line poem indexes; a timeline index; and by a keyword or concordance-keyword search. Hyperlinked notes append each poem, and the original source, composition date, and rhyme scheme are also included. Furthermore, brief biographical profiles outline each poet's nationality, sexual orientation, family relations, education, religion, politics, occupation, residences, and cause of death. Additional features include a glossary of poetic terms, selected poetry criticism in prose and poetry by Burns, Byron, Coleridge, Keats, Peacock, Shelley, and Wordsworth, and an extensive bibliography of poetry anthologies and websites.

Finally, if you can disregard the advertising, the commercial site *Bartleby.com* offers nineteenth- and early twentieth-century editions of works by Austen, Byron, Lamb, Keats, Paine, Scott, Shelley, Wollstonecraft, and Wordsworth. *Bartelby* is also useful for its collection of verse anthologies, including the 1919 edition of *The Oxford Book of English Verse* and the Harvard Classics *English Poetry II: From Collins to Fitzgerald,* that both present poems by many canonical Romantic poets.

Scholars working with non-canonical authors will find that the Web is also an excellent resource for accessing full-text works by less-established authors. Many texts previously restricted to special collections, or available only in microforms are reproduced now online for the researcher's benefit. Reflecting the current interest in expanding definitions of the Romantic canon, several websites highlight works by Romantic-era women writers.

British Women Romantic Poets, 1789–1832, an electronic collection of texts from the UC Davis Shields Library, currently contains poems by more than sixty-five British and Irish writers. This online archive was created to make relatively unknown or not readily accessible texts from the Kohler Collection of British Poetry available to the broader scholarly community. The texts may be browsed by author, or searched by keyword, author, and title. In accordance with the Text Encoding Initiative for the humanities, the poems are encoded in SGML in order to preserve the original formatting and increase search function capability. For these reasons, the archive advises scholars to use the SGML versions which require an appropriate SGML browser. HTML versions of the texts are also provided for greater ease of access. In addition, the archive has partnered with the *Literary Encyclopedia* <http://www.litencyc.com/about.html> to offer links to relevant biographical entries, unfortunately not all of which currently contain information. The archive is notable for including works by recognized authors such as Baillie, Barbauld, Hemans, and Smith, as well as more marginalized authors. Due to its range and unique coverage, *British*

Women Romantic Poets can serve as a general introduction to women writers of the period, or it can be mined for specific critical inquiries.

The *Bluestocking Archive*, maintained by Elizabeth Fay at the University of Massachusetts, Boston is an electronic text resource devoted to women Romantic-era writers. Aiming to highlight "the connections between the phenomenon of the original Bluestocking Circle, the development of sensibility, and the achievements of High Romanticism," when completed this archive will present selected texts by the British Bluestocking members Montagu, Carter, Talbot, Vesey, and Chapone, in addition to texts by second generation "Blues" and members of related circles (e.g., Ladies of Llangollen, Anna Seward, Della Cruscans). From the original circle, currently only texts by Montagu and Carter are available. To place these works in context, Fay provides contemporary eighteenth- and nineteenth-century texts including: writings that encouraged women's intellectualism, works about the slavery debate, predecessor texts, works by related women authors (e.g., Radcliffe, Robinson, Baillie, Dorothy Wordsworth, Smith, Barbauld, Shelley, and Hemans), contemporary critiques by male and female authors, and example texts of High Romanticism by Shelley, Keats, and Byron. For scholars already familiar with the Bluestockings, this site will be useful for its collection of original and related texts. Unfortunately, the absence of an introduction leaves the novice longing for more information about these women and the principals upon which they formed their writers' circle.

The *Chawton House Library and Study Centre* was established to promote the study of English women's writing published during the long eighteenth century from 1600 to 1830. The library collection contains more than nine thousand texts including fiction, poetry, published letters, cookery books, autobiographical writing, educational works, and advice manuals, in addition to related manuscripts. Part of the collection is made available on the Web through *Novels Online*, an ongoing project that currently provides full-text transcripts of forty-three "little-known" novels by both anonymous and named authors, most of which were originally published in the late eighteenth and early nineteenth centuries. Bibliographic information and physical descriptions are offered for each novel, and some entries also include a summary of the text. The novels have not been edited and can be viewed in HTML, PDF, and Microsoft Word formats. Online forums for individual novels and biographical sketches appear to be upcoming features and critical introductions to the novels are planned as well. The library's site also posts information about scheduled lectures, conferences, and events, and includes links to related Web resources.

Aiming to redress the scarcity of Romantic-era women's plays in print, *British Women Playwrights Around 1800* features seventeen full-text plays by Burney, Cowley, Craven, Gore, Inchbald, Harriet and Sophia Lee, Mitford, Plumptre, Polack, Scott, Starke, and Wallace. Plans to include additional plays by Smith, Lefanu, Baillie, and Inchbald are forthcoming. All of the plays are edited by scholars in the field, and many are prefaced with an introductory essay. The site also offers an ongoing bibliography of critical works about Romantic drama and British women playwrights, with links to reviews posted at *Romanticism on the Net*. A chronological list of plays published by British women playwrights from 1770 to 1854, a collection of related scholarly essays, and links to women authors, theatre history, Romantic studies, and electronic editing resources all serve to complement this unique resource.

Although scholarly efforts have focused on bringing women writers into the expanded Romantic canon, writers of Gothic literature also are receiving renewed attention. Scholars working with writers in this genre will find full-text complete and extracted works of Gothic fiction, poetry, and drama by Ainsworth, Beddoes, Byron, Hogg, Lewis, Radcliffe, Mary and Percy Shelley, Smith, and Southey, among others, offered at the *Literary Gothic* website. The library covers works published from 1764 to 1820, as well as related pre- and post-Gothic literature written before 1950. Most of these electronic texts are prefaced with the original date of publication and the source from which the electronic text was reproduced; be aware, however, that not every source is credited. In addition to its own electronic texts, *Literary Gothic* also provides brief biographical notes for numerous Gothic authors and a collection of links to external author websites, texts, and online critical essays and reviews. Furthermore, the "Community" and "Resources" sections offer annotated selections of general Gothic literature resources including: associations, discussion lists, timelines, publishers, critical essays, and reviews of Gothic anthologies and criticism. The *Literary Gothic* is maintained by Jack G. Voller, Southern Illinois University at Edwardsville.

Author Sites

Churchyard, Henry. *Jane Austen Information Page*, at www.pemberley.com/janeinfo/janeinfo.html (accessed 20 November 2004).
Dibert-Himes, Glenn. *Letitia Elizabeth Landon*, at www.shu.ac.uk/schools/cs/landon/index.html (accessed 20 November 2004).

Eaves, Morris, Robert N. Essick, and Joseph Viscomi, eds. *William Blake Archive*, at www.blakearchive.org (accessed 20 November 2004).

Although the *Voice of the Shuttle* author list is extensive, a closer look reveals that sites devoted exclusively to one author are primarily for canonical Romantic figures. These author sites typically provide biographical information, a bibliography of primary and secondary materials, electronic versions of the author's works or links to external editions, and contextual materials such as chronologies, itineraries, portraits, and links to associated places, such as the Lake District, etc. The following selected author sites illustrate this particular type of literary Web resource. Be sure to check the *VoS* list to discover if a site exists for your particular author.

One of the preeminent Romantic author sites is the **William Blake Archive *(WBA)*** which is jointly sponsored by the Library of Congress, NEH, University of Virginia, the University of North Carolina at Chapel Hill, Sun Microsystems, and Inso Corporation. The *WBA* is notable especially for its beautiful and accurate digital reproductions of Blake's illuminated manuscripts that feature text and image search capabilities. Currently the archive provides unified access to electronic copies of Blake's nineteen illustrated manuscripts. Blake's non-illuminated works are also presented, including: commercial book illustrations; separate plates and plates in series; drawings and paintings; and manuscripts, letters, and typographic editions. Detailed descriptions, bibliographic information, and related critical bibliographies of books and journal articles are provided for each work. A searchable electronic edition of David Erdman's *The Complete Poetry and Prose of William Blake*, bibliographies of recommended reference works, standard editions, and general studies, and selected collection lists further enhance the research potential of this site. The *Archive* also includes biographical material, a glossary, and a chronology, as well as selections of Blake, Romanticism, and art history Web resources.

Lacking the heavyweight sponsorship of the *Blake Archive*, the **Jane Austen Information Page** makes quite a different initial impression. Despite its haphazard appearance, however, this site does contain numerous scholarly resources. Arranged into short and longer tables of contents, the continuous list of links can be overwhelming until you realize that the resources are organized thematically around Austen's six novels and juvenilia, with additional categories for biographical, historical, and critical material. Clicking on the title of each novel will take you to a brief description of the work, followed by links to ASCII and occasionally HTML versions of the texts. Extra features vary for

each novel and can include: C. E. Brock illustrations, character geneal-
ogy charts, Penguin Reading Guides, chronologies, maps, and links to
television and film adaptations. Scholars will also find these useful
features: an overview of Jane Austen's life; Lord Brabourne's edition
of Austen's letters to her sister Cassandra and nieces, Fanny Knight and
Anna Austen Lefroy; notes on Austen's literary reputation; background
material on the status and education of women, marriage, and money;
and separate bibliographies of books, articles and dissertations, as well
as Jane Austen sequels. In addition, this site presents related, playful
material ranging from Jane Austen jokes to amusing book illustrations.
Designed originally by Frank Churchyard at the University of Texas,
Austin, the *Jane Austen Information Page* now is hosted by *Pem-
berly.com*, a "haven in a world programmed to misunderstand obses-
sion with things Austen."

As the introduction to the ***Letitia Elizabeth Landon*** website states,
although Landon was an acclaimed writer of her time, nevertheless
"much of her work remains uncollected, misrepresented, and underval-
ued." To redress this neglect, in part, this well-organized site provides a
rotating selection of Landon's poetry, novels, and both fiction and non-
fiction short prose pieces, all of which are drawn from *The Collected
Works of Letitia Elizabeth Landon*, a forthcoming CD-ROM. The creator of this site, Glenn Dibert-Himes from Sheffield Hallam University,
also discusses the work of L. E. L. at length in an introductory essay
that traces her literary career and critical reception through the mid-
nineteenth century. Keeping scholars in mind, the site presents a useful
bibliography of primary and secondary materials, including contemporary reviews, and offers biographical excerpts from nineteenth-century
publications.

Contemporary Newspapers and Journals

The Athenaeum Index of Reviews and Reviewers: 1830–1870, December 1998, at web.soi.city.ac.uk/~asp/v2/home.html (accessed 20
   November 2004).
Batchelor, Jennie. *Lady's Magazine (1770–1800)*, 10 March 2004, at
   www.soton.ac.uk/~jeb/ (accessed 20 November 2004).
The *British Library Newspaper Library Catalogue*, at
   www.bl.uk/catalogues/newspapers.html (accessed 20 November
   2004).
Cutmore, Jonathan, ed. "*Quarterly Review* Archive," *Romantic Circles*,
   forthcoming at www.rc.umd.edu (accessed 10 December 2004).

de Montluzin, Emily Lorraine. *Attributions of Authorship in the European Magazine, 1782–1826*, at etext.lib.virginia.edu/bsuva/euromag (accessed 20 November 2004).

de Montluzin, Emily Lorraine. *Attributions of Authorship in the Gentleman's Magazine, 1731–1868; A Supplement to Kuist*, 13 September 2004, at etext.lib.virginia.edu/bsuva/gm/gm1.html (accessed 20 November 2004).

Hancher, Michael, comp. *British Periodicals at Minnesota: The Early Nineteenth Century*, 17 November 2000, at mh.cla.umn.edu/britper.html (accessed 20 November 2004).

Internet Library of Early Journals: A Digital Library of 18th and 19th Century Journals, 1990s, at www.bodley.ox.ac.uk/ilej (accessed 20 November 2004).

Liu, Alan. *British Newspaper Coverage of the French Revolution*, 2000, at www.english.ucsb.edu/faculty/ayliu/research/around-1800/FR (accessed 20 November 2004).

Penny Magazine, 1995, at www.history.rochester.edu/pennymag (accessed 20 November 2004).

Scholars working with eighteenth- and nineteenth-century periodicals will find several Web resources to supplement their use of the print and microform materials outlined in the preceding chapters. Some of these sources can be used to identify potential journals and newspapers of interest, other resources can be used to search for specific content. ***British Periodicals at Minnesota: The Early Nineteenth Century*** is a hand list to the University of Minnesota's extensive early British periodical collection (excluding newspapers and microforms) arranged by title or by date of first issue. Although not comprehensive, the list can be used as a quick way to identify select journals that began publishing from 1665 through 1850.

The ***British Library Newspaper Library Catalogue*** provides descriptive access to the library's collection of more than 52,000 newspaper and periodical titles, including national daily and Sunday newspapers from 1801 to the present, British and Irish provincial newspapers, and selected papers in European languages from around the world. Keyword searches may be sorted by title, date, or place; thus a search of "Bath" sorted by date retrieves a list of newspapers published in Bath, England from the mid-eighteenth century onwards. The Newspaper Library also features a brief chronology of British newspaper events from the seventeenth through the twentieth century <http://www.bl.uk/collections/britnews.html>.

Although not as prevalent as electronic literary text archives, a few full-text resources exist for contemporary journals on the Web. The most well-known is probably the **Internet Library of Early Journals** project which offers digitized twenty year runs of the *Annual Register* (1758–1778), *Blackwood's Edinburgh Magazine* (1843–1863), *Gentleman's Magazine* (1731–1750), *Notes and Queries* (1849–1869), *Philosophical Transactions of the Royal Society* (1757–1777), and *The Builder* (1843–1852). Unfortunately, the years covered by the project are earlier and later than the main period addressed by this book, but the journal coverage may still be of use to particular research endeavors.

Alan Liu has compiled a small archive of transcribed *London Times* and *Morning Chronicle* newspaper articles at **British Newspaper Coverage of the French Revolution** in order to show contemporary reactions to events from 1792 and 1793. If you are interested in the later Romantic period, University of Rochester presents selected full-text issues of the Society for the Diffusion of Useful Knowledge weekly **Penny Magazine** published during the years 1832, 1833, and 1835.

In addition to these limited full-text resources, the following websites offer access to selected contemporary journal contents. The **Lady's Magazine (1770–1800),** a project derived from Jennie Batchelor's dissertation research, provides an index to essays and poetry published in the *Lady's Magazine; or Entertaining Companion for the Fair Sex* arranged by year. Batchelor also gives a brief overview of the magazine's publishing history, content, and audience, a select bibliography of works about eighteenth-century women's periodicals, the full-text of the magazine's introductory address, and other related materials.

Emily Lorraine de Montluzin has created two searchable databases to assist scholars trying to track down unidentified contributors to the prominent journals, *European Magazine* and *Gentleman's Magazine*. **Attributions of Authorship in the European Magazine, 1782–1826** identifies 2,074 authors of anonymous, pseudonymous, or incompletely attributed works in that periodical, and **Attributions of Authorship in the Gentleman's Magazine, 1731–1868; A Supplement to Kuist** presents four thousand new and corrected attributions of authorship not listed in Kuist's standard work, *The Nichol's File of the Gentleman's Magazine: Attributions of Authorship and Other Documentation in Editorial Papers at the Folger Library*. Since the attribution entries may be browsed chronologically by volume number, these outlines provide an incomplete but intriguing key to each journal's contents. De Montluzin also organizes the entries by contributor, and discusses each journal's publishing history.

Covering the end of the Romantic era, *The Athenaeum Index of Reviews and Reviewers: 1830–1870* features searchable title, author, and reviewer indexes for selected years of the *Athenaeum*. The three indexes are cross-referenced and the contributor entries contain brief biographical sketches. Although the majority of authors reviewed are associated with the Victorian era, you will find reviews of works by Baillie, Keats, Hazlitt, Coleridge, and Wordsworth, among others.

The forthcoming "*Quarterly Review* Archive," edited by Jonathan Cutmore, will soon be posted on the *Romantic Circles* website. Scholars of Romantic literature can anticipate such research tools as an index to the *Quarterly Review* from 1809 to 1824, background material about the journal, a table of publication dates and sales information, and finding aids.

Current Awareness Resources

British Association for Romantic Studies, formally at www.bangor.ac .uk/english/bars/intro.htm and in the process of moving to a new server (attempted access 21 November 2004).

"Cambridge University Press @ Romantic Circles." *Romantic Circles*, at www.rc.umd.edu/bibliographies/CUP/index.html (accessed 21 November 2004).

European Romantic Review, at www.tandf.co.uk/journals/titles/ 10509585.asp (accessed 21 November 2004).

Grimes, Kyle. "Romantic Circles Bibliographies." *Romantic Circles*, at www.rc.umd.edu/bibliographies (accessed 20 November 2004).

Higginbotham, Jennifer, ed. *Calls for Papers*, 1 September 2004, at cfp.english.upenn.edu/ (accessed 21 November 2004).

International Conference on Romanticism, 12 November 2004, at icr.byu.edu/ (accessed 21 November 2004).

International Gothic Association, at info.wlu.ca/~wwwgac/ (accessed 21 November 2004).

North American Society for the Study of Romanticism, at publish.uwo.ca/~nassr/ (accessed 21 November 2004).

North American Society for the Study of Romanticism. *NASSR-L@LISTSERV.WVU.EDU*, at listserv.wvu.edu/archives/nassr-l .html (accessed 21 November 2004).

Romanticism on the Net (RoN), 7 October 2004, at www.ron.umontreal.ca (accessed 21 November 2004).

Wang, Orrin N. C., ed. "Romantic Circles Praxis Series." *Romantic Circles*, at www.rc.umd.edu/praxis/ (accessed 21 November 2004).

The World Wide Web can be, among other things, an excellent vehicle for current awareness. Online bibliographies of recent publications, scholarly electronic journals, online journal tables of contents, and society discussion lists enable scholars to keep abreast of current developments in Romantic literary studies.

The *Romantic Circles Bibliographies* page features separate bibliographies for books (e.g., primary texts, critical editions, current scholarship), Romantic literature journal contents, and Web bibliographies. The book section covers works published from 2000 to 2004, arranged by year, with links for most titles to the publisher's description and *Romantic Circles* reviews, if available. Although tables of contents are provided for eight journals: *Byron Journal, European Romantic Review, Keats-Shelley Journal, Keats-Shelley Review, Romantic Circles Praxis, Romanticism on the Net, Studies in Romanticism*, and *Wordsworth Circle*, the most recent issues profiled are from 2002. Some of the journal contents also provide article abstracts. The Web bibliographies list includes links to associated university presses that publish Romantic scholarship, as well as to *Project Muse* for journal contents.

Featured as a link from the *Romantic Circles Bibliographies* page, **Cambridge University Press @ Romantic Circles** currently offers sample chapters from nine Cambridge University Press Romantic studies publications on such topics as the poetics of spice, women in Romantic British theatre, and pairings between Romanticism and colonialism, the Cockney school, slave narratives, and print culture. A description, table of contents, and bibliographic information are provided for each title; each chapter or work may also be searched in its entirety

In addition to using bibliographies of current publications, you can also stay informed of recent scholarship by consulting electronic journals and online tables of contents for prominent print journals in the field. Although you will still need to use *MLA International Bibliography* or *ABELL* to perform thorough literature reviews, checking recent journal contents will alert you to timely topics in Romanticism.

The peer-reviewed electronic journal, **Romanticism on the Net** (*RoN*) has been publishing full-text critical articles quarterly since February 1996. Each issue presents four to seven essays and selected reviews; most of which are concerned with canonical figures. Several *RoN* volumes are devoted to special topics, including the transatlantic poetess, Robert Southey, textual scholarship in British literature of the Romantic period, and Romanticism paired with religion, science fiction, and sexuality. The website also posts international conference notices, a list of Romantic studies journals with an online presence, and a selection of related general, Romantic author, scholar, online bookstore, academic press, and association websites.

Describing itself as "devoted to using computer technologies to investigate critically the languages, cultures, histories, and theories of Romanticism," *Romantic Circles Praxis Series* offers thematically organized scholarly essays on Romantic studies topics. Past issues have explored book culture and bibliomania in nineteenth-century England, Romanticism and contemporary poetry and poetics, the nineteenth-century play *Obi; or Three-Fingered Jack*, and Shelley's interventionist poetry. Occasional volumes feature interviews with prominent scholars in the field. Each individual volume or the entire archive (1997–present) may be searched by keyword.

Several print journals that cover Romantic-era authors and issues provide their recent table of contents online and frequently offer contents for archived issues as well. For a fairly complete list of relevant journals online, check both the *Romantic Circles Bibliographies* page list and the *RoN* "Journals" page. Contents for numerous scholarly literature journals can also be accessed for free at the *Project Muse* website, described in Chapter 4. One representative example of a print journal with online contents, the *European Romantic Review (EER)*, is concerned with the literature and culture of Great Britain, Europe, and the Americas from 1760 to 1840. Each issue features approximately eight to ten thematically focused essays and four to five book reviews; contents are posted for 2002 to the most current issue and may be searched by keyword. This journal also presents selected papers from the North American Society for the Study of Romanticism (NASSR) annual conference. Recent issues have addressed works by Blake, Baillie, Wordsworth, Austen, and Hemens. Full-text access for *EER* is restricted to subscribers. Even though access to complete articles is typically limited in this way, nevertheless, journal contents alone can be used to assess trends in scholarship and also to identify potentially useful articles for your research.

Another way to stay informed of scholarly debate is to participate in a Romantic literature listserv or to review a listserv's archived postings. The North American Society for the Study of Romanticism sponsors *NASSR-L@LISTSERV.WVU.EDU*, the principal listserv for Romantic studies whose archives may be searched or browsed monthly from May 1997 to the present. Listservs are a forum for participants to ask questions, post calls for papers and conference announcements, and share information. Scanning the recent *NASSR-L* reveals postings about division panels at the upcoming Modern Language Association conference, calls for papers about the figure of the coquette in the long eighteenth century, a request for four recommended "indispensable" journals in the field, and questions about the fate of the online *Quarterly Review Project*.

Many Romantic studies sites maintain conference lists that can be perused both to identify hot topics and to find potential forums for your work. The **North American Society for the Study of Romanticism** website provides NASSR conference descriptions from 1993 to forthcoming conferences through 2007, in addition to related "calls for papers" postings. *Romantic Circles*, *Romanticism on the Net*, and the University of Pennsylvania English Department *Calls for Papers* site also present listings of current and forthcoming conferences. Romantic literature association websites are an additional resource for learning about upcoming conferences, new publications, and recent news. General Romantic associations, such as the **International Conference on Romanticism**, the **International Gothic Association**, the **British Association for Romantic Studies**, and the *North American Society for the Study of Romanticism* post this type of information; you may also want to look at individual author association websites listed in the *Romanticism on the Net* "Romantic Writers" and "Association" categories.

Reference Tools

ARCHON, at www.archon.nationalarchives.gov.uk/archon (accessed 21 November 2004).

Brady, Corey, Virginia Cope, Mike Millner, Ana Mitric, Kent Puckett, and Danny Siegel. *Dictionary of Sensibility*, at www.engl .virginia.edu/~enec981/dictionary/ (accessed 21 November 2004).

British Library Integrated Catalogue, at catalogue.bl.uk (accessed 21 November 2004).

Copac, at www.copac.ac.uk (accessed 21 November 2004).

Corvey Women Writers on the Web (cw³): An Electronic Guide to Literature 1796–1834, at www2.shu.ac.uk/corvey/CW3/ (accessed 21 November 2004).

Craciun, Adriana. *Romanticism: Selective Bibliography*, 11 January 1998, at www.nottingham.ac.uk/~aezacweb/rombib.htm (accessed 21 November 2004).

Halmi, Nicholas. *A Selective Bibliography of British Romantic Poetry and Prose*, 2 August 2004, at faculty.washington.edu/ nh2/biblio.html (accessed 21 November 2004).

Keats-Shelley Journal Current Bibliography, at www.rc.umd.edu/ reference/ksjbib (accessed 21 November 2004).

Library of Congress Online Catalog, at catalog.loc.gov (accessed 21 November 2004).

Mandell, Laura and Alan Liu, general eds. *Romantic Chronology*, at english.ucsb.edu:591/rchrono/ (accessed 21 November 2004).

National Archives, at www.nationalarchives.gov.uk (accessed 21 November 2004).

National Register of Archives, at www.nra.nationalarchives.gov.uk/nra (accessed 21 November 2004).

National Union Catalog of Manuscript Collections (NUCMC), 15 October 2004, at www.loc.gov/coll/nucmc/nucmc.html (accessed 21 November 2004).

New Books in Nineteenth-Century British Studies, 11 June 2002, at www.usc.edu/dept/LAS/english/19c/newbooks.html (accessed 21 November 2004).

"Scholarly Resources." *Romantic Circles*, at www.rc.umd.edu/reference/ (accessed 21 November 2004).

Scottish Archive Network, at www.scan.org.uk/index.html (accessed 21 November 2004).

Scottish Documents.com, at www.scottishdocuments.com (accessed 21 November 2004).

Thomson, Douglass. *Gothic Literature: What the Romantic Writers Read*, at www.georgiasouthern.edu/~dougt/gothic.htm (accessed 21 November 2004).

Watt, R. J. C. *Web Concordances and Workbooks*, at www.dundee.ac .uk/english/wics/newwics.htm (accessed 21 November 2004).

Traditional reference tools, such as library and archive catalogs, bibliographies, chronologies, biographical material, concordances, and dictionaries abound on the Web, including sources designed specifically for research of Romantic literature. Although library catalogs and archival resources are discussed at greater length in Chapters 3 and 9 respectively, you should make note of the following online catalogs. Please consult the catalog and manuscript/archives chapters for more detailed descriptions and comprehensive coverage.

Copac provides unified access to the online catalogs of 26 member research libraries in the United Kingdom and Ireland, including the British Library, Cambridge University, University of Edinburgh, Oxford University, and Trinity College Dublin Library. The database may be searched by author/title, periodical, or a keyword subject search and limited by date published and/or library. The ***British Library*** and the ***Library of Congress*** websites also feature online catalogs to their important collections.

The ***National Archives*** website, launched in April 2003, combines the resources of the Historical Manuscripts Commission and the Public Records Office to form an impressive document collection relating to British history. The catalogue, formally called *PROCAT*, provides descriptive access to central government, courts of law, and other national entities documents. In the "Search Other Archives" section, you can search the *National Register of Archives* indexes to more than 43,000 unpublished lists, as well as to published catalogs and finding aids that describe archive collections in the United Kingdom and abroad. *AR-CHON*, an online directory of participating record repositories, is also accessed in this section.

The ***Scottish Archive Network*** (*SCAN*) features a searchable catalog to the holdings of fifty-two Scottish archives, as well as a directory of participating archives, a selection of related Scottish archival research tools, and a digital archive of historical records. *SCAN* is also responsible for an impressive project which digitized 520,000 surviving wills and testaments registered in Scottish commissary courts and sheriff courts between 1500 and 1901. The index can be freely accessed at the companion commercial site, ***Scottish Documents.com***.

The ***National Union Catalog of Manuscript Collections*** *(NUCMC)* gateway operated by the Library of Congress, enables you to search literary and historical document, public record, and primary source material entries in the Research Library Group and OCLC databases cataloged after 1986. Participating members include libraries in the United Kingdom and the United States, as well as institutions around the world.

In addition to the lists of new publications described in the "Current Awareness Resources" section above, researchers will also find general Romantic, genre, and author-specific bibliographies that cover both current and retrospective scholarship, as well as bibliographies of primary materials. Nicholas Halmi's *A Selective Bibliography of British Romantic Poetry and Prose* features pertinent critical texts on general Romanticism organized in the following topical categories: literary and intellectual history, poetic forms, women writers, the Gothic, the novel, social and political context, sister arts, and reference works. In addition, Halmi offers recommended editions, biographical sources, and selected critical texts for twenty-eight Romantic-era authors, arranged chronologically from Burke to L. E. Landon. The critical bibliography is composed primarily of books, with some journal articles, that range in publication date from the 1930s through 2004. Some of the texts listed receive brief annotations; others link to electronic versions in the case of primary materials or to publishers' websites for more recent publications.

Adriana Craciun's ***Romanticism: Selective Bibliography*** plays a similar role by listing recommended texts by topic, including: traditional approaches and general introductions; modern critical reassessments; reactions to the Romantics; historical and political context; political debate of the 1790s and the French revolution; the novel; women and Romanticism; the Gothic; and sensibility. Craciun also provides selected critical books and journal articles for seventeen authors, and covers Dacre, Hays, and Dorothy Wordsworth who are not addressed by Halmi. Although there is some overlap, it is worthwhile to consult both bibliographies since they cover a few unique topics and authors, and also suggest different texts for topics in common. The resources are not annotated. Unfortunately, Craciun's bibliography has not been updated since 1998 and so it does not reflect recent scholarly contributions.

Although the *Romantic Circles Bibliography* now supercedes the online edition of the *Keats-Shelley Journal* "Current Bibliography," the earlier bibliographies can still be accessed at ***Keats-Shelley Journal Current Bibliography***, which continues to be hosted by *Romantic Circles*. Aiming to be comprehensive in its coverage, this annual bibliography of the Keats-Shelley Association of America presents annotated entries for monographs, collected essays, articles, reviews, and dissertations published during a specific year that are concerned with the later Romantic writers. The entries are arranged alphabetically by author into general and author-specific categories. Reviews are listed separately from the main bibliography, by reviewer, and are not annotated. Additional bibliographies are provided for works addressing Byron, Hazlitt, Leigh Hunt, Keats, Mary Shelley, and Percy Shelley and include hypertext links to related full-text sources if available. The complete bibliographies may be searched (1994–1999), or searches may be limited to either the reviews (1994–1999) or individual author bibliographies (1994/1998–1999). Note that works of general interest to Romanticists or those about the earlier Romantic writers are included in the bibliography, but usually are not annotated. Although the bibliography is no longer published online as a separate entity, the earlier bibliographies can be used to assess lines of critical inquiry for particular Romantic authors, and to identify reviews of those works. The print bibliography continues to be featured annually in the *Keats-Shelley Journal*. Since the online *Romantic Circles Bibliography* lacks the scope and annotations of the *KSJ* "Current Bibliography, you should supplement it with the annual print bibliography for more thorough coverage.

The University of Southern California's ***New Books in Nineteenth-Century British Studies*** used to be a viable resource that compiled works from multiple disciplines addressing British Romantic and Victorian periods. Since the bibliography was last updated in June 2002, however, it has ceased to be a useful current awareness tool. You can still consult the bibliography for information about books published from 1995 to 2000, as well as for the original reviews for selected works.

Drawn from the remarkable Corvey Library collection, the *Corvey Women Writers on the Web (cw³): An Electronic Guide to Literature 1796–1834* presents bibliographic information for 1,071 literary works by 417 Romantic-era women writers and related sources, including: "biographies, bibliographies, contemporary reviews and memoirs, images, synopses and keyword descriptions of texts, as well as new criticism and contextual material." Many of the titles in the collection are rare, and some are found only in the Corvey Library. The bibliography may be browsed by an alphabetical author index, or accessed through a detailed search form. For better-known authors, such as Charlotte Dacre or Joanna Baillie, the entries include title page images and transcribed contemporary reviews. For the majority of authors, however, (who tellingly wrote anonymously) just bibliographic citations are offered. Although very little critical or contextual material is currently available for these authors, look for such features to be added in the future.

Designed to facilitate the "reappraisal of the relationship between the Gothic and the Romantic," Douglass Thomson's site *Gothic Literature: What the Romantic Writers Read* provides an annotated compilation of Gothic works read by Blake, Wordsworth, Coleridge, Byron, Mary and Percy Shelley, and Keats. After introducing each list with a relevant excerpt from the author's own work, Thomson proceeds to note each title and give evidence for the work having been read, either by citing letters, contemporary reviews, critical and biographical works, or in some cases, his own conjecture. Apart from Lewis's *Castle Spectre* and Maturin's *Bertram, The Fatal Revenge: or, The Family of Montorio*, and *Manuel: A Tragedy*, Thomson focuses on works of Gothic fiction rather than drama and offers links to selected online Gothic texts and Coleridge's critical reviews within the bibliographies. An additional guide to online primary and critical resources for studying Gothic literature and a glossary of literary Gothic terms (from "ancestral curse" to "witches and witchcraft") further enhance this specialized bibliography.

An impressive endeavor, *Romantic Chronology* covers literary, political, and cultural events from 1785 to 1851, with select coverage of the seventeenth and eighteenth centuries. Each entry contains a date, a brief event description, and in some cases an assigned topic heading. Forty-six topics are currently traced by the chronology, which cover such issues as abolition, child labor, the Regency crisis, French revolution, colonialism, the Gothic, printing, Ireland, radicalism, and sensibility. A "Details" link for each entry leads you to further information, and, in many cases, to a selection of related Web resources, including any of the following: full-text poems, novels, essays, and critical articles; relevant journals; online lectures; encyclopedia entries; biographical information; and museum and National Trust sites. The chronology may be browsed by date or by the topic catalog; it may also be searched by specific date and keywords, person, or literary work mentioned in the event description. The collection of linked Web resources may also be searched separately. *Romantic Chronology* is edited by Alan Liu, at UC Santa Barbara and Laura Mandell, at Miami University. Special chronologies for Byron, Mary Shelley, and Percy Shelley are posted at the "Scholarly Resources" section of *Romantic Circles*; additional author chronologies can be identified from the *Voice of the Shuttle Romantics* list.

If you are in need of a concordance to a work by the canonical poets, the **Web Concordances and Workbooks**, created by R. J. C. Watt at the University of Dundee, features concordances to selected poems by Shelley published between 1816 and 1821, Coleridge's "The Ancyent Marinere," Keats's *Odes of 1819*, Blake's *Songs of Innocence and of Experience*, and Wordsworth's and Coleridge's *Lyrical Ballads* (1798). For each work, separate frames present an alphabetical wordlist, the concordance entries in their contextual lines, and the original source text. The concordance entries are hyperlinked so that when selected, the text frame scrolls to that part of the text from which the highlighted line is drawn. Unfortunately, only the Coleridge, Blake, and Wordsworth entries contain notes on the original source texts used in preparing the concordances. Additional workbooks for Coleridge, Keats, and Blake provide students with introductory material to the texts, and pose questions about specific words and themes to illustrate how the concordances can assist with literary analysis.

Seeking to provide an "atmospheric view" of the language of eighteenth-century sensibility, the **Dictionary of Sensibility** offers excerpts from selected primary texts to illustrate the various meanings of twenty-four key terms, including: benevolence, virtue, landscape, heart, sympathy, delicacy, sublime, fear, imagination, wit, spirit, melancholy, and taste. A brief introduction to each term discusses the ways in which the term was understood and used in the eighteenth century, and is followed by a list of illustrative literary selections. In turn, each text receives a critical commentary and related key terms are noted. For example, the term "virtue" is represented with excerpts from works by Diderot, Goldsmith, Gray, Hume, Inchbald, Kant, Lewis, Richardson, Rousseau, Mary Shelley, and others. Separate bibliographies of primary sources and critical works complete this engaging reference resource.

Cultural and Historical Resources

Andrews, William L., ed. *North American Slave Narratives*, 9 November 2004, at docsouth.unc.edu/neh/neh.html (accessed 21 November 2004).

Arnowitz, Mark. *British Abolition Movement*, at www.users.muohio.edu/mandellc/projects/aronowml (accessed 21 November 2004).

Censer, Jack R. and Lynn Hunt. *Liberty, Equality, Fraternity: Exploring the French Revolution*, at chnm.gmu.edu/revolution (accessed 21 November 2004).

COLLAGE, at collage.cityoflondon.gov.uk/ (accessed 21 November 2004).

Hacken, Richard. *EuroDocs: Primary Historical Documents from Western Europe: United Kingdom*, September 2004, at www.lib.byu.edu/~rdh/eurodocs/uk.html (accessed 21 November 2004).

Halsall, Paul. *Internet Modern History Sourcebook*, 22 September 2001, at www.fordham.edu/halsall/mod/modsbook.html (accessed 21 November 2004).

Humbul Humanities Hub, 18 November 2004, at www.humbul.ac.uk/ (accessed 21 November 2004).

Images of England, at www.imagesofengland.org.uk/ (accessed 21 November 2004).

Maginnis, Tara. *Costumer's Manifesto: Regency and Empire Fashion Costume Links*, at www.costumes.org/history/100pages/regencylinks.htm (accessed 3 December 2004).

Many cultural and historical websites can be used to place Romantic-era literature in its broader social context. *Voice of the Shuttle: Romantics*, as mentioned above, presents sites on topics as diverse as the French revolution, slavery and abolition, Regency portraits and fashion, and natural history. You can also check other *Voice of the Shuttle* subject categories for pertinent sites, such as history, philosophy, art history, music, religious studies, politics, and science categories. The British gateway **Humbul Humanities Hub** is another good source for identifying key academic resources for a particular subject. The following sites were selected to show the range of contextual Romantics resources available.

EuroDocs: Primary Historical Documents from Western Europe: United Kingdom provides an annotated guide to chronologically arranged English, Scottish, and Welsh document Web resources, with separate sections for historical document collections, legal and governmental documents, and documents related to regional, local, and family history. Note that the links are to documents that have been transcribed, reproduced as facsimiles, or translated. Scholars of Romantic-era literature will find relevant resources in the "1689–1815" and "1816–1918" categories on such topics as Parliamentary reform, the Corn Laws, history of the workhouse, the Peterloo Massacre, and Scottish statistical accounts. *EuroDocs* is maintained by Richard Hacken, European Studies Bibliographer, Brigham Young University.

Liberty, Equality, Fraternity: Exploring the French Revolution serves a dual purpose as both an introduction to the French revolution and an archive of more than six hundred primary texts, images, songs, and maps. Ten essays examine the major themes of the revolution, including social causes, the monarchy, the Enlightenment and human rights, women, slavery and the Haitian revolution, and Napoleon. Illustrative primary documents are integrated into each essay with linked icons to the left of the relevant text. For example, the essay "War, Terror, and Resistance" contains a document on the expulsion of the Girondins, political cartoons and engravings of the Terror, a newspaper account of Marie Antoinette's execution, and a funeral hymn for General Hoche, as well as many other sources. Two additional essays discuss how to read an image critically, and present an overview of revolutionary songs and hymns. In order to be accessible to students, the archive's textual documents have been translated into English; scholars interested in the original text can consult the citation to identify the source document. The archive may be searched by keyword or selected topic (e.g., counterrevolution, economic conditions, nobility, peasants, public opinion, sans-culottes, war), or browsed alphabetically by resource category (e.g., texts, images, maps, songs). Additional features include a timeline of key events, and a glossary. *Liberty, Equality, Fraternity*, edited by Lynn Hunt (UCLA) and Jack Censer (George Mason University), is a collaborative project between the Center for History and Media (GMU) and the American Social History Project (CUNY).

Part of the Documenting the South project at University of North Carolina, Chapel Hill, ***North American Slave Narratives*** is an ongoing bibliography that aims to present a complete list of North American autobiographical, biographical, and fictionalized slave and ex-slave narratives of the eighteenth, nineteenth, and early twentieth centuries published in English. The collection covers broadsides, pamphlets, and books, and can be accessed by either an alphabetical or chronological arrangement. Almost all of the works that are extant and no longer under copyright are presented in full-text HTML and XML/TEI versions. In addition, William L. Andrews, the bibliography's creator, offers an

introduction to the historical context of slavery and to the literary contexts of slave and ex-slave narratives.

The **British Abolition Movement**, originally designed as a student
project, provides a concise historical overview of British attempts to
abolish both the slave trade and slavery, and also offers selected complementary art and literary materials. Excerpts from authors such as
Wordsworth, Cowper, Wilberforce, Blake, Southey, Cuguano, More,
Opie, and Equiano illustrate the ways in which anti-slavery sentiments
were portrayed in poetry, drama, fiction, and prose literature of the late
eighteenth and early nineteenth centuries. The site also features related
images by Blake and others, and concludes with a brief bibliography.

Compiled by Paul Halsall at Fordham University, the **Internet
Modern History Sourcebook** presents source texts and links to external
texts in order to support the needs of teachers and undergraduates in
college history survey courses. To meet this goal, the *Sourcebook* offers a range of texts, including political, cultural, religious, and scientific documents. The "Romanticism" section covers Romantic philosophy, art, and literature. You may also want to review the documents in
other pertinent sections, including nineteenth century Britain, France,
and Germany; nationalism, liberalism, the French revolution; Industrial
revolution; and American independence.

COLLAGE, Corporation of London Library & Art Gallery Electronic, is a searchable image database of twenty thousand prints, drawings, maps, paintings, sculptures, and watercolors selected from the
Guildhall Library and Guildhall Art Gallery London collections. Most
of the images in the collection are concerned with London topography
and life from 1550 to 1990, however, images about the adjoining counties are included as well. An advanced search feature enables you to
retrieve images by date range, keyword, artist/engraver/publisher, particular collection, or medium; thus, for example, you can search for
engravings containing children completed between 1780 and 1830. The
collection may also be browsed by general subject categories, including: abstract ideas, archaeology, architecture, history, leisure, military,
natural world, politics, religion, society, and industry; or by specific
categories, such as: advertisement, caricature, crowd scene, satire, and
seascape. Each image is accompanied by a textual description, and is
linked to related subject headings. *COLLAGE* is an ongoing project that
aims, over time, to add more images from the Guildhall's main collection.

Produced by English Heritage, *Images of England* features several
thousand digital photographs of English Heritage listed buildings (registered for their architectural or historical importance) and will eventu-
ally include photographs of all 370,000 currently listed buildings. A

"Quick Search" option enables you to search for images either by county, building type, or time period, or by associated person. Try a search for buildings from the Georgian/Hanovarian (1714–1837) period, or buildings associated with Wordsworth, Coleridge, Byron, or Keats. Each photograph is accompanied by an architectural description of the building, and some make note of the building's particular historical significance. To take advantage of the "Standard" and "Advanced" detailed search functions requires free registration.

Tara Maginnis, at the University of Alaska, Fairbanks, has compiled a directory of Romantic-era costume resources for the *Costumer's Manifesto: Regency and Empire Fashion Costume Links* page. Here you'll find links to general costume sites for the time period, and resources specifically for women's, men's, and children's dress and accessories, as well as Western European traditional regional dress sources, costume patterns, and related period information. In addition, Maginnis offers scanned fashion plates from *Ackermann's Repository of Arts*, the *Ladies Pocket Magazine*, and other contemporary English, French, German, Russian, and American periodicals. Other features include relevant paintings, selected photographs from museum costume collections, and a bibliography of nineteenth-century costume books.

Conclusion

These are the primary sources and a sample of auxiliary websites available for Romantic-era studies at the time of publication. Since the Web is always changing, inevitably some of the resources listed here may disappear or might no longer be current; likewise new projects devoted to Romantic studies will be developed. Although you can rely on *Romantic Circles* and *Voice of the Shuttle* to keep you informed of most changes in the field, nevertheless you also will need to make your own assessment of a website's reliability and relevance. Remember that the Web is useful as a complementary tool. You still will have to use traditional print materials and online databases. Keep in mind, however, that the Web can provide ready access to works previously only available on microfilm or in special collections, and that it can be your link to the Romantic literature community through online bibliographies, journals, and association sites. Enjoy exploring the various ways outlined in this chapter that the Web can contribute to your research.

Chapter 11
Researching a Thorny Problem

This day is published, handsomely printed in 8 vols. 8vo. price 11.4s.
boards, the third edition of Self-Control. A Novel.

> His warfare is within. There unfatigued,
> His fervent spirit labours. There he fights,
> And there obtains fresh triumphs o'er himself,
> And never-withering wreaths; compared with which
> The laurels that a Caesar reaps are weeds. Cowper.

Printed for Longman, Hurst, Rees, Orme, and Brown, Paternoster-
row; and Manners and Miller, Edinburgh.

"Advertisement,"
The Times, September 12, 1811, Issue 8397, p. 2, col. A

Over the course of this book we have discussed a variety of resources
and best practices for researching questions on Romantic-era literature
and literary figures. Unfortunately, there may be questions for which
there are no clear answers, and which will require the scholar to try a
variety of approaches to solve the problem. Discovering statistics about
publication runs for specific titles is one such question. A student, for
example, who wished to find quantitative data to confirm the anecdotal
evidence that Mary Brunton, who is little known today, was at least as
popular an author as Jane Austen at the beginning of the nineteenth
century would need to use most of the techniques discussed in previous
chapters to accomplish this goal. In the end, the student might not find
anything conclusive, but this question provides us with the opportunity
to review a variety of search techniques discussed in this volume. Mary
Brunton's first novel *Self-Control* was originally published in 1811 by
Longman, and went to a third edition by 1812. *Sense and Sensibility*
was published in 1811 by T. Egerton. What steps would a scholar take
to compare the sales and print runs of these two novels and which resources would prove most valuable for finding this information?

At present, no single source exists which answers the research question posed. What are the best practices to follow? The first step is to brainstorm ideas and identify types of published sources which might be useful, such as books or articles about the publishing history of the author, biographies, letters, diaries, publisher records, and archives. Which of the resources discussed in this volume might be helpful? Are there any directories which may have clues? Are there any biographies about the author? Are there any standard biographical sources which may have information? Have any of the author's letters or diaries been published? Would book reviews prove useful? How about advertisements for new printings? Have standard editions been published which may have information about publication history? What about other secondary research done on the author? Does a scholarly website for the author exist? Does a listserv exist for the author or the time period where a query can be posted for help from other scholars of the author or the literary period? Is there an expert on the author who you can contact? What types of primary source materials might prove useful? Are there any archives for the publisher or for the author?

The purpose of this chapter is not to find the information sought, but to develop a research plan for doing so, taking into account all of the above questions. The answer may be in one of the sources discovered, or in none of them. As reference librarians, the following are the steps we would recommend scholars take to discover if the information sought exists. If it does not, then the scholar will need to make some assumptions based upon any clues, including the anecdotal, found during the process. The following will provide guidance about how to research the publishing history for a literary work.

Although no single reference work exists which provides definitive data on publication numbers, William St Clair has compiled statistics about various aspects of the reading public, from demographics to print runs in the appendices of his study, *The Reading Nation in the Romantic Period*. These appendices, the product of St Clair's research into the culture of reading during the Romantic era, will be valuable for any researcher in need of data about publishing during this time. Researchers interested in the methods used to compile these data must read his valuable Chapter 1, "Reading and It's Consequences," in which he discusses some of his strategies for collecting the data—strategies others interested in this type of research can use as a model. Even more important for the purpose of this book is his statement:

> Since they provide information not previously available or consolidated, the appendices are therefore a resource which can be used for helping to answer questions other than those addressed in the present study. Tabular presentation, although seldom used in traditional liter-

ary history, has many advantages. It enables factual and statistical
material to be presented in non-hierarchical form in ways which reveal long-term historical developments; it provides opportunities for
both my empirical foundation and my provisional results to be assessed, added to, replicated, or modified.[1]

The author intends for the data to be assessed and used by other
scholars, and he is contemplating making his database available as a
Web publication, which would allow for additions and changes.[2] The
database is not currently available to the public, so scholars should
search to see if the status has changed in the future. Because the thirteen appendices provide an invaluable statistical portrait of the demographics of the reading public and publishing industry from the sixteenth century through the nineteenth century, the descriptive titles are
worth listing: 1) Markets, book production, prices, and print runs;
2) Intellectual property and textual controls. Custom, law and practice;
3) Intellectual property. Rights of authors and performers, anthologies
and abridgements; 4) Intellectual property. Popular literature, England;
5) Book costs, prices, and margins. Romantic period and later; 6) The
old canon; 7) Romantic period. Book production arranged by literary
genre; 8) Periodicals; 9) Romantic period. Authors and texts. Publishing histories, prices, print runs, and sales; 10) Libraries and reading
societies; 11) Pirate and radical publishers and publications; 12) Shakespeare; and 13) The romantic poets in Victorian times. At this time, the
volume is unique in the amount of information compiled to provide the
Romantic scholar with a foundation for understanding the literary publishing world of the Romantic era.

St Clair's book was released just as we were completing this chapter, but the steps we took to try to solve this problem would still be required since Brunton is not included in Appendix 9, which lists known
data about prices, print runs, and reprints during the Romantic era. Jane
Austen is included, however, and because the search is a comparative
one between Brunton and Austen, the figures on the latter could shed
some light on the former. St Clair provides the data he discovered researching in secondary sources, published letters, and archival research
which give us as complete an overview of Austen's print runs and sales
figures as is currently available. The print run data on the first three
runs of *Sense and Sensibility*, in 1811, 1813, and 1815, is unavailable,
but the footnotes tell us that for "a first novel published on commission,
the records noted in appendix 5 and elsewhere suggest that a print run
of 500 or 750 was more normal" than the 750 to 1,000 quoted in Austen's letters.[3] Print runs for the reissues done from the 1830s to the
1850s were: 3000 copies in 1832, 1,000 copies in 1837, 1,000 copies in
1846, and 750 copies in 1853. In 1815, St Clair's sources estimate that

2,000 copies of *Emma* were printed because 1,250 copies were sold in the first year, 565 copies still available in 1818, and 535 copies remaindered in 1820—a typical print run which would account for these numbers would have been 2,000. *Mansfield Park*, reissued in 1816, had a print run of 750, with 489 copies remaindered in 1820. If one can argue that comparable numbers of copies were published for each novel for the first edition, then the number of editions could be another point of comparison, for *Self-Control* went to three editions in 1811 while the second edition of *Sense and Sensibility* was not published until 1813. How much this had to do with the popularity of the authors, or with the management of sales by the publishers, cannot be answered through statistics alone—further research into the practices of each publisher may be required to shed light on how first-time authors were promoted and their novels distributed. Although at present the goal is to discover, if possible, data to support the hypothesis that Brunton was indeed equally popular, the researcher should keep aware of the role the publisher played in the success of each author.

Altogether, St Clair provides the publishing data he was able to discover on fifty-four authors, including Blake, Burney, Burns, Byron, Edgeworth, Godwin, Hazlitt, Keats, Lamb, Landon, Maturin, More, Opie, Paine, Porter, Radcliffe, Scott, Mary Shelley, Percy Shelley, Smith, Southey, Wollstonecraft, and Wordsworth. Although no figures for Brunton's novel *Self-Control* were included, information about a variety of authors provides the researcher with known facts, such as standard print runs for first time authors. In addition, the scholar has also been given hints how to make educated guesses about the number of copies in a print run, such as approximate copies of *Emma* in 1815, which differed because Austen had previously been published. The data supplied by St Clair about typical print runs for first novels for a variety of authors may prove exceptionally useful if no solid figures about Brunton can be found. In addition, St Clair has extensive notes which cite the original sources, which should be consulted for the authors he covers. Because our question seeks to compare Brunton and Austen, it would be a valuable step to use the books and articles cited in his notes to see if, in the original sources, women authors who were contemporaries of Austen were discussed.

Because Brunton isn't included in St Clair's study, the scholar needs to try a variety of approaches. The most logical initial search would be to search for books and articles about the publishing history of the author. Search the local library catalog and union catalogs, *MLAIB* and *ABELL*, using keywords to find books and articles on the history of *Self-Control*, or about the author and the publisher. If nothing is found, the search could be broadened to search for books about authors and publishers in the eighteenth and nineteenth centuries, or in the Romantic era, or about publishers and women and the Romantic era. The first two are more precise searches which will either succeed or fail at the point of searching the catalog or index, whereas the last suggestion will retrieve books and articles, which may or may not include Brunton, something that can only be determined through the time-consuming process of examining each book or article. This last step could wait until some of the following strategies are attempted.

Another potential avenue to pursue would be biographies or published letters or diaries of the author, or published histories or correspondence of the publisher, Longman. If no biography of the author exists, or if the biography does not have the information, then try looking for the author's published letters and diaries to see if any references to book sales or print runs have been mentioned. Are there any letters to or from the publisher? Is there reference to a contract between the author and the publisher? It is best to start with the author because generally the relationship between the author and the publisher will be mentioned in some form, while secondary sources on publishers may not address the issues surrounding an individual author. In books about the history of the publisher, examine the index and the list of tables to see if there is information about the author or novel, or if the standard numbers for print runs of first novels have been listed, or if there is information about contracts or references to correspondence with authors. In any of the biographies, histories, diaries, or collections of correspondence, note whether there are any references to archives which may be consulted if the information desired cannot be found in secondary sources. In archives you may be able to find a contract or ledger books of sales and, if you can verify through these secondary sources that such materials exist, you will have much more confidence about pursuing a plan to correspond with the archivist and, if possible, visit the archives.

To find biographies, histories, diaries, and correspondence, search the library catalog and union catalogs for books. For example, do a keyword search on *brunton and (letter* or correspondence)* and on *longman and (letter* or correspondence)* to find specific categories of published materials. A biographical sketch in a reference work may prove useful. Brunton has an entry in the *Oxford Dictionary of National Biography*, which lists the dates of her novels, to whom her book was dedicated, and publishing information which may prove useful: "A seven-volume edition, *The works of Mary Brunton*, came out in 1820. *Self-Control* and *Discipline* were republished in Colburn and Bentley's Standard Novels in 1832, and in cheap editions in 1837 and 1852, an index to their lasting success. A French translation of *Self-Control* ap-

peared in Paris in 1829."[4] We discover that Brunton died of fever in
1818 after giving birth, and that her husband published a memoir of her
in 1819, which may be a source to hunt down in case he discussed the
publishing of her novels. A brief bibliography provides references to
other sources, and her archives are listed under her maiden name Balfour in the Orkney Archives. Other dictionaries or companions which
could prove useful to find concise information about an author, publisher, or literary work include the *Dictionary of Literary Biography*,
the *Oxford Companion to English Literature*, and the *Cambridge Companion to English Literature*. Consult Chapter 2 for more recommendations.

Another approach to finding either statistical or anecdotal information would be to find information about the novel. Basic publishing
information, including title, date of publication, publisher, reprint dates,
and references to contemporary reviews, can be found in the reference
book *The English Novel 1770–1829: A Bibliographic Survey of Prose
Fiction Published in the British Isles*, discussed in Chapters 4 and 6.
The entry on *Self-Control* provides us with this information:

> 1811:25 [BRUNTON, Mary].
> SELF-CONTROL: A NOVEL
> Edinburgh: Printed by George Ramsay & Co. for Manners and
> Miller; and Longman, Hurst, Rees, Orme, and Brown, Lon-
> don, 1811.
> I x, 388p; II 468p. 8vo. 21s (ECB); 24s (ER, 3rd edn., QR,
> 2nd edn).
> ER 18:517 (Aug 1811) [for 3rd edn.]; QR 5:537 (May 1811)
> [for 2nd edn.] WSW I:177.
> BL 1608/742; ECB 526; NSTC B5017 (BI C, E, O).
> Notes. Dedication to Miss Joanna Baillie, dated Jan 1811.
> Further edns: 2nd edn. 1811 (NSTC); 3rd ed. 1811 (NSTC);
> 4th edn. 1812 (Corvey), CME 3-628-48640-8; London 1832
> (NSTC); 1844 (NSTC); [at least 2 more edns to 1850]; New
> York 1811 (NUC); French trans., 1829 [as *Laure Montreville,
> ou l'empire sur soi-meme* (BN)].[5]

Using the Introduction to learn how to read this highly abbreviated record, we can interpret the acronyms, dates, and numbers in the entry.
The *English Catalog of Books* (*ECB*) and the *Nineteenth-Century
Short-Title Catalogue* (*NSTC*) both provide information about publication dates of new editions. The periodicals *Edinburgh Review* and
Quarterly Review were sources of information about prices of the third
and second editions respectively, and Ward's *Literary Reviews in Brit-*

ish Periodicals, 1798–1820, Volume I, has a list of reviews on page 177. The edition examined was in the British Library, shelfmark 1608/742, and other library holdings are included in the *ECB* and *NSTC*. From this source, we have discovered the names of the printers, the number of editions and their publication dates, and a source for book reviews.

Although it is doubtful book reviews about Brunton's novel listed in *The English Novel 1770–1829* and Ward's *Literary Reviews* would have information about sales or print runs, articles about the novel published for later reprints may make anecdotal references to the popularity of the novel when originally published. Was *Self-Control* published in the United States? The entry above indicates that the *National Union Catalog* (*NUC*) listed it was published in 1811 in New York. Would book reviews in American periodicals give us any insights into the publishing history of this novel? How does a scholar find review articles in American periodicals? If there is a bibliography about the author, a list of contemporary reviews or assessments may be included. *Poole's*, discussed in Chapter 7, indexes nearly four hundred American and forty-four British periodicals from 1802 to 1906. Would articles published about the novel a couple of decades later, or throughout the Victorian era prove useful? Perhaps, and therefore locating those articles would be important. *Poole's*, again, could provide references to potential articles. Although the reviews or periodical articles may not provide actual data about the book, these could be good sources of anecdotal information about its popularity at the time it was published, or, articles published later in the century, could provide a historic view of the novel.

A less direct route to the information sought, and a time consuming one, would be the examination of criticism about the author. But, unless the author of the book or article took the time to establish the numbers in a print run or the sales figures of the novel, this will probably not prove to be a worthwhile avenue of exploration. However, a careful scholar always keeps an eye out for any clues such secondary research may provide.

In the end, perhaps there are no secondary sources to help answer the question, so the scholar then needs to turn to primary source materials. We know Brunton's works are in the Orkney Archives under Balfour, her maiden name, from the *Oxford Dictionary of National Biography* entry. If references to an archive had not been found, however, the scholar would then have searched the *National Register of Archives* database under both her married and maiden names, or search for family papers in archives rather than only searching by her name. Once an archive is identified, a search for the archive on the Web may provide a link to information about the archive, including contact information. In some cases it is possible to search the finding aid for the archives online.

In Chapter 8 we discussed microfilm collections and digitization projects which provide access to primary source materials. To find the former, search *WorldCat* for microform collections. For example, do a keyword search on *longman and publishers* and limit the format to *microform* to discover that the *Archives of the House of Longman, 1794–1914* has been published by Chadwyck-Healey as part of the series *British Publishers Archives on Microfilm.* St Clair cautions that publisher data can be very sketchy, so this avenue of exploration may prove fruitless, but the archival material on microfilm usually allows the scholar to explore primary source material without traveling. At present no Web-based digital archives for Longman or Brunton exist.

At the very least a scholar could look for advertisements to make a case for the anecdotal popularity of a novel, a process which could prove time consuming. However, if access to the print, microfilm, or digital versions of newspapers or periodicals exists, it may be interesting to see if the novel is mentioned and if any reference to its popularity included in the advertisement. For example, a search on *Self-Control* (not the author) in *Times of London Digital Archives* found the advertisement we quoted at the beginning of this chapter. According to *The English Novel 1770–1829*, there are references to the advertisements in the *Edinburgh Review* in August 1811 for the third edition and in the *Quarterly Review* in May 1811 for the second edition.[6]

When no reference tool exists which provides an answer to a question, a reference librarian will help guide your search by recommending a broad range of sources to consult. Dead ends can be frustrating, especially because you don't know when to stop looking and determine that the definitive answer doesn't exist, and that you need to make a best guess about the answer with the available information. When in doubt, talk to a reference librarian about your search strategies and sources examined to make sure you didn't forget anything, and ask others in your field for help or advice. Even though your research project is unique, you are not alone; there are librarians and colleagues who can provide you with assistance and advice.

Conclusion

Throughout this volume we have recommended the best approaches for researching literary topics concerning the Romantic era. Although print sources and Web pages may be updated and revised, search engine interfaces modified, and new digital projects undertaken, the basic skills for conducting effective research remain constant. As we conclude this volume we are aware that there are many projects underway which will provide alternative access to some of the resources we recommend. That is the nature of research in the twenty-first century. The Romantic scholar must be prepared for change. In this volume we cannot predict everything that will be available, but we can tell scholars, whether the information sought was published in 1775 or 2004, technology and the Web are increasingly providing access to primary and secondary source materials available online. This is the exciting part of research. Because of new online resources, the Romantic scholar should continue to consult with reference librarians for recommendations. By establishing good research skills and understanding the best practices for conducting research covered in this volume, the scholar can face the constant change and new resources with confidence.

Notes

1. St Clair, William. *The Reading Nation in the Romantic Period.* Cambridge: Cambridge University Press, 2004, 17.

2. St Clair, *The Reading Nation*, 17.

3. St Clair, *The Reading Nation*, 578.

4. Bour, Isabelle. "Mary Brunton," in *Oxford Dictionary of National Biography* (New York: Oxford University Press, 2004), 8:368–369.

5. Garside, Peter, James Raven, and Rainer Schöwerlin. *The English Novel 1770–1829: A Bibliographic Survey of Prose Fiction Published in the British Isles, vol. 2.* (New York: Oxford University Press, 2000), 341.

6. Garside, *The English Novel*, 341.

Appendix
Resources in Related Disciplines

The following is a highly selective list of sources to consult when researching within other disciplines. These recommendations are meant as starting points. In some cases, such as *Historical Dictionary of London* and *Women Playwrights in England, Ireland, and Scotland, 1660–1823*, the sources are included because they are valuable for Romantic scholars, but each also serves to illustrate types of more specialized and potentially useful sources available. We recommend reading through all the sources in this section to help you realize that each discipline has the conventional tools (e.g., dictionaries, encyclopedias, indexes, bibliographies) as well as unique reference tools, just as we do in literature. Browse the reference shelves within the discipline of interest to you for other titles and types of reference sources which may prove valuable in your research.

Use the same skills and practices discussed in this volume when using any reference tool. Remember, whatever the discipline, search the library catalog to find books on the topic. Consult with your reference librarian for additional suggestions.

Both *Encyclopedia of the Romantic Era* and *An Oxford Companion to the Romantic Age: British Culture 1776–1832*, discussed in Chapter 2, provide selected bibliographies for further reading within different aspects of life in the Romantic era, including art, theater, science, medicine, politics, and economics. Consult both Marcuse and Harner, discussed in Chapter 2, for additional relevant research tools in other disciplines and recommended background reading. In the following, the citations under "Guides" will provide you with sources which list the important and specialized research tools available in other disciplines.

General

Guides

Balay, Robert, ed. *Guide to Reference Books*. 11th ed. Chicago: American Library Association, 1996.
The standard guide to general and specialized references sources in all disciplines. Individual branches of study and individual disciplines have their own guides to research sources (see "Guides" in the different sections below), but the Balay and Walford guides listed here are essential tools which reference librarians consult for guidance.

Blazek, Ron and Elizabeth Aversa. *The Humanities: A Selective Guide to Information Resources*. 5th ed. Englewood, CO: Libraries Unlimited, 2000.
Lists important sources and provides helpful evaluative annotations for print and electronic research tools in the general humanities, philosophy, religion, visual arts, performing arts, and languages and literatures.

Walford's Guide to Reference Material. 8th ed. 3 vols. London: Library Association, 1999–.
The British standard version of *Guide to Reference Books*. Volume 1: *Science and Technology*, Volume 2: *Social and Historical Sciences, Philosophy and Religion*, and Volume 3: *Generalia, Language and Literature, The Arts*. The 8th edition of volume 3 has not yet been published.

Indexes and Bibliographies

Academic Search Premier. Birmingham, AL: Ebsco. search.epnet .com/.
An interdisciplinary article database indexing nearly 4,700 general and scholarly journals. Includes full text of articles when available.

Dissertation Abstracts International. Ann Arbor, MI: University Microfilms International. Available online at www.umi.com/ dissertations/.
Both *MLAIB* and *ABELL* (see Chapter 4) index dissertations on literary topics, but coverage is limited to the period of time covered in each and the records don't have abstracts. Search *DAI* to supplement *MLAIB* and *ABELL* and to find abstracts for the dissertations citations found in those two resources, and search *DAI* for dissertations from other disciplines.

Expanded Academic ASAP. Farmington Hills, MI: Thomson Gale.
infotrac.galegroup.com/.
Although similar in scope to *Academic Search Premier* in that it is interdisciplinary, it includes both scholarly and general periodicals, and it provides full text of articles when available, the coverage of the two databases and the full-text content available online does differ, so it is valuable to search both if possible.

Art

Dictionaries, Encyclopedias, and Handbooks

Brigstocke, Hugh, ed. *The Oxford Companion to Western Art*. New York: Oxford University Press, 2001.
Entries include biographical sketches of individuals involved with and definitions and histories of words related to Western art. Selected longer entries provide background and context for artists, art movements, and patronage and collecting. Excludes architecture and non-Western subjects.

Chilvers, Ian, ed. *The Oxford Dictionary of Art*. 3rd ed. New York: Oxford University Press, 2004.
Focuses primarily on definitions for Western European art, including painting, sculpture, printmaking, and drawing from antiquity through the present. Includes biographical sketches.

Turner, Jane, ed. *The Dictionary of Art*. New York: Grove, 1996. Available online at www.groveart.com/.
The standard, scholarly dictionary for art and art history. Entries are lengthy and signed, with bibliographies. For Romantic scholars without access to the full dictionary, either in print or online, extracted articles have been collected in *The Grove Dictionary of Art: From Renaissance to Impressionism*, edited by Jane Turner (New York: St. Martin's Press, 2000).

Guides

Arntzen, Etta and Robert Rainwater. *Guide to the Literature of Art History*. Chicago: American Library Association, 1980.
Marmor, Max and Alex Ross, eds. *Guide to the Literature of Art History 2*. Chicago: American Library Association, 2005.
GLAH and *GLAH2* are essential annotated guides to reference works for art history research, including bibliographies, dictionaries, encyclo-

pedias, histories and handbooks, architecture, sculpture, drawings, paintings, prints, photography, and decorative and applied arts (subdivided by medium). Sections include geographic subdivisions, including Great Britain and Ireland. International in scope, but with an emphasis on Western language resources.

Jones, Lois Swan. *Art Information: Research Methods and Resources.* 3rd ed. Dubuque, IA: Kendall/Hunt, 1990.
A guide to research methods within the discipline of art and art history, and an annotated bibliography of available research tools.

Jones, Lois Swan. *Art Information and the Internet: How to Find It, How to Use It.* Phoenix, AZ: Oryx Press, 1999.
A guide to searching for art information on the Internet and to websites valuable for art and art history research.

Indexes and Bibliographies

Art Index. New York: H. W. Wilson. Available online through various vendors.
Indexes over 450 art periodicals, including art history, architectural history, painting, sculpture, and decorative arts from around the world. If your library subscribes to this index, be aware there are three versions: *Art Index* (1984–present), *Art Abstracts* (1984–present), and *Art Index Retrospective* (1929–1983).

BHA: Bibliography of the History of Art. Santa Monica, CA: J. Paul Getty Trust, Getty Art History Program. Available online at www.rlg.org/.
Much more international in scope than *Art Index*, this source provides indexing to and summaries for books, dissertations, exhibition catalogs, and over 4,000 periodicals covering European and American (post-European arrival) visual arts from antiquity to the present. *BHA* continues *RILA: International Repertory of the Literature of Art* (1975–1989). The online version provides access to both *BHA* and *RILA*.

Historical Sources

Eitner, Lorenz, comp. *Neoclassicism and Romanticism, 1750–1850: Sources and Documents.* 2 vols. Englewood Cliffs, NJ: Prentice-Hall, 1970.
Excerpts from important texts, including translations, about art during the Enlightenment, Romanticism, and early Victorian. Includes writ-

ings by Goethe, Schelling, Constable, and Turner, and even short excerpts of testimonies by artists given to members the House of Commons committee debating the purchase of the Elgin Marbles from Lord Elgin.

Historical Atlases

Cunliffe, Barry, Robert Bartlett, John Morrill, Asa Briggs, and Joanna Bourke, eds. *The Penguin Atlas of British and Irish History: From Earliest Times to the Present Day*. New York: Penguin, 2002.
Using overview and small-scale colored maps, photographs, illustrations, and essays, this atlas explores British and Irish history in five chronological periods: ancient, medieval, early modern, nineteenth century, and modern. Thematic sections within these periods focus on narrower subjects, such as "Enlightenment Edinburgh," "The 18th-Century Empire," and "The Napoleonic Wars." Includes a detailed chronological table, rulers of Britain and Ireland, and a bibliography.

Gilbert, Martin. *Atlas of British History*. 2nd ed. New York: Oxford University Press, 1993.
This atlas features 114 black and white, thematic maps arranged chronologically from 50 B.C. to 1994. Romantic-era maps address agriculture, industry, transport, British expansion in India, wars against France, Napoleon, and the United States, and the British Empire in 1820.

History

Dictionaries, Encyclopedias, and Companions

Arnold-Baker, Charles. *The Companion to British History*. 2nd ed. New York: Routledge, 2001.
This hefty encyclopedia provides entries on all aspects of English, Scottish, Welsh, and Irish history, including their relationships with other countries, from 55 B.C. to 2000. Three appendices: "English Regnal Years"; "Selected Warlike Events"; and "Genealogies and Diagrams."

Cannon, John, ed. *The Oxford Companion to British History*. Rev ed. New York: Oxford University Press, 2002.
Like other Oxford companions, this source presents brief entries for people, places, institutions, events, and concepts of English, Irish, Welsh, and Scottish history. An emphasis on "local history" is illus-

trated by entries for counties, provinces, ancient kingdoms, modern regions, and important towns (vii). Includes maps, genealogies, and a subject index.

Connolly, S. J., ed. *The Oxford Companion to Irish History*. 2nd ed. New York: Oxford University Press, 2002.
This companion covers Irish individuals (none living), events, and institutions throughout the twentieth century. The second edition expands the treatment of Irish prehistory, the arts, and literary figures. Includes historical maps and a subject index.

Hornblower, Simon and Antony Spawforth. *The Oxford Classical Dictionary*. 3rd rev. ed. New York: Oxford University Press, 2003.
A standard reference work for ancient Greek and Roman history and culture. The third edition is more interdisciplinary; introduces and expands coverage of ancient sexuality, the history of women, and the Near Eastern world; and includes more thematic entries. Use this source for references to classical historical and mythological figures and events.

Loades, David, ed. *Reader's Guide to British History*. 2 vols. New York: Fitzroy Deaborn, 2003.
This guide aims to introduce readers to recommended works of secondary scholarship, in order to trace the "main themes, changes, [and] controversies in interpretation and presentation" (vii) in the history of the British Isles from the earliest times to the present, excluding the republic of Ireland since 1922. Beginning with a bibliography, each entry then proceeds to discuss the selected works within the context of the topic. Sample topics related to the Romantic era include "Radicalism in Politics, later 18th and 19th centuries," poetry and fiction of the period, and essays on the slave trade and anti-slavery movement. See the complete list of thematic topics for the Modern period, 1783–1914 (xxii-iii). Includes alphabetical and thematic lists of entries, as well as a comprehensive bibliography.

Lynch, Michael, ed. *The Oxford Companion to Scottish History*. New York: Oxford University Press, 2001.
This Oxford companion provides entries on the following themes and elements of Scottish history: events; biographies; politics; government; economic life; social life; religion; peoples and families; demographics; physical environment and material culture; places; culture; relations with Britain, Ireland, Europe, and the world; ethnographies; and historians, historical sources, and heritage. See, for example, the essay on

Scottish culture during the Enlightenment (1660–1843), which discusses philosophy, art, language, literature, the novel, music, and medicine.

Newman, Gerald, ed. *Britain in the Hanoverian Age, 1714–1837: An Encyclopedia.* New York: Garland, 1997.
Featuring more than 1,000 articles, this encyclopedia presents information about Hanoverian British historical events, religion, government, politics, military, wars, empire, cities, business, economics, transportation, labor and trades, science, thought and scholarship, professions, education, general social phenomena (e.g., adultery, childrearing, working conditions, smallpox, wigs), pastimes and amusements, literature, arts, styles and trends, and women, as well as entries on individuals and family groups.

Panton, Kenneth J. *Historical Dictionary of London.* Lanham, MD: Scarecrow Press, 2001.
Following an introductory overview of London's history, the dictionary presents brief entries on "the people, institutions, political forces, economic trends, and social values that gave the metropolitan area its shape and focus" (xiii), as well as entries for the city's districts (e.g., boroughs, hamlets, suburbs). Additional maps, chronologies, London government contact information, organization Web addresses, and an extensive bibliography complete this handy reference work.

Williams, Neville. *Chronology of World History, vol. 3, 1776–1900, The Changing World.* Santa Barbara, CA: ABC-CLIO, 1999.
A good general chronology. Brief entries covering annual events in politics, government, economics, science, technology, medicine, arts, education, culture, religion, sports, and births and deaths. For more detailed entries about chronological developments in science, consult that section of this appendix.

Guides

Fritze, Ronald H., Brian E. Coutts, and Louis A. Vyhnanek. *Reference Sources in History: An Introductory Guide.* 2nd ed. Santa Barbara, CA: ABC–CLIO, 2004.
Arranged in fourteen chapters by type of resource, this guide provides annotations for 930 print and electronic historical reference works, covering all time periods and geographical areas. Resources discussed include standard reference sources (e.g., guides, bibliographies, periodical guides and core journals, periodical indexes and abstracts,

dissertations), in addition to geographical sources and atlases, historical statistical sources, archives, and microforms. Sources specifically for British history are presented in the relevant categories throughout the guide.

Indexes and Bibliographies

Brown, Lucy M. and Ian R. Christie, eds. *Bibliography of British History: 1789–1851.* Oxford: Clarendon Press, 1977.
An annotated bibliography of contemporary through twentieth-century publications covering the following subjects: general reference works; political, constitutional, legal, ecclesiastical, military, navel, economic, social, and cultural history; local history, including Wales, Scotland, Ireland, and the British empire.

Historical Abstracts Online. 1954–present. Santa Barbara, CA: ABC-CLIO. serials.abc-clio.com/.
The principal bibliographic database for historical research. Indexes books, journal articles, and dissertations published from 1954 to the present addressing the history of the world after 1449, excluding the United States and Canada, which are covered in the database *America: History and Life.* Includes international coverage of key historical journals, in addition to selected journals in the social sciences and humanities. The advanced search permits limiting by decade(s) or century (e.g., 1790, 1800–1899) and subject terms (e.g., romanticism, Luddites). Use this database to research a wide range of subjects within a historical period, including popular culture, science, medicine, and so forth.

Webb, R. K. "Britain and Ireland since 1760" in *The American Historical Association's Guide to Historical Literature.* 3rd ed., gen. editor Mary Beth Norton. New York: Oxford University Press, 1995.
A selective annotated bibliography of the "best contemporary historical scholarship" (xi) published primarily from 1961 to 1992. Includes general studies, politics, law, government, urban and regional history, economic, social, labor and working class, religion, intellectual and cultural, science and medicine, diplomatic and military, and regional histories for Ireland, Scotland, Wales, and the British empire/commonwealth.

Historical Sources

Aspinall, A. and E. Anthony Smith, eds. *English Historical Documents: 1783–1832.* Vol. XI, *English Historical Documents*, gen. ed. David C. Douglas. New York: Oxford University Press, 1959.
This source presents documents from the Romantic period, including laws, speeches, letters, diary entries, debates, treaties, reports, and statistical tables, arranged in the following categories: executive branch; parliament; administration of justice; local government and poor law administration; economic development; social and religious life; the empire; and wars and foreign policy. Each of these sections begins with an introduction and bibliography. Also includes borough maps of England, Scotland, and Ireland.

Baxter, Stephen B., ed. *Basic Documents of English History.* Boston: Houghton Mifflin, 1968.
This anthology provides transcriptions of selected legal documents of English history from the Anglo-Saxon dooms to twentieth-century documents (e.g., excerpts from the Seditious Meetings Act, 1795; the Abolition of the Slave Trade, 1807 and 1833; the Corn Laws Amendment Act, 1815; and the Catholic Emancipation Act, 1829).

Music

Dictionaries, Encyclopedias, and Handbooks

Latham, Alison, ed. *The Oxford Companion to Music.* New York: Oxford University Press, 2002.
The latest edition reflects the current scholarship, particularly about Western classical music, and includes entries on individuals, instruments, movements, and definitions of musical terms.

Randel, Don Michael, ed. *The New Harvard Dictionary of Music.* Cambridge, MA: Belknap Press of Harvard University Press, 1986.
Basic reference source with international coverage and all styles and forms of music.

Sadie, Stanley, ed. *The New Grove Dictionary of Music and Musicians.* 2nd ed. 29 vols. New York: Grove, 2001. Available online at www.grovemusic.com.
A core reference resource with scholarly, authoritative entries on all aspects of music, including composers, performers, genres, movements,

and theories. The entry on "Romanticism" provides a short discussion of the history of the term as used in literature as opposed to music; the Romantic era in music is later, starting roughly in the post-Beethoven era of 1830.

Guides

Duckles, Vincent H., Ida Reed, and Michael A. Keller, eds. *Music Reference and Research Materials: An Annotated Bibliography*. 5th ed. New York: Schirmer Books, 1997.
An important guide for music scholarship and research which includes selected bibliographies, indexes, dictionaries, companions, chronologies, catalogs, websites, and other types of reference published through 1995.

Indexes and Bibliographies

The Music Index: A Subject-Author Guide to Music Periodical Literature. Warren, MI: Harmonie Park Press. Available online at www.hppmusicindex.com.
Index to about 700 popular and classical music periodicals. Print index covers years 1949–present and online version from 1979–present.

RILM Abstracts of Music Literature. New York: RILM. Available online at www.rilm.org/.
An international index with abstracts to all aspects of music literature: periodicals, books, dissertations, reviews, films and videos, and commentaries from 1969 to the present.

Sources and History

Grout, Donald Jay and Claude V. Palisca. *A History of Western Music*. 6th ed. New York: Norton, 2001.
Standard history of music survey from antiquity through the twentieth century. Chapters covering the Romantic literary era include "Late Eighteenth Century: Haydn and Mozart" and "Ludwig van Beethoven."

Philosophy

Dictionaries, Encyclopedias, and Handbooks

Audi, Robert. *The Cambridge Dictionary of Philosophy*. 2nd ed. New York: Cambridge University Press, 1999.

Substantial entries providing definitions of philosophical terms, movements, and concepts, and biographical information on philosophers from all ages. The second edition expanded upon non-Western philosophies and living philosophers, so both first and second editions will be valuable to the Romantic scholar.

Craig, Edward, ed. *Routledge Encyclopedia of Philosophy*. 10 vols. New York: Routledge, 1998. Available online at www.rep .routledge.com/.
Standard encyclopedia with lengthy, scholarly signed essays and bibliographies. The entry for Romanticism is focused on German romanticism. Use the detailed index in volume 10 to find all references to the British philosophers and intellectual thinkers included.

Dematteis, Philip B. and Peter S. Fosl, eds. *British Philosophers: 1500–1799*, vol. 252, *Dictionary of Literary Biography*. Detroit: Gale Group, 2002.
Dematteis, Philip B., Peter S. Fosl, and Leemon B. McHenry. *British Philosophers, 1800–2000*, vol. 262, *Dictionary of Literary Biography*. Detroit: Gale Group, 2002.
Part of the *Dictionary of Literary Biography* series (Chapter 2). Biographic essays about the writings of British philosophers, including Bentham, Burke, Paley, Priestley, Wollstonecraft, and Godwin.

Honderich, Ted, ed. *The Oxford Companion to Philosophy*. New York: Oxford University Press, 1995.
A companion with brief, signed entries and bibliographic references, covering individuals (such as Bentham, Coleridge, Paine, Wollstonecraft), movements, ideas, and theories. Entry for "romanticism, philosophical" provides brief, general overview about the movement and the thinkers and philosophers who contributed to the idea of Romanticism, including Coleridge.

Horowitz, Maryanne Cline, ed. *New Dictionary of the History of Ideas*. 6 vols. New York: Charles Scribner's Sons, 2005.
A new edition of the classic reference tool. In-depth, lengthy, signed essays provide overviews about all aspects of intellectual history, including such concepts as aesthetics, revolution, slavery, political protest, and other surveys of ideas and thought which will be of interest to the Romantic scholar. Includes chapter on "Romanticism in Literature and Politics."

Zalta, Edward N., principal ed. *The Stanford Encyclopedia of Philosophy*, 1995. Online at plato.stanford.edu (accessed 12 December 2004).

A free, online scholarly encyclopedia with entries contributed and reviewed by experts. Although started in 1995, many of the entries are still in process. Content is selective at present: Godwin has an entry but no entries for Romanticism, Goethe, or Coleridge are listed as available or in process. The "dynamic" encyclopedia entries can be updated by the authors as new research becomes available.

Guides

Bynagle, Hans E. *Philosophy: A Guide to the Reference Literature.* Englewood, CO: Libraries Unlimited, 1997.

An invaluable annotated bibliographic guide to the reference sources available for scholarly research in philosophy, including dictionaries, encyclopedias, bibliographies, indexes, companions, websites, and others.

Indexes and Bibliographies

The Philosopher's Index: An International Index to Philosophical Periodicals and Books. Bowling Green, OH: Philosopher's Information Center. Available online through various vendors.

International coverage of books, book reviews, and over 550 journals from 1940–present.

Religion

Dictionaries, Encyclopedias, and Handbooks

Eliade, Mircea, ed. *Encyclopedia of Religion.* 16 vols. New York: Macmillan, 1987.

A core, standard encyclopedia for religions from around the world. Second edition due to be published in 2005.

Guides

Blazek's volume (see under "General" category above), *The Humanities: A Selective Guide to Information Resources* is a helpful, supplementary source for all humanities, including religion.

Johnston, William M. *Recent Reference Books in Religion: A Guide for Students, Scholars, Researchers, Buyers, and Readers.* Rev. ed. Chicago: Fitzroy Dearborn, 1998.
A evaluative guide to over 300, mainly print, reference resources published since 1970 through 1997 covering Christianity, Judaism, Asian religions, Buddhism, and other religions worldwide, as well as mythology, the social sciences of religion, and philosophy of religion.

Indexes and Bibliographies

Religion and literature are covered by *MLAIB* and *ABELL*. The history of religion is included in *Historical Abstracts.*

ATLA Religion. Chicago: American Theological Library Association. Available online via various vendors.
Indexes articles and book reviews from religious and theological journals from 1949 to the present, with an ongoing project to selectively index journals prior to 1949, and essays in multi-author works. The print versions of this database *Religion One* (periodicals) and *Religion Two* (multi-author works).

Sciences and Medicine

Dictionaries, Encyclopedias, and Handbooks

Bynum, William F., E. Janet Browne, and Roy Porter. *Dictionary of the History of Science.* Princeton, NJ: Princeton University Press, 1981.
A dictionary to the ideas of science throughout the history of Western science rather than the individuals involved. Useful bibliography, divided by broad science subject categories, at the beginning of the book.

Bynum, W. F. and Roy Porter, eds. *Companion Encyclopedia of the History of Medicine.* 2 vols. New York: Routledge, 1993.
Seventy-two essays cover all aspects of the history of medicine, including: theories of life, health, and disease; medicine and society and culture; diagnosis; education; nursing; and the hospital. Includes a chapter on "Medicine and Literature."

Rosner, Lisa, ed. *Chronology of Science from Stonehenge to the Human Genome Project.* Santa Barbara, CA: ABC-CLIO, 2002.
Chronology of scientific advances and discoveries in astronomy, biology, chemistry earth sciences, ecology, mathematics, and physics.

Trautmann, Joan and Carol Pollard. *Literature and Medicine: An Anno-*
   tated Bibliography. Rev. ed. Pittsburgh: University of Pittsburgh
   Press, 1982.
An annotated bibliography of literary works in which medical themes
or issues are explored. Chapters include "18th Century" and "19th Century," and an index by topic includes abortion, death, evil doctors,
madness, medical ethics, science fiction, and suicide.

Indexes and Bibliographies

For articles on the history of social sciences, sciences, and medicine
during the Romantic era, use *Historical Abstracts*. The interdisciplinary
coverage of both *Academic Search Premier* and *Expanded Academic
ASAP* make them valuable starting points as well.

Web of Science. Philadelphia, PA: Institute for Scientific Information.
   isi10.isiknowledge.com/.
An interdisciplinary index to articles in over 8,000 international science
and social sciences journals. If available, years of coverage depends
upon the library's subscription.

Sources and History

Hessenbruch, Arne, ed. *Reader's Guide to the History of Science*. Chicago: Fitzroy Dearborn, 2000.
A guide to recommended and important readings about individuals,
disciplines and institutions, and themes relevant to the history of science, technology, and medicine. The list of sources are reviewed and
compared in one- to two-page essays. The entry for *Romanticism* concentrates largely upon German Romanticism and science, but there are
some references to Britain.

Kiple, Kenneth F., ed. *The Cambridge World History of Human Disease*. New York: Cambridge University Press, 1993.
Essays and statistical data provide historical overviews of medical practices, public health concerns, and major diseases from around the world
and throughout the ages.

Knight, David M. *Science in the Romantic Era*. Brookfield, VT: Ash-
   gate, 1998.
Reprints of articles and books chapters written from 1967 to 1996 by
Knight, a historian of science and an expert about science during the

Romantic era. He approaches the topic through his research on Humphrey Davy and on the importance of chemical theorizing. Knight explores the development of science in response to new discoveries as well as its relationship to society, culture, religion, and the philosophical and political ideas of the era.[1]

Knight, David M. *Sources for the History of Science, 1660–1914.* Ithaca, NY: Cornell University Press, 1975.
Knight, who wrote the essays included in *Science in the Romantic Era*, here describes the methods for conducting research in the history of science. Although much has changed since 1975 in terms of the sources available, the discussions about the challenges historians of sciences face in identifying relevant resources, the advice for approaching the discipline and the historic context of the types of resources available (e.g., manuscripts, journals, scientific books, non-scientific books, and physical objects) are invaluable.

Lindberg, David C. and Ronald L. Numbers. *The Cambridge History of Science.* New York: Cambridge University Press, 2003–.
Volume 4, *Eighteenth-Century Science* and Volume 5, *Modern Physical and Mathematical Sciences*, of this series provide scholarly essays describing a wide range of topics about the role of science during the eighteenth, nineteenth, and twentieth centuries. The chapters are very readable and extremely valuable for the Romantic literary scholar needing to understand the development of different sciences over time, and to be able to put into context the developments which occurred at the end of the eighteenth and beginning of the nineteenth centuries. (See the "Social Sciences" section of this appendix for another volume in this series.)

Social Sciences

Guides

Herron, Nancy L., ed. *The Social Sciences: A Cross-Disciplinary Guide to Selected Sources.* 3rd ed. Greenwood Village, CO: Libraries Unlimited, 2000.
Lists relevant print and electronic sources and provides evaluative annotations for research in the general social sciences, political science, economics, business, history, law, anthropology, sociology, education, psychology, geography, and communication.

Indexes and Bibliographies

For articles on the history of social sciences, sciences and medicine during the Romantic era, use *Historical Abstracts*. The interdisciplinary coverage of both *Academic Search Premier* and *Expanded Academic ASAP* make them valuable starting points as well.

Web of Science. Philadelphia, PA: Institute for Scientific Information.
        isi10.isiknowledge.com/.
An interdisciplinary index to articles in over 8,000 international science and social sciences journals. If available, years of coverage depends upon the library's subscription.

Sources and History

Lindberg, David C. and Ronald L. Numbers. *The Cambridge History of Science*. New York: Cambridge University Press, 2003–.
Broader in scope than just the Romantic era, Volume 7 of this series, *Modern Social Sciences*, provides valuable scholarly essays about the history of various social sciences, including economic theory, education, psychology, ethnography, and political science. Some issues addressed include ideas of class, the invention of race, and scientific ethnography and travel. Part one concentrates on social sciences to the end of the nineteenth century, but information valuable to the Romantic scholar, especially in what forms various social sciences existed during the time period, is scattered throughout the book. (See the section on "Sciences and Medicine" in this appendix for two more volumes in this series.)

Theater

Literary research tools often include drama and dramatists. The following represent some conventional and some unique types of resources available to researchers in theater.

Dictionaries, Encyclopedias, and Handbooks

Hartnoll, Phyllis, ed. *The Oxford Companion to the Theatre*. 4th ed. New York: Oxford University Press, 1983.
Basic reference source with short entries for actors, dramatists, directors, theaters, and definitions of terms. Does not reflect the scholarly research of the last twenty years, but is still valuable as a place to check facts and find condensed information.

Highfill, Philip H., Kalman A. Burnim, and Edward A. Langhans. *A Biographical Dictionary of Actors, Actresses, Musicians, Dancers, Managers, and Other Stage Personnel in London, 1660–1800.* 16 vols. Carbondale, IL: Southern Illinois University Press, 1973–1993.

The title of this important biographical reference work accurately reflects the content of this source. A major undertaking to identify and provide information about everyone involved in the performance of a play, excluding dramatists unless the playwright was also an actor, manager, or involved in the production of the play in some other way.

Mann, David and Susan Garland Mann. *Women Playwrights in England, Ireland, and Scotland, 1660–1823.* Bloomington: Indiana University Press, 1996.

This volume contains brief biographical entries for roughly 600 women playwrights and individual entries for the plays they wrote. A chronology concludes the volume.

The entry for each play has references to modern print and microform versions available. For example, the Larpent Collection at the Huntington Library, part of the *Three Centuries of English and American Plays* microform collections discussed in Chapter 8, was one of the sources for this book; the microform numbers for titles in that collection are referenced as available editions. *Women Playwrights* was published prior to the digitization projects covered in Chapter 8, so texts might be available online through projects, such as *ECCO* for the late eighteenth-century plays. In addition, be sure to check your library catalog and union catalogs to discover if a modern edition has been published since this volume was written.

Guides

Simons, Linda Keir. *The Performing Arts: A Guide to the Reference Literature.* Englewood, CO: Libraries Unlimited, 1994.

Annotated bibliography to theatrical research sources encompassing theatre and dance but excluding music. Includes bibliographies, catalogs, indexes, dictionaries, encyclopedias, companions, biographical sources, and libraries and archives.

Indexes and Bibliographies

MLAIB and *ABELL* are both excellent indexes for scholarly research about theater during the Romantic era.

Stratman, Carl J. *A Bibliography of British Dramatic Periodicals, 1720–1960*. New York: New York Public Library, 1962.
The list of English, Scottish, and Irish periodicals is arranged chronologically by the initial date of publication. Periodicals included in the list focused on drama; periodicals which simply had a column about drama are excluded.

Sources and History

The London Stage: 1660–1800: A Calendar of Plays, Entertainments, and Afterpieces, together with Casts, Box-Receipts, and Contemporary Comment. Compiled from the Playbills, Newspapers, and Theatrical Diaries of the Period. 6 pts. in 12 vols. Carbondale, IL: Southern Illinois University Press, 1966–1979.
A chronological, day by day, list of plays performed in London each season, including cast (if known), and, if available brief contemporary comments. The amount of detail in each entry various according to the amount of information which could be discovered about the performance.

Trussler, Simon. *The Cambridge Illustrated History of British Theatre*. New York: Cambridge University Press, 1994.
A survey of British theatre from Roman Britain to the end of the twentieth century. Chapters of interest to Romantic scholars include "From Manners to Melodrama 1776–1814" and "The End of the Monopoly 1814–1843."

Note

1. Hamm, E. P. Review of *Science in the Romantic Era*, by David M. Knight. *Annals of Science*, 57, no. 2 (April 2000): 201–203; Oldroyd, David. Review of *Science in the Romantic Era*, by David M. Knight. *ISIS: Journal of the History of Science in Society*, 90, no. 4 (December 1999): 816–817.

Bibliography

Altick, Richard D. and John J. Fenstermaker. *The Art of Literary Research.* 4th ed. New York: W. W. Norton, 1993.

Balay, Robert. *Early Periodical Indexes: Bibliographies and Indexes of Literature Published in Periodicals before 1900.* Lanham, MD: Scarecrow Press, 2000.

Beetham, Margaret. *A Magazine of Her Own? Domesticity and Desire in the Woman's Magazine, 1800–1914.* New York: Routledge, 1996.

Bellardo, Lewis J. and Lynn Lady Bellardo, comps. *A Glossary for Archivists, Manuscript Curators, and Records Managers.* Chicago: The Society of American Archivists, 1992.

Biscoe, Walter S. "The Improvement of Poole's Index." *American Library Journal* 1, no. 8 (April 30, 1877): 279–281.

Black, Jeremy. *The English Press, 1621–1861.* Thrupp, Stroud, Gloucestershire: Sutton, 2001.

Bond, Richmond. "English Literary Periodicals to form New Microfilm Series." *Library Journal* 76, no. 2 (January 15, 1951): 125–128.

Bour, Isabelle. "Mary Brunton." Vol. 8. *Oxford Dictionary of National Biography.* New York: Oxford University Press, 2004.

Burke, Frank G. *Research and the Manuscript Tradition.* Lanham, MD: Scarecrow Press, 1997.

Cohen, Laura B., ed. *Reference Services for Archives and Manuscripts.* New York: Haworth Press, 1997.

Donoghue, Frank. "Colonizing Readers: Review Criticism and the Formation of a Reading Public." Pp. 54-74 in *The Consumption of Culture 1600–1800: Image, Object, Text,* eds. Ann Bermingham and John Brewer. New York: Routledge, 1995

Fader, Daniel and George Bornstein. *British Periodicals of the 18th and 19th Centuries.* Ann Arbor, MI: University Microfilms, 1972.

Fisher, Steven, ed. *Archival Information: How to Find It, How to Use It.* Westport, Conn.: Greenwood Press, 2004.

Frazier, Patrick, ed. *A Guide to the Microform Collections in the Humanities and Social Sciences Division of the Library of Congress.* Washington, DC: Library of Congress, 1996.

Garside, Peter, James Raven, and Rainer Schöwerling, eds. *The English Novel 1770–1829: A Bibliographical Survey of Prose Fiction Published in the British Isles.* 2 vols. New York: Oxford University Press, 2000.

Guide to the Contents of the Public Record Office, vol. 2, *State Papers and Departmental Records.* London: Her Majesty's Stationery Office, 1963.

Hamm, E. P. Review of *Science in the Romantic Era*, by David M. Knight. *Annals of Science* 57, no. 2 (April 2000): 201–203.

Harner, James L. *Literary Research Guide: An Annotated Listing of Reference Sources in English Literary Studies.* 4th ed. New York: Modern Language Association of America, 2002.

Johnson, Peter. "Printed Indexes to Early British Periodicals." *The Indexer: Journal of the Society of Indexers* 16 (April 1989): 147–155.

McCalman, Iain, ed. *An Oxford Companion to the Romantic Age: British Culture, 1776–1832.* New York: Oxford University Press, 1999.

O'Neill, Michael, ed. *Literature of the Romantic Period: A Bibliographical Guide.* Oxford: Clarendon Press, 1998.

Oldroyd, David. Review of *Science in the Romantic Era*, by David M. Knight. *ISIS: Journal of the History of Science in Society* 90, no. 4 (December 1999): 816–817.

Poole, William Frederick. "Preface." Vol. 1, pt. 1. *Poole's Index to Periodical Literature.* Rev. ed. 1891. Reprint, Gloucester, MA: Peter Smith, 1963.

Roper, Derek. *Reviewing Before the Edinburgh, 1788–1802.* Newark, NJ: University of Delaware Press, 1978.

Rosenbaum, Barbara, comp. *Index of English Literary Manuscripts*, vol. 4, pt. 2. *1800–1900 Hardy-Lamb.* London: Mansell Publishing, 1990.

Thorpe, James. *The Use of Manuscripts in Literary Research: Problems of Acccess and Literary Property Rights.* 2nd ed. New York: Modern Language Association of America, 1979.

Vann, J. Don and Rosemary T. VanArsdel, eds. *Victorian Periodicals: A Guide to Research.* New York: Modern Language Association of America, 1978.

Williamson, William Landram. *William Frederick Poole and the Modern Library Movement.* New York: Columbia University Press, 1963.

Index

NOTE: This index includes author-specific resources that were used as examples in the research guide. Consequently, the author subject entries feature a representative and not comprehensive resource list. A lowercase f or t following a page number indicates a figure or table reference, respectively.

About the Authors

Peggy Keeran is an associate professor and the arts and humanities reference librarian at the University of Denver Penrose Library.

Jennifer Bowers is an assistant professor and a reference and instruction librarian at the University of Denver Penrose Library.

The authors are coeditors of the Scarecrow Press series, *Literary Research: Strategies and Sources*.